DATE			

The Moral Meaning of Revolution

THE MORAL MEANING
OF REVOLUTION

Jon P. Gunnemann

New Haven and London   Yale University Press

1979

Published with assistance from the foundation
established in memory of Amasa Stone Mather
of the class of 1907, Yale College.

Designed by John O. C. McCrillis
and set in Press Roman type.
Printed in the United States of America by
The Murray Printing Co., Westford, Massachusetts.

Published in Great Britain, Europe, Africa, and
Asia (except Japan) by Yale University Press,
Ltd., London. Distributed in Australia and
New Zealand by Book & Film Services, Artarmon,
N.S.W., Australia; and in Japan by Harper & Row,
Publishers, Tokyo Office.

Library of Congress Cataloging in Publication Data

Gunnemann, Jon P.
  The moral meaning of revolution.

  Includes index.
  1. Revolution (Theology) 2. Revolutions—Moral
and religious aspects. I. Title.
BT738.3.G86   1979   261.7   79-10219
ISBN 0-300-01997-1

For Karin

Contents

Preface

This book is a critique of the idea of revolution. In part it was born out of the conviction that revolution cannot be everything that has been claimed for it, and especially that it cannot be a substitute for moral judgment. In this vein, it rejects the notion that revolution is the most fundamental of human activities; and it therefore rejects also the possibility of permanent revolution as well as recent attempts in theology to construe Christian activity as revolutionary activity.

But I hope it is evident in these pages that I take the idea of revolution with utmost seriousness. All of the persons and movements I discuss were chosen because of the powerful challenge they pose for moral analysis, and the purpose of the critique is to extract and understand the essential points of that challenge. Perhaps most important is the awareness at points in history that in the pursuit of certain goals, often ostensibly moral, things have gone desperately wrong and that to continue on the same course is insanity. This negative revelation, a sense of abyss and dead-endedness, lies at the heart of revolutionary change. It is also a theme that appears in Christian thought as the failure of the law or the failure of the ethical, a failure that drives the individual to despair but also paves the way for conversion and faith. This parallel to religious conversion is essential to understanding revolution.

Of special interest is the account of the transformation of despair into hope, of the recreative process whereby human activity is set on a sane course. On this count there is little agreement. My own conclusions are basically three: (1) that revolution cannot be justified in the usual sense of what it means to justify an act; (2) that the very possibility of revolution depends on a particular understanding of moral activity and the "normal" (as opposed to revolutionary) work of the tradition expressing that understanding; and (3) that this tradition, broadly defined as Judeo-Christian, is in principle open to the possibility of having revolutions (but this is quite different from any notion of the necessity of revolutions). The first two conclusions derive from an analysis of the structure of revolutionary change, using in part the work of Thomas Kuhn on scientific revolutions. The third conclusion derives from the same analysis but also from theological considerations about the nature of evil and the structure of human response to evil.

In a year that I spent in Japan, a student asked me how I could be a Christian and not be a Marxist. The answer has turned out not to be so easy as I then imagined, nor so easy as I suspect my Japanese friend imagined. It is a question that has occupied much of my attention in the many years that have followed and this book is an attempt to give my answer as best I can. It is fitting that Marx is at the center of the book, not so much as the midpoint of a tradition but as the center in which the issues receive their fullest and most subtle expression, giving coherence to the whole.

My indebtedness to teachers, friends, colleagues, and students is immense and I cannot mention them all. Friends among students and faculty at Doshisha University in Kyoto, Japan, are responsible for starting my thinking about issues of modernization, conversion, revolution, and the Christian churches. They also provided the friendship and marvelous environment to nurture this thinking. The year spent there, 1964-65, was formative in a way that no other year has been. The Board for World Ministries of the United Church of Christ made that year possible with its Internship Abroad program. This book might not exist but for that.

In its first form the book was a doctoral dissertation for the Department of Religious Studies at Yale University. James Gustafson and David Little, my teachers, formed my early thinking on the topic. Mention must be made of the patience of the department and of James Dittes, then Director of Graduate Studies, who never ceased expressing confidence that it would, someday, be completed. It was written, however, while I was teaching at the Pennsylvania State University, and the Department of Religious Studies there, and especially Luther Harshbarger, have my gratitude for their support and for giving me a reduced teaching load to facilitate the writing.

Many persons have read portions or all of the manuscript at various stages but I have benefited especially from the helpful criticisms of George Hunsinger, Paul Harrison, George Lindbeck, and Gene Outka.

Four persons have had such an intimate connection with the work as to require special mention. Hans Frei helped me in focusing attention on persons and issues when the dissertation was still an idea. He read it as a completed dissertation and while I was revising it for publication. His encouragement and critical insight have been a continual source of help. Ernest Lowrie read each chapter as it was being written and again read the whole with a literate and critical eye. He was and is my constant theological partner and friend. Charles Powers assumed the task of advising the dissertation when I left Yale. There is no other person with whom I have more continuous and important dialogue on the moral life. His contribution to the whole, both direct and in ways unknown, is immense. Sheldon Wolin made detailed comment and criticism on the entire manuscript; it is thereby immeasurably improved.

To all of these, and to students who have taught me in my classes on the subject, I express gratitude. At the same time I tender them all the customary right of disclaimer for all persistent defects. In addition, I want especially to thank Marian Neal Ash of the Yale University Press for her patience and encouragement in bringing the book to completion. Her early expression of interest in the manuscript has been followed by long and faithful support. Joan Rosenstock has done what is possible to improve my prose and has often improved the intelligence of the argument. Barry Seltser not only offered critical comments but helped to check footnotes and sources. Nona Jenkins worked late into the night to type revised portions of the text. A grant from the A. Whitney Griswold Fund, administered by Yale's Council on the Humanities, has covered the cost of manuscript preparation and of the index.

No one has been more important to my work than my wife, Karin, to whom I dedicate the book. She and our two boys, Robin and Martin, have endured every stage of its process and have often seen family plans and promises disrupted or deflected by it. They have maintained patience and humor throughout. But for Karin's love and self-sacrifice, this book would not be.

North Haven   J. P. G.

1

Introduction

Wars and revolutions . . . have thus far determined the
physiognomy of the twentieth century.

Hannah Arendt, *On Revolution*

The twentieth century has been called a revolutionary century, and
those who live in it are sometimes moved to reflect upon the per-
manence of change. The term *revolution* has been applied to so
many kinds of change—to sudden transfers of political power, social
upheavals, and economic shifts; to long-term economic and social
changes such as the industrial revolution; to fundamental transformations within intellectual and cultural domains such as science,
literature, and art—that the question is whether the word has lost all
meaning.

Revolution is an extraordinary rather than an ordinary phenomenon, not easily subject to the kind of ethical or social scientific
analysis used to construe ordinary human affairs. More precisely,
political and social revolutions have certain features that are pre-
moral or presocial in character, which is to say that revolution resembles the real or imagined process of the emergence of society, or
of a social contract or covenant. Since most ethics and most social
science assume the existence of the social grouping, the language and
categories of these disciplines are often ill-suited to revolution.

In religious language, revolution resembles conversion. Like conversion, it brings a radical change of perspective with regard to ultimate questions, along with a change in the pattern of life. The
ultimate question at stake in revolution, I shall argue, is the cause of
evil and suffering, although revolutionary change has to do as well
with the social order predicated upon a particular understanding of
evil. As a result, revolution cannot be justified in the usual sense of
what it means to justify an act. This does not mean that all revolutions are by nature unjust, although in a certain very limited sense,
that is true. It is rather that the language of justification seems as

1

unsuited to revolution as it does to conversion: it offends our sense of what is appropriate to ask whether a conversion is justified or unjustified. Conversions can, of course, be evaluated in other ways. We may speak of authentic and inauthentic conversions and even of the adequacy of the content or direction of someone's conversion. We may also reasonably make moral judgments about the consequences of conversion and the actions of those who stand in some relation to the converted person. But in none of these cases are we weighing the justice of the conversion itself, and the person who is converted would find it strange indeed if the question were raised.

The conversion aspects of revolution emerge in the implicit and sometimes explicit claim that for those who undergo the transformation revolution is its own justification. This claim achieves its clearest expression when revolutionaries speak of the inevitability of revolution (too often interpreted by others as a form of historical determinism); when they explicitly reject moral adjudication of the revolutionary conflict; and when they use religious language, especially of conversion and apocalypse, to interpret their conflict. Any moral analysis of revolution must take these claims seriously and determine exactly what kinds of moral judgments can be made in relation to revolution. Further, it must take into account the fact that revolutions are more complex than conversions, involving not only more persons but many different kinds of actors, not all of whom undergo the same transformations. And, the preceding claims notwithstanding, revolutionaries do use moral language freely. The task we have, then, is to clarify the relationship between revolutionary practice and moral reasoning.

Much of the recent enthusiasm for revolution on the part of many Christian thinkers has its roots, conscious or unconscious, in the religious character of revolution. Unfortunately, this enthusiastic correlation between Christian and revolutionary practice has often obliterated precisely the distinctions that might have served to give powerful direction to a specifically Christian response to revolution. Theologies of liberation, of revolution, and of hope have claimed that Christians *ought* to be involved in revolutionary change because the Gospel is a message of liberation; that the church is in a unique position to participate in and "correct" revolutions; that the Gospel is *the* permanent revolution; that the virtue of hope and the eschatological elements of the Gospel are revolutionary in implication; that

God is where revolution is, humanizing the world, or vice versa; that Christians have unique insight into the direction and quirks of history. The easy equation of words like revolution, liberation, and humanization not only begs many theological questions, it also creates a connection between Christian practice and revolution that glosses over profound difficulties. Most of these claims turn out to be slogans which, under inspection, do little more than qualify attitudes to Christian practice. Much worse, they cannot be a guide to Christian practice in revolution because in their generality they fail to recognize many of the fundamental claims being made by the revolutionaries.

Thus it is not surprising to find theological views of revolution that seem to bear little resemblance to revolution in the minds of its practitioners. Here, for example, is what one Christian writer has said about Christian participation in revolutions: Christians ought "to discern the direction in which western history may be moving" and to "strive for reconciliation in the midst of diversity and tension." By doing this,

> Christian faith can provide the resources for being authentically revolutionary. . . . Our western world needs cadres of men and women who are as seriously concerned as the Marxists in China or earlier in Eastern Europe, to bury the dead, violate the old and create the new . . . the distinctiveness of the Christian witness does not lie in its emphasis upon the values to be preserved from the past, but rather in the freedom it offers to bury the dead without remorse. . . .[1]

Here is what one of those earlier Eastern European Marxists had to say about the authentic revolutionary:

> The revolutionary is a doomed man. He has no pity for the state nor for the privileged and educated world in general, and expects no pity for himself. Between the two there exists, whether openly or secretly, a continuous and irreconcilable war for life and death. . . .
> Merciless toward himself, he must be merciless towards others.

1. Richard Shaull, "Christian Faith as Scandal in a Technocratic World," in *New Theology No. 6,* ed. Martin Marty and Dean Peerman (London: Macmillan, 1969), pp. 127, 129, 131.

A single, cold passion for the revolutionary cause must suppress within him all tender feelings for family life, friendship, love, gratitude, and even honor. For him there exists only one pleasure, one consolation, one reward, and one satisfaction—the success of the revolution. Day and night he must have one single purpose: merciless destruction. To attain this goal, tirelessly and in a cold-blooded fashion, he must always be prepared to be destroyed and to destroy with his own hands everything that hinders its attainment.[2]

One can argue about what constitutes an authentic revolutionary, but only a hopeless romantic could believe that the revolutionary of the first passage would last one day in the ranks of the revolutionary Nechayev describes. Granted that the "Catechism of a Revolutionary" is considered an abhorrent aberration by some Marxists (it was most frequently cited by anticommunists during the cold war), it nevertheless reveals one kind of revolutionary thinking—one move toward reconciliation with the enemy would surely be grounds for liquidation. So much for burying the dead without remorse.

We ought not, however, to dismiss such muddled theological thinking as fruitless. For one thing, much of the theological writing on revolution and liberation reflects critical problems faced by Christians and by churches engaged in various contemporary struggles: Third World struggles for justice and political emancipation; the Christian-Marxist dialogue in Europe, Asia, and Latin America; and the failure of many Western democracies to establish racial, political, and economic justice. Furthermore, such writing, in spite of its shortcomings, serves to recover a dimension of the Christian faith often obscured by premature attempts to treat revolution as simply another kind of political change or activity.

TWO TYPES OF REVOLUTION

Almost no one disputes that there is a strong case in the Christian tradition for resistance to and even active rebellion against political authority. Already in the twelfth century John of Salisbury had established the principle that kings are subject to the laws of God

---

2. Sergei G. Nechayev, "The Catechism of the Revolutionary," paragraphs 5 and 6, in Basil Dmytryshn, ed., *Imperial Russia: A Source Book, 1700-1917* (Hinsdale, Ill.: Dryden Press, 1974), p. 304.

and had worked out a justification for tyrannicide. Similar arguments were put forth by Thomas Aquinas. The justification in both cases rested on a conception of the *lex naturae* which reflected the divine will and ordered all dimensions of human existence. In political life this ordering implied that each sovereign derived his legitimacy not from his own strength but from God's law; if he violated that law, he ceased to be sovereign. In practice this meant that sovereignty lay only with God and, by derivation, with his people. All human conflict, including conflict between sovereigns, and between sovereign and people, could be adjudicated in theory by reference to the *lex naturae.*

The consequence of this view was the careful working out of a theory of the just war together with a theology of the state that specified the extent and limits of the right to resistance. To be sure, the latter was generally more limited than extensive, but through the work of John Calvin, and even more of his followers, the right of political resistance was enlarged until it culminated in the great political upheavals of the seventeenth century in England and later in the American colonies.

It would seem that the obvious starting point for an inquiry into the ethics of revolution would therefore be this tradition of natural law and the just war. But a reading of the literature on revolution and particularly the literature of the Marxist tradition (which is *the* revolutionary literature of the modern world) shows that any attempt to apply the categories of the just war tradition would involve a fundamental distortion of what the Marxists mean by revolution. Natural law assumes a fundamental structure to the world and human society, an overarching "ideal" human community in which all peoples and nations participate, even if distantly (thus, the close relationship between the *lex naturae* and the *jus gentium*). Even in conflict, the fundamental moral community of the human race is assumed. A political revolt has its justification in the claim that this moral community (or the natural law) has been violated; those who revolt act in its name to restore justice and peace.

In contrast, the Marxist tradition makes no claim for the prior existence of a moral community, nor does it justify the revolutionary impulse with an appeal to an immutable moral structure. This reflects not merely a different moral viewpoint but also a very different conception of what revolution achieves. In effect, the Marxist maintains that a revolution brings into being a mode of human existence that has no precedent. The revolution is not for the purpose of restoring justice in the face of a contemptible violation of God's law but rather to change fundamentally the relations people have with one another.

The difference may be illustrated in the following manner. I am an active citizen—to use the language of political science, I show a relatively high degree of political participation. In our democratic system I may have a high level of tolerance for injustice provided that political leaders on all levels continue to redress these injustices (even if imperfectly) and I and my fellow citizens are not excluded from the relevant decisions. But it is quite plausible that my tolerance would become strained to the point of active resistance and even rebellion if the fundamental principles of the republic were endangered. Even more drastic: if there were a military coup that suspended our constitution, I should have no qualms about taking up arms to restore the constitution. Through all of this my most cherished political convictions do not change, even though the nature of my political activity does.

In contrast, we must imagine a Third World peasant who is illiterate or semiliterate, who has certainly never heard of John Locke, who barely ekes out a living on a third of an acre of land, and whose political participation has been confined to the paying of a burdensome tax on his meager yearly harvest. In a year of almost no rainfall, and with the growth of large, mechanized farms around him (owned, no doubt, by a large American food company), the tax becomes irrelevant as finding food for his family becomes problematic. There seems to be no way out other than to join the movement of his neighbors who are leaving their small plots to work on the large farms, or to go to a nearby city and work in one of the new factories. Neither solution is good in his eyes because each involves abandoning a way of life that has been transmitted through countless generations. But a friend in similar circumstances persuades him to attend a meeting of local farmers and small truckers out of which grows a plan for a strike (by the truckers) coupled with sabotage against one of the large farms. The issue is to force the government into land reform. Our peasant is reluctant to join in; such activity has not been part of his life. But the first effects of action exhilarate him. For the first time in his life he sees himself in company with friends refusing to accept conditions imposed by others. He thrives on the confidence solidarity creates and begins to see the future as something within his control, rather than as something that controls and even threatens him. A revolutionary is born. The question of success is irrelevant for the moment. He has undergone a transformation of consciousness that entails seeing his world in a new way. He has moved from political passivity to political activity.

Despite our different ways of life, it is likely that the two experiences I have just described would have some things in common. I am not likely to go through a major political upheaval without some changes in consciousness, and the peasant is not likely to find his new mode of existence totally discontinuous with the past. Nevertheless, the distinction between the two kinds of political activity, both of which may be called revolutionary, is important. When Marxists speak of revolution they tend to refer to something approximating the peasant's transformation rather than my rebellious instincts as a citizen. And although it may be necessary in the last analysis to look carefully at the overlap between these two kinds of revolution, I have chosen to focus on the revolution for which the peasant's transformation is the model.[3] It is essential to understand what this transformation is, and what is claimed for it by others, if theology and ethics are to talk about revolution with any rigor.

It would be convenient to distinguish between these two modes of revolution by using the terms *revolution* and *rebellion* for the peasant and the citizen, respectively. Unfortunately, even when such a distinction is made in the literature on revolution there is no consensus on the appropriate nomenclature. Therefore, I will limit the term *revolution* to those political revolutions in which at least some actors undergo a transformation of consciousness to the point where they actually experience some form of discontinuity with their previous mode of consciousness. It remains to determine the nature and extent of that transformation.

My decision to focus on the kind of revolution for which the peasant's transformation is the model ought not to be construed as a

3. Marx regarded the rebellion of the citizen as similar to the revolution of the peasant. The reason for this is that he was interpreting the eighteenth-century revolutions in which bourgeois citizens first came to political power. Thus he was interested in the birth of civil society, not in revolts that reestablished violated principles of already existing civil society.

rejection of the moral reasoning that has built up around the revolution of the citizen who attempts to restore lost rights or to defend fundamental political principles. This tradition has a powerful capacity to address a variety of contemporary political issues ranging from civil disobedience limited to reforming a democratic society to more active and extensive resistance and even violence in the face of totalitarian regimes. The reader needs to keep this point in mind, since when I argue that revolutionary violence cannot be justified under any circumstances I am referring to a kind of revolution for which the category of justification is not appropriate. Resistance to a Hitler, on the other hand, does not fall under that kind of revolution. I accept, then, without arguing for or against, the possibility of justifying Christian resistance to tyrannical or radically unjust forms of government. At the same time, what follows *is* in part a polemic against premature attempts to subsume all kinds of revolutionary change under this model of a citizens' rebellion against tyranny. Thus, while a natural law tradition or a contract tradition based on a notion of natural rights may well be able to justify peasant resistance or rebellion in the face of a violation of traditional peasant rights, they are less able to deal with a peasant movement in which the peasants no longer wish to be peasants.

2

Revolution and the Problem of Evil

> The love of fairplay is a spectator's virtue, not a principal's.
>
> George Bernard Shaw

The aim of revolution is to bring about fundamental changes in political, social, and economic affairs. It is possible therefore to see revolution simply as one kind of political activity among others, albeit a special one. Many social scientific inquiries proceed along these lines, first establishing the nature of political structure, activity, and change and then locating revolution as a specific kind of political change. Such an approach ignores almost entirely the claims made by one western revolutionary tradition, having its origin in the apocalyptic movements of Christianity and culminating in Marxism, that sees in revolution either a divine intervention in the normal course of history or the most fundamental of human activities: the practice by which men break with alienating structures and thereby establish genuine human history. The first view understands revolution as a political concept, derivative and even aberrational in character. The second view understands revolution as the manifestation of divine power or historical energy, working to undo the political structures that tend to resist the divine or the movement of history.

The choice between these two contrasting views of revolution is fateful for both social science and ethics, for while the terms in which I have presented them suffer from the weaknesses of all large generalizations, it is nevertheless the case that moral judgments about revolution tend faithfully to reflect one or the other. Those who begin with political inquiry tend to see revolution as at best a last resort in response to political failure. Moral and political energy is to be devoted to maintaining the political system, to making politics responsive to new needs and challenges; in short, to preventing

9

the conditions that could lead to revolution. If revolution does thrust itself forward as a possibility, the moral task is to delimit the conditions that would justify revolution rather than some other remedy. But those who begin, for example, with Marxist premises champion revolution as the activity whereby human beings express their humanity. For them, revolution is easily equated with liberation and humanization, and there is no perceived need for special justification. On the contrary, the burden of justification lies with those who promote the political and social institutions that alienate men from their world-shaping capacities.

It is important to take seriously the claims of those who refuse to reduce revolution to another kind of political activity. The first task is to understand the structure of the revolutionary process as they would have it (even though at crucial points they may differ among themselves). Having done this, I shall argue that the issue at stake in a revolution is theodicy, or the explanation of evil in a society; that the structure of a revolution deprives one of a neutral vantage point from which to adjudicate the conflict (except perhaps in hindsight); and that consequently revolution is better understood as an apocalyptic event, or as a religious conversion, than as a moral act.

DEFINING REVOLUTION

Revolution as Social Innovation

In his comprehensive study of revolution, Chalmers Johnson begins by noting that one cannot understand revolution apart from the social system as a whole and asserts that we need a paradigm of the functional society. The paradigm he offers is a modification of the Parsonian model, the "portrayal of society in a state of homeostatic equilibrium."[1] The implication that revolution will be presented as a problem of dysfunction is soon confirmed when Johnson states that "the study of society and revolution is somewhat analogous to the study of physiology and pathology" and that "the problem of conceptualizing revolutions is closely analogous to the problem of conceptualizing mental illness."[2]

This propensity to conceive of revolution by analogy to disease is

1. Chalmers Johnson, *Revolutionary Change* (Boston: Little, Brown, 1966), p. xii.
2. Ibid., pp. 3 and 7.

characteristic of much American social scientific writing on the subject. Even the relatively dispassionate Crane Brinton is unable to
avoid the fever analogy in his classic work.[3] And despite the rejoin-
der that fever can be understood as a healthy reaction to disease on
the part of the physical organism, the problem remains that any
pathological characterization of revolution suggests that health depends upon a restoration of the organism as it was before the disease
set in. The reader of Johnson's exhaustive analysis learns almost
nothing of the intentions of the revolutionaries themselves; everything is understood in terms of equilibrium and "dissynchronization
between value structures and patterns of environmental adaptation"
(the cause of either politically sanctioned or revolutionary change).[4]
The revolutionaries remain the foreign bodies that raise the tempera-
ture of the organism.

I have chosen to examine Johnson's approach to revolution because he distinguishes, much as I have, between two kinds of revolution, calling a revolt in the face of violated political principles a
rebellion and a revolt that involves transformation of consciousness
a revolution.[5] The former, he notes, are "renovative" while the latter
are "innovative."[6] This distinction could easily become the basis for
an analysis of revolution from the standpoint of the revolutionaries
and of the theme of innovation in revolution. But instead Johnson
refers all variants of his typology of revolution back to the social
system as a whole.[7] The significance of his approach may be made
clearer by looking at his conception of violence in connection with

3. Crane Brinton, *The Anatomy of Revolution* (New York: Vintage, 1965),
p. 16.

4. Johnson, *Revolutionary Change*, p. 166.

5. Ibid., chap. 7.

6. Ibid., p. 149.

7. Ibid., pp. 143ff. A full discussion of the alleged ideological bias of functional analysis appears in Robert Merton's *Social Theory and Social Structure*,
rev. ed. (New York: Free Press, 1968), pp. 91–100. While I find Merton's
comparison of the Marxist and functional methods illuminating, the history
of the use of these methods renders his argument less compelling, which in
any case is not relevant to other parts of Johnson's definition discussed in the
text. A fascinating work that views Marxist theory as an early form of functional analysis is Alfred B. Meyer, *Marxism: The Unity of Theory and Practice*
(Ann Arbor: University of Michigan, 1963). See also Arthur L. Stinchcombe,
Constructing Social Theories (New York: Harcourt, Brace and World, 1968),
pp. 91–98.

revolution. He begins by quoting the well-known passage from Max Weber on "social action": action is "all human behavior when and in so far as the acting individual attaches a subjective meaning to it," and "action is social in so far as by virtue of the subjective meaning attached to it by the acting individual (or individuals), it takes account of the behavior of others and is thereby oriented in its course."[8] At this point a discussion of the subjective meaning attached to violence on the part of revolutionaries could be forthcoming. But instead Johnson abstracts the notion of subjective meaning from individual acts and talks of the social system as a system of meanings within which human behavior is oriented. But Weber's notion of orientation is thereby transformed into conformity to the system. Revolutionary activity is then understood as action that disrupts this sytem of meanings, and violence is defined in this fashion:

> We may define violence as action that deliberately or unintentionally disorients the behavior of others. Violence is either behavior which is impossible for others to orient themselves to or behavior which is deliberately intended to prevent orientation and the development of stable expectations with regard to it. . . . Violence is "antisocial action," and in a political context dependent upon the prior existence of a system of social action within which it takes place.[9]

This is, I think, an interesting and useful definition of violence, but as it stands, it neglects entirely the possibility that from the standpoint of the revolutionary violent acts may have a meaning that *does* orient the behavior of others, namely, the members of a revolutionary party, or of a marginal group, or of a social class; or it may represent the attempt on the part of such groups to bring into being a new system of meaning for the society as a whole. Revolutionary violence disorients only those who remain committed to the estab-

8. Johnson, *Revolutionary Change*, p. 8. The quote is from Max Weber, *The Theory of Social and Economic Organization* (New York: Free Press, 1964), p. 88.
9. Johnson, *Revolutionary Change*, p. 8.

lished order or those against whom the violence is directed. This point becomes crucial when revolutionaries claim that certain social systems are in themselves violent, that is, the social structure itself prevents some people from orienting themselves.[10] Although such claims demand critical evaluation, they should not be excluded by a definition of violence that ignores them.

It is fundamental to Johnson's approach that he sees revolution as something to be avoided, something that can in fact be avoided by "creative political action."[11] The issue here is not whether this view is right or wrong but rather whether it is capable of comprehending, for example, Karl Marx, who would find talk of avoiding revolution tantamount to depriving man of his most unique characteristic, historical energy.

The problem is to find an approach to revolution that takes into account positions similar to Marx's without losing analytical rigor. I propose to move in this direction by utilizing the work of Thomas

10. Johnson's neglect of the possible positive subjective meaning attached to revolutionary activity is exacerbated by his abstract treatment of meanings on the level of the system as a whole. This predilection stands in contrast to much of Weber's work. Weber's definition of social action drove him to analyses of human behavior which took account of relatively personal statements and reflections on the meaning of certain kinds of action. Thus in *The Protestant Ethic and the Spirit of Capitalism* (New York: Scribner's, 1958) we are not given an analysis of a social system or meanings but rather are introduced to flesh and blood people who reflect on the meaning of certain actions both systematically (Calvin and Luther) and aphoristically (Benjamin Franklin). Not all of Weber's studies of religion deal with this level of meaning, however. In his studies of the religions of China and India, for example, he focuses on the subjective meaning attached to the actions of various social classes, castes, and religious groups, but even here he does not analyze total social systems. As Reinhard Bendix has pointed out, the shifting focus of his analysis reflects Weber's different interests: *The Protestant Ethic* and *Ancient Judaism* (Glencoe, Ill.: Free Press, 1952) contain studies in "the sociology of innovation," whereas the studies of religion in China and India serve as "vantage points for the analysis of the Western development" by concentrating on "the perpetuation of established beliefs and traditions." See Bendix, *Max Weber* (Garden City, N.Y.: Doubleday Anchor, 1962), pp. 265–66 and n. 13 on p. 265. It is precisely the possibility that revolution is a form of social (and religious) innovation that a definition of revolution must protect.

11. Johnson, *Revolutionary Change*, pp. xiv and 166ff.

Kuhn on the structure of scientific revolutions.[12] Kuhn has borrowed ideas from other fields, especially political theory, in interpreting scientific revolutions. This borrowing has been the cause of much of the criticism leveled at his work (by those who are convinced that development in science is not analogous to development in other fields of human endeavor), but it has also created the possibility of applying his theses to the fields from which his ideas originally came. Kuhn has warned that the practice of science and the scientific community are strikingly different from their counterparts in other fields.[13] Nevertheless, it is because he has used political analogies that his reformulations may be helpful in understanding political revolutions quite independently of the adequacy of the same formulations in relation to science. And it is not surprising that Kuhn's contributions seem original and provocative, for frequently the transfer of an idea or set of ideas from one field to another reveals patterns and contours which were not obvious in their original setting, perhaps because too much was assumed or taken for granted.

The outline of Kuhn's position is as follows: Science is generally carried on in the mode of "normal science," that is, "research firmly based upon one or more past scientific achievements, achievements that some particular scientific community acknowledges for a time as supplying the foundation for its further practice."[14] In his introduction he calls this "the tradition-bound activity of normal science" (note here and in some of what follows a language that recalls Max Weber's). At certain critical historical points, however, the scientific tradition is "shattered" in such a way that the entire framework of scientific investigation is altered before normal science can again be

12. Thomas S. Kuhn, *The Structure of Scientific Revolutions*, 2d ed., enlarged (Chicago: University of Chicago Press, 1970). The first edition was published in 1962. Johnson, *Revolutionary Change*, mentions Kuhn in his first chapter (p. 22) and at one later point (p. 112) but makes no systematic use of his work. An extensive use of Kuhn's theses and terminology for political and social revolutions can be found in Isaac Kramnick's treatment of recent writing on revolution, "Reflections on Revolution: Definition and Explanation in Recent Scholarship," *History and Theory* 11 (Middletown: Wesleyan University Press, 1972), pp. 26–63. I discuss Kramnick's views in the text. An entire literature has grown up around Kuhn's book, making it something of a modern classic.

13. Kuhn, *Scientific Revolutions*, pp. 208–09.

14. Ibid., p. 10.

carried on. This shattering of the tradition amounts to a change in world view[15] and constitutes a genuine revolution in science. What is important for Kuhn is that science progresses by means of these revolutions (he singles out, of course, the Copernican and Einsteinian revolutions), and the kind of progress entailed could not have come about merely through "normal science." This is owing to the very logic of scientific inquiry, the understanding of which is dependent upon Kuhn's notion of a "paradigm."

A paradigm in science refers to "accepted examples of actual scientific practice—examples which include law, theory, application, and instrumentation together—[that] provided models from which spring particular coherent traditions of scientific research."[16] Solving problems and puzzles, articulating hypotheses suggested by the paradigm, making theoretical predictions—all such research is basically cumulative in character, since it remains within the limits posed by the paradigms themselves. This science is extraordinarily useful, of course, both for solving problems that might not have been solved (or at least not well solved) under other paradigms and for achieving technological advances. But in the process of doing normal science, of fact-finding, of paradigm articulation, scientists frequently discover anomalies, that is, findings which make them aware "that nature has somehow violated the paradigm-induced expectations that govern normal science."[17] Some anomalies go unattended for a while, some can be accounted for by adjustments within the paradigm. But there are times when the accumulation of anomalies becomes great enough, and their character of such a kind, that paradigm adjustment no longer does the job. (The classic example from our history of science courses was the attempt by astronomers just before Copernicus to account for the retrograde motion of planets by positing epicycles within epicycles until the entire Ptolemaic paradigm threatened to fall of its own weight.) When this happens, there is a crisis in the scientific community, a crisis which can be resolved only by the emergence of a new scientific paradigm with its concomitant theory. Such a new paradigm is illegitimate in terms of the old one, for while both attempt to account for the same set of "facts," their vantage points are incommensurate. The old paradigm

15. Ibid., chap. 10.
16. Ibid., p. 10.
17. Ibid., pp. 52–53.

eventually yields to the new, but only the latter is able to give a more adequate interpretation of the facts. The logic of scientific inquiry, then, requires paradigms as the basis of its normal work, which is *cumulative* in character; but the very pursuit of paradigm-based research yields results that eventually undermine the paradigm, so that *at key points, science progresses not through cumulation but through revolution*.

It is not difficult to see a happy marriage between this view of scientific revolutions and revolutions in other areas of human endeavor. The pattern of a period of normalcy culminating in a crisis that calls into question the legitimacy of the "normal" state of things, forcing the development of a new structure or set of norms, fits neatly with interpretations of revolution from a variety of other perspectives (it has a sort of Hegelian logic to it which may please even the Marxists). Isaac Kramnick notes that Kuhn's conception is "strikingly similar" to the work of the philosopher Paul Schrecker, who conceives of revolution in any field as involving

> a fundamental change in the basic constitutive norms or generative principles of that area of endeavor. These basic norms or generative principles are those that give legitimacy, legality, or appropriateness to all lower level norms and principles. Revolution refers to change which reaches the fundamental norms; and since it changes those norms which themselves give legitimacy, the revolutionary change is itself considered illegitimate from the perspective of the previous set of basic norms. Revolution is, in short, an illegal change in what are considered the fundamental principles of legality. The political use of the term, then, is quite clear; it is a change in the fundamental laws or conventional norms of a political system, which change is itself considered illegitimate by the norms it abolishes.[18]

As with so many marriages that begin smoothly, however, problems lie just below the surface. The major problem here is the loose

18. Kramnick, "Reflections of Revolution," pp. 31–32. The article he discusses is Paul Schrecker, "Revolution as a Problem in the Philosophy of History," *Revolution*, ed. C. Friedrich (New York: Atherton, 1967) *Nomos VIII*, Yearbook for the American Society of Political and Legal Philosophy; pp. 34–35. The quote is from Kramnick.

way is which "paradigm" has been translated as "constitutive norms," "generative principles of legality," and the like. While we may be fairly certain of what a scientific paradigm is, do we know what the constitutive principles of a society are? A second problem emerges in the discussion of crisis. According to Kramnick, a crisis occurs in political systems as a result of challenges to the "ruling political paradigm."[19] But is this the same thing as the discovery of anomaly, and how can we know unless we are fairly precise about what we mean by the "political paradigm"? Third, there is perhaps implicit in this entire scheme the notion that progress takes place through revolution. Kuhn discusses the notion of progress in science with some care, and it is necessary to do the same in connection with political and social revolution if our definition is not to be weighted toward a Marxist view from the start.

Revolution as a Change in the Paradigm of Evil

For Schrecker, the generative principles of legality are simply those norms that are at the summit of a hierarchy of norms found in every society. In some states this is the constitution, but he admits that "it is difficult to give a discursive and explicit expression to this constitutive and persistent norm."[20] He tries to do so by contrasting revolutionary change with legal change: the latter is "a change sanctioned by a legitimate methodology," just as some constitutions carry within themselves the procedures by which they may be amended; whereas the former is "a mutation of the conditions of legality."[21] Even with this clarification, however, the notion of constitutive norms remains hazy, for there are countries in which there are no constitutions, where it would be difficult to specify the summit of the hierarchy of principles governing the culture as a whole.

Some relief may be had by returning to Kuhn's discussion of a scientific paradigm. Since the ambiguity in his use of the term has evoked criticism, in the revised edition he notes that he used "paradigm" in two ways:

On the one hand, it stands for the entire constellation of beliefs,

19. Kramnick, "Reflections of Revolution," p. 33.
20. Schrecker, "Revolution as a Problem," p. 39.
21. Ibid., p. 42.

values, techniques, and so on shared by the members of a given community. On the other, it denotes one sort of element in that constellation, the concrete puzzle-solutions which, employed as models or examples, can replace explicit rules as a basis for the solution of the remaining puzzles of normal science.[22]

As Kuhn notes, the second meaning of paradigm is philosophically "the deeper of the two" and is the most novel contribution of his book.[23] This meaning of paradigm as "shared exemplar" accounts for the fact that the ability to solve problems in science is not acquired merely by learning a set of scientific methods or rules: a student can learn a theory and some rules about its application and still not be able to solve problems to which the theory applies. Yet somehow "the student discovers, with or without the assistance of his instructor, a way to see his problem as *like* a problem he has already encountered." He then is able to proceed by analogy, using the original problem for "signaling the gestalt in which the situation is to be seen." Once an exemplar has served this purpose, the student can confront a variety of problems and situations and see similarities that were not obvious before. "For him they are no longer the same situations he had encountered when his training began. He has meanwhile assimilated a time-tested and group-licensed way of seeing."[24]

There is a distinct similarity between Kuhn's description of the process of scientific paradigm assimilation and the process called "socialization" by social scientists. In the latter, individuals (particularly children) are led to see certain social events, relationships, and even crises in terms of earlier experiences of the larger social group and especially in terms of thought-structures that have evolved out of social experience. These thought-structures, of course, exist on many different levels and occur in different forms; some are conscious whereas others are unconscious. They include religious symbols and myths, national symbols, cultural clichés, and the telling of

22. Kuhn, *Scientific Revolutions*, p. 175. For a fuller discussion of the meaning of paradigm see Margaret Masterman, "The Nature of a Paradigm," in *Criticism and the Growth of Knowledge*, ed. Imre Lakatos and Alan Musgrave (London: Cambridge University Press, 1970), pp. 59–90, as well as the response by Kuhn in the same volume.
23. Kuhn, *Scientific Revolutions*, pp. 175 and 187ff.
24. Ibid., p. 189.

fairy tales to children, as well as many of the very subtle structures embedded in social custom and in language. As with scientific communities, most of these structures go unquestioned in the course of everyday life. They are convenient ways of quickly organizing the complexity of lived experience and they give cohesion to the social group that shares them.

What Kuhn has done, beyond merely describing the process of scientific socialization, is to suggest that within the total constellation of scientific values and beliefs there are specific puzzle-solving paradigms that uniqely define a particular scientific community and that are key in scientific revolutions. What changes dramatically in a scientific revolution is not the entire belief structure of scientists—for clearly many scientific commitments and values persist through revolutionary turmoil—but rather a specific puzzle-solving paradigm that had given coherence to a scientific community and its research.[25]

Every society has a "paradigm" solution to the problem of evil as a part of its total constellation of symbols, beliefs, norms, and values. My thesis is that in a revolution it is this paradigm that is called into question, that is the focus of the crisis. *Political and social revolutions are innovative responses to the problem of evil,* and a full revolution can be said to have occurred only when a new paradigm solution to the problem of evil has emerged.

This interpretation of a social paradigm and its role in revolution differs from that suggested by Schrecker and Kramnick. Their emphasis was on constitutive norms or generative principles of legality, suggesting both that we can discern a fairly consistent and clearly articulated hierarchy of legal and moral principles in a society and that we will find at the top of this structure principles that generate or legitimize the whole. The societal solution to the problem of evil is probably not a norm or a principle (although it may entail such). It is more likely to be embodied in religious symbols or myths, such as the Christian myth of the Fall and the doctrine of Original Sin. These myths or symbols are the shared

---

25. This clarification by Kuhn (that a scientific revolution focuses on a specific problem-solving paradigm rather than on the total belief-structure of scientists) in the second edition of his book has helped to answer the charge by some of his critics that he does not give enough attention to the continuities of science throughout revolutionary change. See, for example, Ian Barbour, *Issues in Science and Religion* (New York: Harper Torchbooks, 1971), p. 156.

exemplars in light of which whole cultures interpret and give meaning to their experiences of death, suffering, human injustice, and so on. Since they do serve to give meaning and structure to the crises of life, to the events that threaten both the personal and social organism, they also serve to legitimize particular social structures. Using slightly different language but making essentially the same point, Peter Berger suggests that the

> implicit theodicy of all social order, of course, antecedes any legitimations, religious or otherwise. It serves, however, as the indispensable substratum on which later legitimating edifices can be constructed. It also expresses a very basic psychological constellation, without which it is hard to imagine later legitimations to be successful. Theodicy proper, then, as the religious legitimation of anomic phenomena, is rooted in certain crucial characteristics of human sociation as such.[26]

If Berger is correct in his understanding of the importance and priority of theodicy in understanding legitimation, his work supports the choice of the problem of evil as a starting point for understanding any social order or its disruption, including revolution.[27] There is a sense in which the demonstration of this thesis is the purpose of the entire essay, and the reader will be convinced only to the extent that it proves to illuminate the nature of revolution and the moral issues involved. But it is possible at this point to suggest the usefulness of this formulation for handling recurring problems in discussions of revolution, and to make a preliminary statement on the analogy between the discovery of anomaly in science and the discovery of anomaly in relation to the problem of evil.

26. Peter Berger, *The Sacred Canopy* (Garden City, N.Y.: Doubleday Anchor, 1969), p. 55. All of chapter 3, "The Problem of Theodicy," is directly relevant to the thesis I advance here and has been useful in formulating some of the following points.

27. Berger is of course not the first to see the importance of this focus; his work constitutes a refinement of Max Weber's, especially *The Sociology of Religion* (Boston: Beacon, 1963) and Weber's important essay, "The Social Psychology of the World Religions," in H. H. Gerth and C. Wright Mills, eds., *From Max Weber: Essays in Sociology* (New York: Oxford, Galaxy, 1958), pp. 267–301.

A Preliminary Definition of Revolution

One of the persistent difficulties encountered in the literature on revolution arises from the attempt to distinguish revolution from other types of change, particularly evolutionary change and "rapid change." There are times, of course, when the distinction is not made at all, but when it is, the extent of change and its rapidity are frequently selected as the characteristic marks or revolution (as is violence, a point I shall take up later).[28] To focus on the extent of change is imprecise, since it is a commonplace that even in revolutions institutions and social patterns from the past not only persist but are indispensable in providing a foundation for the new order. Many commentators have pointed out that the differences and antagonisms that separate the Soviet and Chinese systems of communism (and which at times seem to move one or the other closer to friendship with the U.S.) can be understood only as the consequence of particular historical traditions and institutions, traditions and institutions that have given a distinctive stamp in each of these two societies to communism. Even if we could determine the institutions, strata, or dimensions of a given society that would undergo extensive change in a revolution, we would find ourselves caught in a game of social mathematics, with the line between revolutionary change and nonrevolutionary change a very fuzzy one.

A similar argument can be made against focusing on rapidity of change. The switch in England right after the war to a socialist government could hardly have been more rapid—it was the consequence of one day's voting. Yet few if any historians refer to it as a revolution. The industrial revolution, which, though not political or social, was understood to have revolutionary political and social consequences, took place over a period of a century or more depending on the political and geographic borders established for discussion. Rapidity of change is not a precise parameter for a definition of revolution.

While it cannot be denied that extent and rapidity of change seem intuitively connected to revolution, it is possible to reach a better understanding of the role played by these factors by locating revolution in a sharp shift of certain crucial "shared exemplars" of a social

28. Kramnick, "Reflections on Revolution," pp. 30ff., discusses some of the literature that defines revolution chiefly in terms of the extent of its impact.

group and, especially in the case of social and political revolutions, in a shift in the symbol or myth structure having to do with the problem of evil. This approach helps to account for several circumstances.

1. Many prerevolutionary institutions, social patterns, and values not only persist in postrevolutionary societies but are invaluable in building the institutions of the new society. Kuhn is especially careful to note the importance of this point in scientific revolutions. The entire scientific structure is not overthrown, nor are all the tools of the former mode of normal science. Continuities are present. What happens in the shift from one critical shared exemplar to another is that many of these tools and techniques are recast or understood in a new light.[29] While it is true that institutions from the past frequently persist unintentionally, they do nevertheless persist. And in some cases the continuity is intentional. As I shall show, Marx uses the Hegelian term *Aufhebung* to account for both break and continuity in revolution.

2. What makes revolutions appear rapid or extensive in effect is their radical nature. I use *radical* here in its etymological sense: going to the root or source of something. If Berger's assertion of the priority of theodicy in relation to social legitimations is correct, then a change in theodicies is indeed radical. But it is wrong to suppose that such a radical change involves an annihilation of the entire superstructure erected upon it. That would be the case only if a particular symbolic structure logically entailed an entire cultural system. I know of no one who has argued for such a position. Theodicies may indeed logically entail certain moral requirements, but it is more precise to say that a theodicy engenders some elements of a social and cultural system, limits some elements, and interprets others. What happens in a revolution, then, is that some new elements are engendered, some are ruled out, and others are reinterpreted. Kuhn notes that in a scientific revolution the shift from one shared exemplar to another resembles what some psychologists call a "gestalt shift," in which the same set of data is seen as one thing on

---

29. See n. 25. Johnson, *Revolutionary Change*, p. 112, also tends to see Kuhn's paradigms as the equivalents of all the values of a society rather than listening to Kuhn's point that in a revolution only certain paradigms are called into question.

one occasion and as something else on another.[30] So also in a social revolution a shift in the theodicy paradigm causes people to interpret data (which themselves do not change) in a different way. The discovery and accumulation of anomalies is central to Kuhn's discussion of the revolutionary process. In science an anomaly is an empirical finding that disrupts the "paradigm induced expectations." Is there an equivalent in the process that precedes social and political revolutions? (It is worth remembering at this point that Kramnick finds an analogy in "challenges" to the ruling paradigm, without specifying what these challenges are. Since in any society there are many challenges to any political paradigm, this is too vague.) It will not do to say that suffering is an anomaly that creates a crisis in the ruling paradigm of the problem of evil, for suffering itself is that dimension of the human condition for which a theodical paradigm offers an explanation. Nor can we say that increased suffering creates a revolutionary crisis. On the contrary, increased suffering frequently, perhaps most of the time, brings apathy or a turning toward religious pursuits that legitimate suffering. Thus peasants in Brazil, finding that the purchasing power of their income from the sugar industry has been cut in half by modernization, have turned increasingly to the fatalism of Pentecostalism, which promises them salvation in the life to come, rather than to the political activism advocated so strongly by the Roman Catholic archbishop of Olinda and Recife.[31] This well-documented phenomenon[32] has several possible explanations. First, in the case of the most severe suffering (I think here of starvation in sub-Saharan Africa and in portions of India and Pakistan), sheer exhaustion and incapacity prevent revolution. Even where the suffering is not so acute physically, the power of existing theodicies to accommodate increased suffering is remarkable. And as Berger notes, even when theodicies are subjected to

30. Kuhn, *Scientific Revolutions*, pp. 111ff.

31. Marvine Howe, "Brazil Peasants Find Their Plight Worsens," in the *New York Times*, November 27, 1972.

32. Perhaps the most direct treatment of this issue is by J. C. Davies, "Toward a Theory of Revolution," in *American Sociological Review* 27 (1962): 5–19. His hypothesis (which is one of the few about revolutions that admits of empirical verification) is that revolutions occur not when suffering is terrible but rather after a period of relative well-being, when expectations have been raised but not met. Then there is the fear that ground gained after a long struggle will be quietly lost.

"empirical disconfirmation" there are "various cognitive and psychological mechanisms to rationalize empirical counterevidence."[33] What, then, creates the revolutionary crisis? One answer may be drawn from the study by Norman Cohn of millenarian revolutionaries in the Middle Ages when there were many groups that drew on the eschatological and apocalyptic tradition of Judaism and Christianity to legitimate violent social and political activity. In spite of their wide variety, they shared certain fundamental traits: they were collective in nature and believed in a miraculous, total transformation of life on this earth.[34] As Cohn demonstrates, the vast majority of them were from among the poor, but they were not merely poor. Rather, they were from among the "disoriented poor," that is, from among those who were dramatically affected by rapid social and economic change, particularly around growing industrial centers. The distinction is critical: the Middle Ages were rife with poverty, but most of the poor lived in relatively stable social conditions where peasant and village life was sustained by custom, religious celebrations, and "communal routine."[35]

> The network of social relationships into which a peasant was born was so strong and was taken so much for granted that it precluded any very radical disorientation. So long as that network remained intact peasants enjoyed not only a certain material security but also—which is even more relevant—a certain sense of security, a basic assurance which neither constant poverty nor occasional peril could destroy. Moreover such hardships were themselves taken for granted, as part of a state of affairs which seemed to have prevailed from all eternity.[36]

One might point out further that in the Middle Ages the church taught that poverty was a holy state, and the poor peasant could thereby understand his condition as blessed.

Nascent industrialism spawned another kind of poor: those who

33. Berger, *Sacred Canopy*, p. 70. Berger cites here the work of Leon Festinger on the psychology of "cognitive dissonance." Cf. n. 30, p. 195.

34. Norman Cohn, *The Pursuit of the Millennium*, rev. ed. (New York: Oxford, 1970), pp. 15ff.

35. Ibid., pp. 53ff.

36. Ibid., p. 56.

left the security of the villages and of manorial relationships to become free men in new urban centers. Some of them improved their condition, but those who failed not only found that their poverty was as bad or worse than before but also suffered from massive disorientation:

> There was no immemorial body of custom which they could invoke in their defence, there was no shortage of labour to lend weight to their claims. Above all, they were not supported by any network of social relationships comparable to that which sustained a peasant.[37]

Most of the revolutionary millenarians and anarchists came from this group. The new kind of experience they were having could not be assimilated under the old legitimations for suffering. Or, to use the language of Kuhn, there was no way in which they could see these new experiences of suffering in light of the shared exemplars of the peasant village. The new urban experience together with its abject poverty constituted the anomalies that could not be handled by the old paradigm: they became the empirical evidence that jarred the paradigm-induced expectations. Furthermore, not only did the disoriented poor discover anomalies that could not be interpreted in light of the old paradigm—it was also the case that they had ceased to practice the communal customs and routines that had given meaning to their former suffering. I make this point so that it is clear that the theodicy of a given social group is not an abstractly held position (even though it can be and frequently is abstractly stated by the intellectuals among them) but is rather part of the fabric of social norms, expectations, and action.

Even with the discovery of anomaly, however, the disoriented poor would not be moved to revolutionary activity. As in science, a revolution does not occur until a new paradigm emerges to compete with the old in the interpretation of anomaly. In the case of the millenarians this new paradigm was provided by the self-appointed messiahs who drew on Jewish and Christian apocalyptic myths to evoke a dualistic world in which one group or another (including the rich, kings, the pope and clergy, the Jews) was portrayed as the

37. Ibid., p. 59.

Antichrist, the mythical figure of the Book of Revelation who was to epitomize evil before the Second Coming of Christ. These charismatic leaders had sufficient education to read and to interpret the Scriptures, and they provided for the disoriented poor what the traditional customs and teachings of the church could not: a coherent metaphysic and a view of history that structured the new urban experience and laid at the feet of various other groups the responsibility for the new suffering. Armed with this, the poor could again find meaning in their poverty and suffering, this time not as a sign of godliness but as a sign that they were the warrior-saints who would defeat the hordes of Antichrist:

> The resulting phantasy could easily be integrated into the old eschatology derived from the Johannine and Sibylline traditions; and in this form it became a coherent social myth. The myth did not of course enable the helpless masses to overcome their dilemmas, and it often prompted them to courses of action that proved downright suicidal. But it did hold their anxieties at bay, and it did make them feel both immensely important and immensely powerful. That gave it irresistible fascination.[38]

That these social myths frequently drove their adherents to suicidal action warns us that not all theodicies are equally capable of providing the kind of social organization needed for revolutionary success. In chapter 3 I shall try to show that moral dualisms (that is, theodicies that divide the world into realms of good and evil) which are too rigid to be tempered by any other solution to the problem of evil doom their revolutionary adherents (if any) to almost certain failure. (Although, paradoxically, almost every revolution must have an element of dualism in order to succeed.) A sharp moral dualism does not provide an organizational ethic for "after the revolution."[39]

The fact that revolutions can fail suggests that there is no reason for considering them to be either intrinsically progressive or intrinsi-

---

38. Ibid., p. 88.

39. Max Weber was, of course, most interested in studying moral systems and theodicies that were especially effective in organizing human behavior, that is, systems capable of being institutionalized. This is clear from much of Weber's work, but see especially Talcott Parson's introduction to *The Sociology of Religion*, pp. xxix–xxx.

cally nonprogressive. Kuhn's discussion of this issue is instructive. While he admits that seen from within specific scientific communities there is a kind of progress in knowledge, he is not willing to admit that science is "the one enterprise that draws constantly nearer to some goal set by nature in advance." "We may, to be more precise, have to relinquish the notion, explicit or implicit, that changes of paradigm carry scientists and those who learn from them closer and closer to the truth." The notion that science does carry us closer and closer to the truth Kuhn calls "evolution-toward-what-we-wish-to-know," and he suggests that we need to substitute for this the notion of "evolution-from-what-we-do-know."[40] The analogy is Darwin's substitution of a nonteleological theory of evolution for the earlier goal-directed theories of Lamarck and others, for whom "progress" meant movement toward a goal inherent in the process of evolution. "Progress" after Darwin, if the term may be used at all, referred to movement from specific beginnings or previous states to present states as a consequence of competition and natural selection. While Kuhn warns against pushing the analogy too far, he suggests that his theory of scientific revolution points to

> the selection by conflict within the scientific community of the fittest way to practice future science. The net result of a sequence of such revolutionary selections, separated by periods of normal research, is the wonderfully adapted set of instruments we call modern scientific knowledge. Successive stages in that developmental process are marked by an increase in articulation and specialization. And the entire process may have occurred, as we now suppose biological evolution did, without benefit of a set goal, a permanent fixed scientific truth, of which each stage in the development of scientific knowledge is a better exemplar.[41]

Independently of the question of the adequacy of this view of science (and again this is one of the more controversial aspects of Kuhn's analysis), the conclusions do follow from Kuhn's articulation of revolutionary change. It indicates that the model of revolution I have been developing does not entail a progressive view of

40. Kuhn, *Scientific Revolutions*, pp. 171. and 170.
41. Ibid., pp. 172–73.

history in the usual sense of progress and therefore does not tip the balance in favor of a Marxist view of history. On the contrary, the definition of revolution I have suggested here allows for viewing something like the Nazi accession to power in Germany as a kind of revolution, a substitution of one theodicy for another, a view that Marxists abhor because of their teleological assumptions. In short, the model of revolution I have proposed is able to account for the claims of novelty and innovation made by many revolutionaries without giving novelty and innovation in themselves the positive connotation that a progressive teleology would imply.

The matter of progress in revolution may be raised in a different fashion. Kuhn's analysis of revolution does not entail a preference for revolutionary science over normal science. Nothing would be more foolish, even impossible, than for scientists to attempt to engage in revolutionary science as a matter of course, because the crises that occasion revolution would not occur without the work of normal science. It is the work of normal science, in its efforts to solve further problems and articulate its fundamental paradigm, that engenders the discovery of anomalies. This interdependency between normal work and revolutionary crises is a perplexing problem for those who advocate revolution, and the concept of permanent revolution advocated by some Marxists must be assessed accordingly. For now it can be said that the emphasis on the innovative character of revolutions, whether scientific or social, does not of itself imply a preference for revolution over against the attention to normal or ordinary pursuits.

Closely related to the question of progress in revolution are the interconnected themes of necessity, inevitability, irresistibility, irreversibility, and the like. Revolutionary literature abounds with such language—for example, Alexis de Tocqueville:

> It is evident to all alike that a great democratic revolution is going on among us, but all do not look at it in the same light. To some it appears to be novel but accidental, and, as such, they hope it may be checked; to others it seems irresistible, because it is the most uniform, the most ancient, and the most permanent tendency that is to be found in history.[42]

42. Alexis de Tocqueville, *Democracy in America* (New York: Vintage, 1945), 1:3. Cf. p. 6.

Tocqueville goes on to say that the tendency to equality is "a providential fact," thereby endorsing a teleological view of the progress of history. But the various terms he uses do not mean the same thing. Thus, the model of revolution I have proposed does not entail a teleological view, nor does it entail a view that revolution is necessary in a deterministic sense. But the model does not clearly avoid notions of inevitability, irresistibility, and irreversibility. Indeed, the reader of Kuhn's book gets the sense that scientific revolutions have not only been inevitable in the past but are inevitable in the future.

It is clear that the model of revolution here proposed does entail some notion of the inevitability of revolutions but in a weak sense that moves away from any idea of necessity and toward the idea of irreversibility. The reason for this is rooted in the cognitive and even perceptual basis of Kuhn's analysis. Kuhn likens the shift in paradigms to a gestalt shift. Once a gestalt shift has taken place, there is no simple return to the earlier perception. Five dots perceived as five dots are forever altered in the perceiver's mind once they are seen as a pentagon or a five-pointed star. So in a revolution there is no simple return to an earlier theodicy once it has been challenged by a competitor that claims to explain anomalies. This is not to say that a shift in theodicies must proceed in any specific direction, nor that a direction once taken will not be discovered as inadequate. But the earlier perception, the earlier theodicy, cannot be embraced in cognitive innocence. For those undergoing a transformation of consciousness in a revolution, this irreversibility takes on all the characteristics of irresistibility and even of necessity, although my analytical framework makes it possible to embrace the former without the latter.

To summarize, my purpose is to provide a view of revolution that specifies the radical character of revolutions (a change in the view of evil), that holds open the possibility of innovation in revolution, and that accounts for the intentions of revolutionaries. It should be noted that this approach is not primarily etiological, although it has etiological implications. I shall proceed by looking more closely at the relationship between theodicies and evil in human society, and at the radical nature of a change in theodicies. It will also be essential to look carefully at the social and political equivalents of the discovery of anomaly in science, and at the relationship between the emergence of anomalies and the theodicy they call into question.

Theodicies and the Problem of Evil

Max Weber characterized the problem of evil as "the incongruity between destiny and merit."[43] A theodicy is the religious interpretation and even justification of such incongruity. The problems of evil and theodicy are not, however, linked simply as question and answer. Rather, they interpenetrate each other both in consciousness and in social configurations.

Evil, Suffering, and Disorder

The "incongruity between destiny and merit" has both an objective side and a subjective side. There is actual misfortune and suffering in human life, and there is interpretation of that suffering. What one merits cannot be objectively fixed, and therefore the perception of incongruity between destiny and merit depends in part on cultural norms and world views. In short, the sense of injustice presupposes in part a solution to the problem of evil.

On the objective side, Weber and others who follow him have attempted to give more specificity to the sources of human suffering, to the critical "breaking points"[44] or "anomic phenomena"[45] that threaten man's physical and psychocultural existence. Thomas O'Dea, for example, locates three contexts in which men experience evil acutely. The first of these is the uncertainty context or the experience of contingency, that is, the frustration and disappointment experienced when human ventures and careful plans run afoul of "fate" or unforeseen circumstances. The second is the impossibility context or the experience of powerlessness, that is, the experience of finitude in the face of death, illness, and natural disasters. The third is the scarcity context or the experience of deprivation that results from limited resources. These include not merely material resources but also human skills, wisdom, sexual fulfillment, leadership qualities—in short, scarcity may take both quantitative and qualitative forms.[46]

It is interesting that none of these contexts includes (at least necessarily) moral evil and disorder, that is, willful injury done by

43. Weber, "Social Psychology of World Religions," p. 275.
44. Thomas O'Dea, *The Sociology of Religion* (Englewood Cliffs, N.J.: Prentice-Hall, 1966), p. 5.
45. Berger, *Sacred Canopy*, pp. 53ff.
46. O'Dea, *Sociology of Religion*, pp. 4–7.

man to man. Thus a fourth context must be added to the list, the perversity context or the experience of willful evil by men.[47] This alerts us to an important point: any of these four contexts of evil can be understood in terms of one or more of the others; alternatively one of the contexts may be considered fundamental to the others. For example, scarcity, contingency, and powerlessness can be considered consequences of perversity, so that one possible reading of the Garden of Eden story in Genesis is that all of man's natural sufferings, including pain at childbirth, hard labor, and death, are the wages of sin. Or, man's suffering at the hands of other men can be understood as the consequence of scarcity, one possible reading of Marxism. It is also possible to view all the other contexts as derivatives of powerlessness or finitude, a plausible reading of the main poem portion of the Book of Job. A similar claim could be made for the fundamental role of contingency or fate, for example in astrological religions.

The fact that O'Dea does not include perversity as a source of disorder perhaps indicates that he considers moral wrongdoing to have a derivative character. But this point also reveals a fundamental ambiguity about the term theodicy. Theodicy proper belongs to the Judeo-Christian tradition. It means "the justification of God," the need for which can arise only in a radically monotheistic tradition that also claims that God is good. If God is good, why has he permitted suffering in the world? In the Christian tradition that question has been worked out in connection with specific understandings of evil and sin. Other religions may pose the question of suffering, but if they are not radically monotheistic, if there is no God (Buddhism), or if there is also an evil power (dualism), then suffering is easily explained, and there is no need to justify God. Furthermore, suffering itself may not necessarily be called evil (as it is not in Buddhism) or be connected with sin.

Most sociologists have followed Weber in giving the term theodicy a much broader application, referring it to the portions of religious belief-systems that attempt to construe experiences of suffering and disorder, including the suffering and disorder connected with inequality and patterns of domination. The use of "theodicy" to refer to these psychocultural phenomena has profound consequences, the

47. I owe this point and terminology to David Little.

most important being that the terms evil, suffering, and disorder become synonomous. But in fact these terms mean very different things in different religions. Furthermore, the functional-sociological appropriation of a theological category in this manner almost always has the consequence of translating moral evil into issues of disorder and suffering. The problem of theodicy from a sociological perspective is not justifying God but justifying evil and legitimating social inequities.

There are compelling theological reasons, then, for wanting to distinguish between the highly articulated theological construct known as theodicy and psychocultural attempts to legitimate suffering. But the revolutionary tradition I am discussing for the most part does not make the distinction (we may come to see why) and for present purposes I shall bracket the problem. Until the last chapter I shall follow sociological practice, with all of its ambiguity, and use the term theodicy to refer to general cultural attempts to structure disorder and suffering.

Theodicies

In spite of continual threats from the contexts of disorder, human society manages to survive. It does this not only by attending to biological necessities but also by creating a world of culture—including economic, political, and familial institutions—which serves to order the world in the face of threats. Political authority, markets, and various hierarchical arrangements like the division of labor serve to order the experiences of scarcity, contingency, powerlessness, and perversity and to distribute the burdens they impose. Yet, following Weber, these institutions are not self-legitimating, if for no other reason than that they themselves entail inequality; not everyone, for example, can have equal authority. Further, certain forms of suffering, such as illness and death, seem to lie beyond the contrivances of human institutions. The function of theodicy, and one of the functions of religion, is to give human institutions, and experiences of suffering not encompassed by these institutions, a place within a cosmic or sacred order of meaning. Religion, and especially the element of theodicy, explains human suffering and inequities by reference to a sacred order that legitimates human institutions and accounts for the "incongruity between destiny and merit." As such, theodicy helps to "maintain" the world.[48]

According to Weber there are only three rationally developed, pure types of theodicy: "the Indian doctrine of Kharma, Zoroastrian dualism, and the predestination decree of the *deus abscondidus*."[49] In *The Sociology of Religion* Weber divides the third type, characteristic of Judeo-Christianity, into two further types, one that sees the justification of the inequities of this world in a world to come, and one that sees the ultimate justification in a future transformation of this world—that is, an otherworldly and a this-worldly solution.[50] This classic division of theodical types is sufficiently well known to obviate their further explication, but several points are relevant to the issues here.

First, these "pure types" admit of considerable variation within the historical traditions that may be said to represent them. For example, the Augustinian doctrine of Original Sin, which was formulated within the predestination type, tends to transform theodicy into anthropodicy.[51] And the Christian tradition contains elements of dualism owing to the influence of Gnosticism and other dualistic religions in the Hellenistic period. Second, although a given type of theodicy fits more comfortably with certain views of the origin or cause of evil and suffering than with others, there is room, especially in the predestination type, for differing views of the source of human suffering. Third, it seems evident on the face of it that a revolution does not entail a movement from one of these pure types of theodicy to another. In fact, as often noted, revolutions have tended to take place within traditions characterized by the predestination type of theodicy, sometimes combined with elements of dualism. If, then, revolution does involve a shift in a

48. Berger, *Sacred Canopy*, chaps. 2 and 3.
49. Weber, "Social Psychology of World Religions," p. 275.
50. Weber, *Sociology of Religion*, pp. 139ff.
51. Berger, *Sacred Canopy*, pp. 77–78. More precisely, St. Augustine divided the problem of evil into two parts, natural and moral. Natural evil, including natural disasters, was understood to be a feature of finitude, one that would be seen to contribute to ultimate good if man had divine perspective. Moral evil was the consequence not of finitude but of the willful disobedience of man, rooted in pride and concupiscence.

society's view of evil, we must look for that shift within the predestination type.

Berger has developed the Weberian line of thought in a way that is most instructive on this issue. He first points out that underlying every theodicy, no matter how rationally articulated, is a fundamental attitude that is itself quite irrational, "the surrender of self to the ordering power of society. Put differently, every nomos entails a transcendence of individuality and thus, ipso facto, implies a theodicy."[52] In primitive societies, where there is little theoretical elaboration of a theodicy, one finds a "transcendence of self brought about by complete identification with the collectivity."[53] Here, the happiness and misfortune of the individual is completely merged with that of the tribe or clan. But the willingness to submit to the explanatory and justifying power of a highly articulated theodicy also involves a "pretheoretical" surrender of the self to a higher order.

This self-surrender, "a certain denial of the individual self and its needs, anxieties, and problems,"[54] is present not only in relation to the overarching system of meaning but also in the institutions and patterns of interaction that make up human culture. Only because of this self-surrender are many if not most members of a society able to accept positions of subordination and the "prevailing inequalities of power and privilege." This attitude Berger calls "masochism," using the term in a Sartrean rather than a Freudian sense, that is, to describe a psychosocial necessity rather than a pathological syndrome:

> Masochism, typically in conjunction with its complementary attitude of sadism, is a recurrent and important element of human interaction in areas ranging from sexual relations to political discipleship. Its key characteristic is the intoxication of surrender to an other—complete, self-denying, even self-destroying. Any pain or suffering inflicted by the other (who, of course, is posited as the sadistic counterpart to the masochistic self— absolutely dominating, self-affirming, and self-sufficient) serves as proof that the surrender has indeed taken place and that its

52. Ibid., p. 54.
53. Ibid., p. 60.
54. Ibid., p. 55.

intoxication is real. . . . The important point for our immediate considerations is that masochism, by its radical self-denial, provides the means by which the individual's suffering and even death can be radically transcended, to the point where the individual not only finds these experiences bearable but even welcomes them.[55]

Thus a theodicy, which must legitimate patterns of unequal power and privilege, entails an attitude of masochism on the part of the powerless and deprived and an attitude of sadism on the part of the powerful and privileged. A given theodicy may legitimate both the suffering of one group and the happiness of another—or, as Weber has suggested and Berger notes, a society may have two discrete theodicies to handle both suffering and happiness.[56]

The key to the definition of revolution I have put forward is now clearer: the transformation of consciousness that takes place in a revolution has fundamentally to do with the roles of masochism and sadism in a society. To the extent that every society has certain masochistic-sadistic configurations, a revolution involves the reconfiguration of those patterns. As such, it almost surely entails a shift in the view of the source of evil as well as a shift in society's articulated theodicy. But the fundamental change, the focus of the revolution, is in the patterns of domination and subordination. In nonrevolutionary situations many people are not only willing to accept positions of subordination together with what may appear to an external observer as an inordinate amount of suffering; they may also welcome such a position and find in it a great deal of meaning— perhaps not always the religious intoxication described by Berger but something at least closer to it than to frustration and disenchantment.

It must be made absolutely clear that masochistic subordination in no fashion creates revolutionaries. On the contrary it may be understood as preventing revolution, inasmuch as the person in such a position finds ultimate meaning in his or her suffering. That is the significance of masochistic-sadistic configurations. For similar reasons, increased suffering, or natural disasters, are not necessarily

55. Ibid., pp. 55–56.
56. Ibid., p. 59.

causes of revolution. Instead, people may find that such experiences confirm the system of meaning that legitimates their position and may even lead them to elaborate an aesthetic of suffering.[57] On the other hand, catastrophic events and increased suffering may be catalysts for a revolution if they are of a kind that cannot be made intelligible by an existing theodicy and the prevailing patterns of masochism-sadism; or if these patterns have for some reason dissolved, so that people have no social structure to give meaning to suffering or disaster. In such situations, suffering and disaster pose not merely a threat of anomie or disorder but actually create them.

In short, if we are to find the political and social equivalents of the scientific anomalies that create revolutionary crises, we must look for such anomalies in relation to the masochistic-sadistic patterns of a society, or its patterns of domination and subordination. It is these patterns that are the nexus between articulated theodicies and the actual experience of suffering—they are the genuine ordering paradigms in a society's attempt to resolve the problem of evil. A revolution may be said to involve a reconfiguration of these patterns of domination. Or, we may say that a revolution is an acute debate about who is to suffer and who is to be happy, provided we do not forget that suffering can be welcomed and that both suffering and happiness have no fixed meanings. A revolution does not necessarily entail the eradication of patterns of domination (although we must examine closely revolutions that do claim this), but it does involve at least their reconfiguration.

Excursus: The Problem of Evil and the Problem of Order

It is possible to follow Weber by approaching revolution and radical social change as a special instance of the problem of order. This is most often done in connection with the Puritan revolution in England, since Weber himself devoted so much attention to this event. For example, in spite of significant differences in their assessments of the role of Calvinism in the English revolution, both David

---

57. See the example I cited of the peasants in Brazil whose suffering confirmed their Pentecostal beliefs.

Little and Michael Walzer[58] start with an interest in the way religious ideas and institutions can underwrite or legitimate a break in the traditional social order.[59] Further, they address themselves to the relationship between Calvinist ideas and values on the one hand and the development of modern (and what Weber calls legal-rational) institutions on the other hand. Like Weber, they are interested in the process of modernization and the role religious values and ideas play in legitimating and giving shape to it, but whereas Weber concentrated on the economic order,[60] Walzer and Little test and revise the Weber thesis by applying it to political institutions.

Now it should be clear from what I have already said and from my brief references to Weber that the problem of order and the problem of evil are interconnected: they are, as it were, two sides of the same coin. Every social order and every new legitimation has an explicit or implicit theodicy, the latter being contained in a society's patterns of domination and submission. Therefore there must be similarities between the approach to revolution taken by Little and Walzer and that taken here. Nevertheless, I think the differences outweigh the similarities. The experience of evil precedes any explanation of it—Berger says it is "pretheoretical" in character, and Paul Ricoeur has called it "pre-reflexive,"[61] in spite of the fact that it is difficult to separate raw experience from interpretation in the human appropriation of the world. The assumption here is that we can speak of a primordial experience of evil, an experience of the abyss of existence, which not only requires the development of theodicies but persists

58. David Little, *Religion, Order, and Law: A Study in Pre-Revolutionary England* (New York: Harper Torchbooks, 1969); Michael Walzer, *The Revolution of the Saints* (New York: Atheneum, 1969).

59. The difference in assessments may be laid to two causes; Walzer is not theologically trained and consequently makes some remarkably arbitrary decisions about what is theological and what is not; see, for example, *Revolution of the Saints*, p. 27, where theology is said to have to do only with a concern to escape this world. This position leads to critical distortions of Calvin. Second, Little appreciates better than Walzer the institutional innovations that emerged from the inner tensions of Calvinist theology and ethics. Nevertheless, both books are highly useful.

60. Especially in *The Protestant Ethic and the Spirit of Capitalism* and *The Theory of Social and Economic Organization*.

61. Paul Ricoeur, *The Symbolism of Evil* (Boston: Beacon, 1969).

as a threat to their validity. To focus on the problem of evil rather than the problem of order is to take seriously the primordial experience of evil before considering human reflection on it, or at the institutions built upon such reflection. The latter must be done, but if our understanding of revolution is correct, an analysis of the changes it brings to the institutions of a society does not do sufficient justice to the experience of the abyss which seems so prevalent in the writings of participants in revolution.

The choice of the problem of evil as the key to understanding revolution is based on the inner demands of revolutionary phenomena. If revolution is an innovative response to the problem of evil, and if the problem of evil is, as Berger suggests, antecedent to social legitimations, then the process of revolution resembles the actual or imagined emergence of human association itself—it is not simply the transition from one form of social order to another. Revolution is, of course, a transition from one form of social order to another, but it has features that distinguish it from other forms of social transition, features that we at least imagine to have been present at the beginning of human association. It is for this reason that the language of apocalypticism has been so often associated with revolution. In the apocalyptic world view we do not merely evolve from one order to another; rather, the old order is torn asunder, there is a "new heaven and a new earth," there is divine intervention in the affairs of men. Apocalyptic language tears our attention away from the possibilities for transforming the world through labor and moral diligence and directs our attention instead to the necessity of a new creation, which we are made to see as a repetition of the original creation of social order. Apart from the ultimate validity of this point of view, the focus on the problem of evil is intended to keep us sensitive to this dimension of the revolutionary experience.

REVOLUTION AND ETHICS

It is essential that we understand the nature of the relationship between order and the break that is called revolution, and that we understand the moral concerns involved when order becomes an issue for those enmeshed in the anomic character of revolution. I shall begin with a preliminary account of the difficulties posed for moral reflection by the radical nature of revolutionary change.

In the introduction I suggested that revolution could not be justified in the usual sense of what it means to justify an act. The difficulties in justifying revolution can be demonstrated by, first, showing that for those who are revolutionaries, there is no neutral ground for adjudicating the justness of a revolution; second, extending this argument by comparing revolution to civil disobedience and war; and third, indicating the moral dilemmas for those who may want to stand outside the revolutionary fray.

The Absence of Neutral Ground

The usual response to the question of how an act can be justified involves the establishment of rules or principles of justification that can be agreed upon by the persons involved. But the rules or principles of justification operating in any social group are called into question the moment the theodicy that underlies the social structure is challenged. This of course is obvious if one raises only the legal question: all revolutions are by definition illegal when viewed from the perspective of the existing order. Kramnick and Schrecker are surely correct in their view that a revolution is a change in the conditions of legality, just as a new scientific paradigm is illegitimate from the standpoint of the ruling paradigm.

The question is whether one can appeal to a higher moral order that stands in judgment over the legal order. Historically this is what many revolutionaries have often done, appealing to natural law, or to the Word of God (this appeal may be made in more than one way), or to some apocalyptic vision demanding the eradication of evil. But the fact that such appeals are made does not necessarily help us, since similar appeals are made for any political act, whether revolutionary, liberal, conservative, or reactionary. The problem runs deeper than the inconvenience of the fact that appeals to the divine span the political spectrum—we could probably sort out the legitimacy of these appeals with reference to some norm. But does such a norm exist? If the paradigm I have suggested for revolution is accurate, the validity of a religious or moral norm is called into question whenever a theodicy is called into question, which implies that revolutions are not merely political events but are religious in character. What is threatened in a revolution is not just a political structure but the theodicy underpinning that structure. It is not by accident that Marx claims that the criticism of religion is the beginning of all criticism and that revolutions have so often been accompanied by powerful protests against all divine order—what Camus has called "metaphysical rebellion."[62] Revolutions are religious events. This is true of revolutions that claim to be antireligious and of those that go under a religious banner. In the case of the former the emergence of a new theodicy may be latent rather than manifest, while in the latter case the theodicy is almost surely manifest. But each new theodicy is unalterably opposed to the sacral order of the preceding political regime and therefore refuses to accept any appeal to a "higher order" that could be construed as related to that regime.

Now it is true that a revolutionary may attempt to justify his action by appealing to an earlier tradition that he considers normative, or by trying to return to a purer or truer interpretation of this tradition. But if his opponents share the same tradition in name, we may assume that their interpretation of it is so radically different from the revolutionaries' interpretation that no adjudication is possible: that is why there is a revolution. Hence, we shall see that millenarian revolutionaries frequently share Christian beliefs with their opponents but on almost every theological point make directly opposite application of these beliefs. Since a theodicy is not merely a belief-structure but includes the psychocultural patterns of domination in a society, those who occupy different positions may be led to make very different interpretations of the same tradition.

Revolution poses a kind of moral dilemma that undercuts the usual starting points for developing a political ethic. For example, a Christian political ethic frequently starts with a theology of the state, utilizing Biblical passages, perhaps a natural law tradition, a doctrine of the "orders of creation," and the like. But a theodicy as I have defined it may be understood to underlie all of these, and they fall, or are perceived to fall, with the theodicy. It is in this sense that revolutions are truly primitive social phenomena—I have suggested that they resemble the real or imagined emergence of human association itself, and that the language used by revolutionaries is often the language of "new creation" or its secular equivalents. An appeal to orders of creation or to natural law will not be persuasive to those who believe that creation and nature are about to be

_____

62. Albert Camus, _The Rebel_ (New York: Vintage, 1958), chap. 11.

transformed radically. This is not to say that we must ultimately bow to revolutionary claims, but they must be taken seriously if an appropriate response is to be made.

The difficulty of justifying revolution may be made clearer by comparing it to the justification of two other comparatively "primitive" social actions: civil disobedience and war. Both share features with revolution, but both can be justified in a way that revolution cannot.

Revolution, Civil Disobedience, and War

Civil disobedience is a phrase that has been used to cover a broad spectrum of illegal acts committed as a form of protest against a legal system or part of it. But as James Childress has shown, civil disobedience is an identifiable mode of political resistance different in kind from political protest, rioting, or revolution.[63] He defines civil disobedience as "a public, non-violent, submissive violation of law as a form of protest."[64] This definition of civil disobedience is "reformative," that is, it assumes that the intention is not to dismantle the entire legal structure but to reform it from within. In the terms I used earlier, civil disobedience is not normally aimed at changing the principles of legality or the constitutive norms of legitimacy— although some acts of civil disobedience may imply that.[65]

Childress is fundamentally interested in the logic of justification for civil disobedience in the context of a relatively just and democratic political order (although he certainly does not intend his analysis to be inapplicable to other political situations), and therefore he takes the appropriate starting point for analysis to be "a theory of political obedience, its basis and limits."[66] He finds the structure for

63. James Childress, *Civil Disobedience and Political Obligation* (New Haven: Yale, 1971). See especially pp. 1–21.

64. Ibid., p. 11.

65. Ibid., pp. 17–21. Childress cites the Schrecker article I have discussed and notes that some forms of civil disobedience are revolutionary. He therefore states that in terms of "the logic of justification" the two cases "are not totally unrelated" (pp. 20–21). But he seems to have in mind here revolution in the first sense of my "threshold distinction" rather than revolution as a fundamental transformation of consciousness.

66. Ibid., p. 42.

this theory in two sources: a Christian theology of the state and independent theories of political obligation, including especially the notion of "fair play" as developed by John Rawls and others.[67] Now, both of these sources are independent of the political structure itself; and they are independent of the point of view of the person contemplating civil disobedience. That is, each represents a court of appeal which can stand in judgment over both a political system and a person contemplating action in disobedience to the system. They provide, as it were, rules of the game, limiting what can be done. For example, Childress notes that fairness is a "fundamental moral notion" and suggests that it is a constitutive principle of political morality and especially of a democratic society, although its content may vary in different cultures and in different times and places. Quoting David Lyons, he points out that "one who acts unfairly is to that extent not a responsible human being, not a responsible member of society, not a social creature."[68]

Childress's discussion of the theory of political obligation and the notion of fair play places limits on acts of civil disobedience; for example, the person who resists in this mode must be willing to submit to the penalty of the law he disobeys (although the form of this submission may vary according to circumstances). This willing submission not only shows a respect for the law as a whole, it also recognizes that both the law being resisted and the act of resistance must come under the judgment of a higher moral order and the formal principle of fairness; and it shows a willingness to permit adjudication of the rightness of either the law or the act by a process that includes public opinion, the courts, the legislature, and so on. In other words, what limits the act of civil disobedience is the assumption that there is a moral order or a moral community that transcends both the law in question and the act of disobedience itself.

The revolutionary, in contrast, makes no such assumption about the society in which he lives, and the first principle to fall in a revolution is almost always the duty of fair play—witness the acts of

---

67. See ibid., pp. 21–27 and 123–49. In general, however, the two sources are discussed in chapters 2 and 3, respectively.

68. Ibid., p. 129; David Lyons, *Forms and Limits of Utilitarianism* (Oxford: Clarendon, 1965), p. 177.

terrorism that almost inevitably accompany political revolution. This is not owing to any peculiar perversity on the part of the revolutionary (although revolutions contain at least their share of perverse minds) but to the fact that the revolutionary, rightly or wrongly, perceives no moral community to which he can appeal, or at least no moral community that includes the enemy. If a theodicy has lost its plausibility for the revolutionary, so has the entire structure of morality based upon that theodicy. The revolutionary then will always reject any appeal to fairness (or morality in general) in somewhat the fashion that Marx's proletariat dismisses law, morality, and religion as "so many bourgeois prejudices."[69] A theodicy justifies the happiness of the powerful and the suffering of the powerless. A revolution is not about the relative justness of a given law or given laws—it is about the question of who will dominate and who will be dominated, or it aims at the end of domination. These questions do not permit adjudication, since they refer to the very terms on which moral adjudication is based.

This point is made abundantly manifest in the literature on revolution. The one thing a revolutionary cannot tolerate is compromise or adjudication by a third party (we shall see this especially in Marx's utilization of Hegel's master-slave analysis and in Frantz Fanon's discussion of the colonial situation). Both compromise and third-party adjudication imply residual confidence in the existing theodicy, and the revolutionary loses his case merely by submitting to such a process. This is not to pronounce judgment on the rightness of revolutionary action or the correctness of the revolutionary's perception of the moral situation; I am only trying to show the difficulty of determining a logic of justification for revolution when it is this very logic that a revolution calls into question.

The issues may be further illuminated by comparing revolution with war—an activity that seems to share with revolution the characteristic of being socially primitive. Like revolution and unlike civil disobedience, a war seems on the face of it to be a complete breakdown of human association between the warring parties, a refusal to permit either adjudication or compromise. Wars are said to occur

69. Karl Marx, "The Communist Manifesto," in Marx and Engels, *Basic Writings on Politics and Philosophy*, ed. Lewis S. Feuer (Garden City, N.Y.: Doubleday Anchor, 1959), p. 18.

when political processes and moral expectations have failed. But is this the case? Theologians have been able to articulate a careful set of criteria for the "just war," and most nations subscribe to some international agreements limiting the means of warfare. In both cases there is an assumption of an overriding moral order which applies to all of the parties involved.

It is a mistake to assume that international agreements limiting the means of war are the consequence solely of the threat of global destruction residing in modern weaponry. They issue rather from a fundamental fact of warfare recognized by most heads of state: most wars are fought over finite issues that are subservient to other goals and are therefore to some extent negotiable. The point of waging war is to force the opponent to see the necessity of negotiating. When Clausewitz said that war is the last resort of foreign policy, he was also saying that there is an overriding policy for which war is only a means. (These statements are not, of course, true of all wars. Racial wars in particular share characteristics with revolution). Wars so conceived are waged only insofar as the cost can be borne—and negotiation is frequently perceived as the goal of war. In this sense, wars do resemble a game, and rules, including notions of fairness (even if primitive), do apply.[70] Or, to use the jargon of game theorists, most wars are not zero-sum games.

In contrast, revolutionary war does resemble a zero-sum game: it is either win or lose. The object of the revolutionary is not to gain parity with the enemy but to replace him. To fail to replace him is not a finite loss but a total loss, since a compromise situation still leaves him with the original theodicy, the structure that was for him disorienting and intolerable. And there are no rules of the game that he can share with the enemy.

A look at the Christian "just war" criteria is helpful in this connection. There have been few careful applications of these criteria to revolution,[71] probably because they do not work well. They have

70. The extent to which the rules of the game can be elevated almost to an aesthetic level even in war has been beautifully explored by Jean Renoir in his great movie, *Grand Illusion*. Another of his movies exploring similar social rituals, but not in war, is entitled *The Rules of the Game*. The fact that Renoir considers such rules an illusion does not undercut the point that they are perceived to exist.

71. Paul Ramsey, in *War and the Christian Conscience* (Durham, N.C.: Duke

been given various formulations, but all of the formulations assign criteria to three categories: cause, conduct, and ends. I shall deal with each in turn. (It should be noted at the outset that all these criteria are necessarily imprecise, some much more than others. The imprecision usually arises in the area of what is to be allowed rather than of what is proscribed—that is, while the criteria rule out certain kinds of war activity, they may be imprecise in designating what is permitted. In any case, I hope to show that when the criteria are applied to revolution, their lack of precision is not merely intensified but is of a different order.)

JUST CAUSE

To satisfy the requirements of this category, a war is considered just only if it is defensive in character, that is, if it is waged as a last resort, that is, after all peaceful means to end the dispute have been exhausted; and if it is waged by legitimate authority.

In wars it is probably possible to distinguish between accidental or temporary injury on the one hand and deliberate or systematic injury on the other. Can similar judgments be made in a revolutionary situation? An example illustrates the difficulties: the hierarchical structure of medieval feudalism may appear unjust by twentieth-century standards, and some might contend that feudalism was a systematic injury done by the haves to the have-nots. Yet from within the feudal structure, it is unlikely that those either on the top or bottom conceived of the domination as a systematic injury. Traditional societies legitimate their domination in a variety of ways. In addition, the medieval structures were never static, and the increased role of merchants in the thirteenth and fourteenth centuries, together with the monetization of society, not only transformed the feudal bond from one of personal loyalty to a monetary contract; it also led to changes in perception, so that the attempts by feudal lords to maintain their domination came more and more to be seen as acts of willful injury.

As we shall see, it is this pattern of transformation of internal

University Press, 1961), chap. 6, discusses the historical application of just war criteria to political resistance to tyranny and to the emergence of democracy. See also Richard J. Neuhaus, "The Thorough Revolutionary," in Peter Berger and Richard Neuhaus, eds., *Movement and Revolution* (Garden City, N.Y.: Doubleday Anchor, 1970).

relations that Marxists use to characterize the revolutionary situation. And while it is possible that historically some wars have been caused by analogous changes of relations, it is nevertheless the case that conflicts between established political entities (such as nation-states) permit an analysis of injury and defensiveness in a way that the transformation of relations between social classes does not. In part this is because nations have historically and geographically established identities which make violation of a people or a territory much more visible. As a minimum we can say that just war criteria are modeled on conflicts between established political entities rather than the dynamic transformation of class identities and relations.[72]

Closely connected to the "visibility" of nations (in contrast to social classes or other revolutionary groups) is the question of legitimacy. In wars between nations the criterion of legitimacy is meant to rule out a war waged by a government without the consent of the people and to rule out all mercenary adventures. In revolutionary wars the question of legitimacy is most thorny. On technical legal grounds every revolution is illegitimate, so that any claim to legitimacy by a revolutionary group must rest on other ground. But what should it be? The consent of the people? An appeal to consent would make almost any revolution unjust because of several factors. If consent is understood in terms of numbers, historically very few, if any, revolutions have been waged by a majority against a minority. Rather, a minority has carried out the revolution, utilizing mass and perhaps majority dissatisfaction at key points but not actually claiming majority consent. If consent is understood to be implicit rather than actual, the question is simply begged, for who is to decide what implicit consent consists of? Most revolutions have taken place in countries where the vast majority of the people are politically unsophisticated and could not give political assent except in terms of immediate needs such as physical safety and food. Therefore the "battle for the hearts and minds of the people" is almost always fought on the level of physical necessity. This does not mean that political education does not take place, but when it does, it amounts

72. The Marxist claims, of course, that wars among nations are best understood by analogy to the revolutionary situation, that they are in fact extensions of class conflict and shifting class identities. It is not essential to deal with that contention here. We need only establish that traditional just war criteria do not reflect the dynamics of historical class conflict.

to "spiritual meddling"—that is, to fundamental education about the origin of and solution to the problem of evil, much in the same way that missionaries meddle spiritually when they take Christianity (or another religion) to a new culture.[73] The best the revolutionary can do is to talk about a *potential* legitimacy, the proof of which comes only in the winning.

JUST CONDUCT

Under the category of conduct, a war is considered just only if the means used are just and if the principle of proportionality is observed. In a war between armies, the principle of just means has usually been interpreted to require noncombatant immunity: you aim your guns and bombs only at the opposing soldiers and military hardware, never at civilians. In spite of the difficulty of observing this principle within the context of modern weaponry, the principle is still meaningful: it occasioned some first-rate moral writing on antipersonnel weapons, saturation bombing, and the like in Vietnam. But in revolutions the principle is much harder to apply and uphold. For one thing, the injury being defended against is not likely to be an invasion of borders by weapon-bearing soldiers. If the enemy is an economic structure, against what do you strike? It is true, of course, that troops may eventually be brought into play, but the armed forces themselves do not adequately represent the enemy threat in a revolutionary situation. The battle is in large part psychological and therefore the tactics of terrorism can be (but are not necessarily) indispensable. And it may be that in order for the revolution to succeed, the government must be provoked into sending the troops out.

More important, however, is the principle of proportionality: the damage done in waging the war must not be greater than the damage that would have been suffered if the injury had not been defended.

73. The phrase "spiritual meddling" may sound pejorative. I use it as a consequence of having discovered in discussions with students that it opens them to see connections they would otherwise miss. Many students politically left of center find missionary movements to be abhorrent because missionaries seem to assume they know more about the ultimate interests of, say, an African than the African himself knows. But this is not different in kind from the claim of Russia and Cuba to know the best interests of Angola and Zaire, or even of liberal students to know the best interests of South Africa.

This has always been the most imprecise of the just war criteria: the morass created by the balancing and weighing that had to be done to determine proportionality in Southeast Asia is an excellent test case. But imprecision becomes impossibility in revolutions, for what is at stake (if my model is correct) is not territorial rights, or trading routes, but the intelligibility of the world. It is not a question of weighing relative benefits and relative deprivations but of one world view against another. I suspect that the willingness to die in a war and the willingness to die in a revolution are fundamentally different: in war death is partly a manner of honor, partly patriotism, and always a matter of self-sacrifice for the benefit of one's country or social group. In a revolution one's death is not a matter of duty but a desperate act for an intelligible world—and the community one dies for is not an experienced reality of the past but a hope that emerges from the very act of revolution itself. The risks are therefore tremendous, because in weighing the benefits to come from revolution it is not possible to look at the land which has given the soldier life and which he is now defending: instead the revolutionary again must look to a potential community, to something he hopes for but has not so far experienced. Yet paradoxically the risk is not great, because if he does not die he has no land at all—he has everything to gain and nothing to lose.

JUST ENDS

To satisfy the requirements of this third category, a war is considered just only if it aims to establish a more just order and if there is a reasonable hope of success. The "more just order" criterion rules out the intention to punish the enemy and places on the defensive war maker the obligation to pursue more than mere victory: in the aftermath of bloodshed there must be reconstruction. But there must also be a reasonable probability that victory will lead to reconstruction—otherwise the bloodshed has not been worth it. Now it would be most helpful if those contemplating war could approach this criterion simply as a counsel of prudence. Unfortunately most wars are waged not under the banner of prudence but under the banner of divine providence, or manifest destiny, or the logic of history. But if prudence in judging one's chances in war is difficult, it is even more difficult to make similar judgments about revolutionary success. Alexis de Tocqueville and Hannah Arendt, among others, have pointed to the remarkable sense of inevitability that pervades every revolutionary movement.[74] Like the scientist who knows that his newly discovered paradigm will inevitably win the day (the old is simply wrong and once unmasked it will go down to defeat), the revolutionary knows that the old order will not hold. His guarantee of success lies not in superior military might or strategy but in the incapacity of the old paradigm, the ancien régime, to maintain its dominion over the world.

If any of this seems overstated, I think the error is in the direction of suggesting that wars admit of "just war" analysis more easily than they in fact do. There are wars that do resemble revolutions in critical respects; I suggested that racial wars are among them. But it can be argued that the just war criteria are designed precisely to prevent wars from becoming like revolutions—and that revolutions do indeed represent the kind of break in moral communities that prevents just war analysis. A logic of justification assumes the possibility that the participants in a moral conflict can agree upon some ground rules or some procedure for adjudicating these differences. A revolution is waged in my view because such ground rules cannot be agreed upon, and war becomes like a revolution when one of the participants refuses to recognize any such ground rules. If the United States had decided to destroy Vietnam no matter what the Vietnamese did, if our position there had been totally nonnegotiable, the war would have been by definition unjust. Similarly, to the extent that there is nothing negotiable in a revolution, a revolution is always unjust.

If the logic of revolutionary change supplies no grounds for its own justification, we must recognize that actual revolutions are much more complex than the rather neat radical shift I have described. A revolution in a Third World nation may involve a battle against both imperialism and traditional modes of social organization or residual tribalism; and the revolution may be waged by a combination of Marxists, elite nationalists, anarchists, and so on. This may seem compelling reason to try to establish grounds for moral evaluation of revolution from outside the process, taking into account the motivations, means, and goals of the various parties in order to choose among them. Such an attempt may seem especially attractive

74. Alexis de Tocqueville, *Democracy in America,* 1:6, and Hannah Arendt, *On Revolution* (New York: Viking, 1965), p. 41.

to Christians who believe that they belong to a community that transcends all political communities and conflicts.

In fact, I shall try to show that even those who have claimed to be revolutionaries sometimes adopt a stance that places them outside the revolutionary dialectic between oppressor and oppressed, into the role of directors or adjudicators of the process. If one has such a position, then something like the just war principles may seem useful both in evaluating the actions of revolutionaries and their oppressors, as well as in guiding one's own involvement. But it must be carefully marked that in this case the person outside the process *intervenes* in that process and uses moral principles not to decide whether he has a right to defend himself against oppression (as just war criteria might be used by a nation that has been attacked) but to evaluate others who are in such a position or to decide whether to intervene on their behalf.

Of course, most moral principles can be used to evaluate both one's own acts and the acts of others. But the logic of revolutionary change suggests that those undergoing revolutionary transformation and those observing from without are not at all comparable. And those in the revolutionary tradition itself, including recently many Christians, claim not only that the external observer of necessity misconceives what happens in revolution but also that there is no such thing as a neutral vantage point. This lies behind Hegel's critique of Kant and behind all dialectical criticisms of moral thought that attempts to establish universal or ideal principles for human conduct. I want to take this claim seriously but not uncritically in analysis of the revolutionary tradition.

If the criteria of a just war do not apply well to revolutions, they nevertheless serve admirably for constructing an analysis of revolution itself, by focusing attention on cause, means (or conduct), and ends, elements that enter into any human act.

3

Revolutionary Dualism

The fact is that soon we shall have had seven years of
crimes in Algeria and there has not yet been a single
Frenchman indicted before a French court of justice for
the murder of an Algerian. In Indo-China, in Madagascar,
or in the colonies the native has always known that he
need expect nothing from the other side. The settler's
work is to make even dreams of liberty impossible for
the native. The native's work is to imagine all possible
methods for destroying the settler. On the logical plane,
the Manicheism of the settler produces a Manicheism of
the native. To the theory of the "absolute evil of the
native" the theory of the "absolute evil of the settler"
replies.

Frantz Fanon

In his chapter on violence in *The Wretched of the Earth*, Frantz
Fanon frequently uses the term "Manichaean" to describe the colonial world.[1] This Manichaeism is an artifact of the settler's presence,
but its effect on the native's psychic structure is devastating, and it is
what makes violent revolution a necessity from the native's point of
view. The importance of Fanon's choice of words cannot be over-
stressed: he is a psychiatrist working in a partial Marxist framework,
a secular man engaged in clinical description and analysis, yet at the
most critical juncture of his analysis of the psychosocial structure of
colonialism he resorts to religious symbolism. Further, the religious
symbolism he finds most fruitful and powerful is one of the oldest
forms of dualism in the Western world. In this chapter I shall explore
the relationship between religious dualism and revolution by examining several key examples of dualistic revolutionary thinking and the
moral issues posed by dualistic revolutionary movements.

1. Frantz Fanon, *The Wretched of the Earth* (New York: Grove Press,
1968), pp. 35–106. The quote at the head of the chapter is on pp. 92–93.

A dualism is any philosophical or religious position that divides the world into two irreducible categories. Religious and moral dualism makes that division in terms of the two irreconcilable powers of good and evil. In fact, there have been few absolute dualisms, at least in Western religious experience. Even Zoroastrian dualism, which usually serves as the historical example closest to the pure type, posits an ultimate victory for the power of good (although the victory is not complete in the sense that not everything is redeemed). But in general, religious dualism exacerbates the conflict between good and evil to the point that, for man, the ultimate victory is problematic. The kind of uncertainty varies so that, for example, in Christian dualism what is of special interest is the extent of the ultimate victory of God over the power of evil. Frequently, the power of evil is only provisional, that is, it characterizes a period of history rather than being a defining characteristic of the cosmos as a whole.

The revolutionary dualisms discussed here are of a provisional kind. What makes them revolutionary is precisely the conviction that evil can be overcome. They are genuinely dualistic in that the ultimate victory is problematic for some portion of history and in that good and evil are discontinuous, that is, admitting of no translation from one to the other. What is excluded by this last point is any notion that evil is a privation of good or ontologically dependent upon the good for its existence (such as one finds in the classical Augustinian formulation of good and evil). It follows that good and evil are powers external to man, rooted in the structure of the cosmos or history. For this reason, the solution to the problem of evil, the victory of the good, is often seen as deliverance or salvation, the consequence of divine intervention. Men may participate in the transformation, they may further the revolution, but victory is accomplished apocalyptically. There is a radical discontinuity between the structures and processes of the old world and those of the new.

We can assume that the moral dilemmas posed by revolutionary dualism are not acute for those who are strongly committed to the faith. The "virtue" (perhaps I should say "advantage") of dualism is its simplicity: to the extent that evil can be isolated and identified, there can be no moral compunction about its total eradication, by violence or any other means. I once asked a theologian friend of mine why he was so fond of American Western movies. He replied that if he could just once stand face to face with pure evil and by pulling a trigger eradicate it, he would be profoundly happy. Serious moral questions arise only out of moral ambiguity, and we shall find that the dualists on the whole live unambiguous lives, or at least try to. But I cannot leave the dualists with that observation for at least two reasons. For one, I have already suggested that almost every revolution has some dualistic characteristics, which necessitates some understanding of the dualistic syndrome. Second, the fact that no serious moral dilemmas confront the adherents of dualistic beliefs does not mean that dualism cannot be ethically instructive. In fact, it is one of my underlying hypotheses that dualistic revolutionism, by its stark simplicity, throws into sharp relief issues that must be faced by any adequate moral analysis of revolution.

The revolutionaries I have chosen to consider, the millenarians and Frantz Fanon, are by no means alike. Millenarianism is a religious belief-system that has produced or been closely associated with countless revolutionary movements throughout history.[2] It is considered by many scholars to be present in some form in every genuinely revolutionary movement, including Marxism. Its unique relationship to the Judeo-Christian tradition makes it of special interest to the Christian ethicist, and its close links with the Christian doctrine of eschatology makes it mandatory as background for those whose theology centers on eschatology.

Frantz Fanon was for some years the intellectual father of young revolutionaries in Europe and America. Moreover, he addresses two key issues not fully addressed by Marx and his followers: the impact

2. In choosing to write about millenarians as a group, I have had to deviate from the rule I have otherwise observed of depending on primary sources. Here I will rely almost entirely on secondary sources, partly because the widespread character of millenarianism makes it desirable to utilize the considerable body of secondary literature available, and partly because millenarians have not, on the whole, produced theoreticians, although to some extent the writers of the "radical Reformation" like Thomas Müntzer are an exception to this generalization. Some scholars include aspects of the Puritan revolution in the seventeenth century in the millenarian category. Cf. Guenter Lewy, *Religion and Revolution* (New York: Oxford, 1974), chap. 6. Although millenarian ideas were clearly present in the Puritan revolution, a full understanding of its capacity for organization (a virtue not found in most millenarian revolutions) requires strict attention to the nonmillenarian elements in the theology of Calvinism. Lewy ignores this point.

of colonialism on revolutionary movements and the role of race in revolutionary consciousness. On both issues he claims to go beyond Marx. I discuss Fanon before Marx because I am more interested in his unique contribution to the problem of evil in revolution than in the use he has made of Marxist thought.

Fanon's modification of Marx emerged from his psychological observation and analysis of colonial and racial conflict. This is of course not surprising, since he was a psychiatrist, but it is also the case that dualistic revolutions lend themselves to psychosocial analysis. Put another way, the etiology of dualistic revolutions almost always becomes the psychology or social psychology of revolution. This is not to say that writers on the subject show no concern for economic and other causes, but even contemporary Marxist scholars make an issue of the millenarian cast of mind. This emphasis on social psychology has both strengths and weaknesses. It is helpful in ethical analysis because it focuses sharply on the moral outlook of the revolutionaries, but it also runs the risk of interpreting millenarianism pathologically—and the fact that millenarians rarely, if ever, succeed in their pursuits increases this risk. Furthermore, because so much of the writing in this area is etiological, it easily becomes reductionist.

It may in the last analysis be impossible to avoid reductionism in discussing revolutionary dualists but it is possible to concentrate on the ways in which their claims illuminate revolution in general. The main part of this chapter will explore the moral issues raised by millenarian revolts and by Frantz Fanon under the three categories of cause, conduct, and ends, concluding with a critique of dualistic violence.

THE MILLENARIAN REVOLUTION

The hope for a terrestrial age of justice and peace, inaugurated by a divine act through the agency of a messianic figure which would forever destroy the forces of evil and create equality, abundance, and harmony, has motivated men to violent revolution from the time of the Maccabean revolt to the twentieth century, in places as diverse as Palestine, China, Melanesia, Africa, and southern Italy. This apparent cultural diversity is deceptive, however; there is almost unanimous agreement among scholars of all persuasions that millenarian revolutions take place only among groups that have been touched directly or indirectly by the apocalyptic tradition of Judeo-Christianity.[3]

The characteristic features of Judeo-Christian apocalyptic beliefs are well known: as expressed in the Revelation of John, many early Christians believed that Christ in his Second Coming (the Parousia) would establish a one-thousand-year period of justice and peace before the Last Judgment. This messianic kingdom would take in all those who believe in Christ, including the resurrected apostles and saints. But before the millennium these same believers and saints would suffer at the hands of the forces of evil, culminating in the apparent triumph of evil in the person of the Antichrist, a figure who would claim to rule in God's name but would in fact rule as the apostle of Satan. It is this kingdom of evil that is destroyed by Christ in his Second Coming, and the

3. See, e.g., Yonina Talmon, "Pursuit of the Millennium," in Barry McLaughlin, ed., *Studies in Social Movements* (New York: Free Press, 1969), pp. 400–27, especially p. 416. Cf. E. J. Hobsbawn, *Primitive Rebels* (New York: Norton, 1959), p. 57. Lewy, *Religion and Revolution*, is ambivalent on this point. On p. 257 he states, "Revolutionary millenarianism, we can conclude, can be motivated by a great variety of messianic beliefs. Judaic-Christian messianism is undoubtedly the most widespread of these beliefs, but it is not the only one. . . . Certain religious belief systems more than others are conducive to the emergence of messianic ideas, but sometimes millenarian movements can develop even in the framework of a cyclical, world-renouncing cosmology." Lewy's empirical evidence does not support this general claim. All the millenarian "revolts" he reports on, except two, are directly influenced by the Judeo-Christian tradition. Of the two exceptions, one is Islamic and therefore more closely related to Judeo-Christian ideas than Lewy shows. The other exception is presented in chapter 3, "Heterodoxy and Rebellion in Traditional China," where (pp. 61–62) he *loosens* the definition of millenarian to include any belief-system that strives after "an age of eternal bliss," although he concedes that "Chinese rebels shared with their antagonists basic cosmological and political assumptions such as the belief in Heaven as a spiritual force that conferred upon the virtuous the mandate to rule. The eyes of the rebels were fixed upon the past, and as soon as they triumphed they set about restoring and continuing the traditional socio-political order" (pp. 66–67). Since Lewy's general statement about finding revolutionary millenarianism outside Judeo-Christianity is based on this one Chinese example, further comment is hardly needed on this muddied thinking, except to note that the general comment already quoted (p. 257) begins talking about "revolutionary millenarianism" and ends up talking about "messianic ideas" as if they were the same thing.

suffering of Christians is vindicated as they become first while the first become last.

These apocalyptic beliefs have undergone various transformations throughout history and as a result of their importation into non-European settings, but wherever they take hold and whatever superficial transformations may occur, certain key features remain. Abstractly stated, millenarian beliefs have a linear view of time and history: history moves towards a final end or future state; change is not gradual but the outcome of abrupt, decisive events; the present time as well as the immediate past is totally corrupt—in fact, the present represents the most remarkable concentration of evil and suffering in history; evil is almost always clearly and visibly concentrated in a particular ruler (the Antichrist), a particular group (the hordes of Antichrist), or a social institution; the overcoming of evil is a decisive historical event, unique, radical, and irrevocable—the power of evil is totally eradicated; the critical event is usually occasioned by a messianic figure; the new kingdom is collective, with an emphasis on equality and justice—and those who suffer in the present are the chosen of the future.[4]

It is not at all difficult to see why millenarian beliefs have held such a powerful fascination for students of revolutionary movements. I have already used the millenarian example to explicate and support a view of revolution derived first from an analysis of scientific revolutions, and the parallels are obvious. Yet the study of revolutionary millenarians can yield very different results, depending on one's purpose. While my interest is in the moral problems posed by millenarian revolutionaries, Norman Cohn, whose work has been cited several times, focuses on the psychological features of millenarians and concludes that the revolutionary movements are outlets for "collective paranoid fantasy." E. J. Hobsbawm, a Marxist historian, views such beliefs as fairly reasonable responses to almost intolerable social conditions and as providing "a connecting link between prepolitical and political movements."[5] Ernst Bloch, a Marxist of a dif-

4. I have used a variety of sources in compiling this list of millenarian features. Cf. especially Hobsbawm, *Primitive Rebels*, pp. 57–65; Cohn, *Pursuit of the Millennium*, pp. 15–18 and passim; Talmon, "Pursuit of the Millennium," pp. 406–13.

5. These characterizations are from Talmon, "Pursuit of the Millennium," pp. 417–21.

ferent color, finds in millennial dreams the origin of Marxist hope,[6] whereas critics can dismiss Marxism as a heretical offspring of Christian eschatology.

The Problem of Cause: Unmasking the Beast of the Apocalypse

Millenarian ideas take root only in deprived groups. But the term "deprivation" is relative and by itself can neither explain these revolutionary movements nor give us an understanding of the human beings involved. Norman Cohn fastens on the disorientation of certain groups of poor as the key to their susceptibility to millenarian beliefs, the disorientation that followed the movement of peasants to the new industrial urban centers in medieval Europe.[7] E. J. Hobsbawm draws similar conclusions from the "cataclysmic consequences" of the introduction of "capitalist legal and social relationships" into traditional and agrarian societies.[8] Others have noted the role of contingencies and disasters—plagues, fires, droughts, wars, economic depressions—as catalysts of the disorientation.[9] But whatever the causes the effect is clear: cultural disintegration.

Cultural disintegration can be given a specific meaning: it entails the loss of social customs and rituals which give structure to time and the critical events of life, such as birth, puberty, and death. It means the destruction of what Cohn calls the "network of social relationships" which assure "a certain material security but also— which is even more relevant—a certain sense of security, a basic assurance which neither constant poverty nor occasional peril could destroy."[10] It creates social isolation by destroying cohesive primary groups. It undercuts the traditional goals and values of a society, the norms and ends that permit self-definition and choice of vocation (to the extent that "choice" can be said to exist in such societies).

6. This theme is sounded in Bloch's three-volume *Das Prinzip Hoffnung* (Frankfurt: Suhrkamp Verlag, 1959). See also his earlier *Geist der Utopie* (Frankfurt: 1964; Munich: Duncker & Humbolt, 1918).

7. See the discussion of Cohn's thesis in chapter 2.

8. Hobsbawm, *Primitive Rebels*, pp. 80 and 96.

9. Cf. Talmon, "Pursuit of the Millennium," p. 413; Hobsbawm, p. 96; and Michael Barkun, *Diaster and the Millennium* (New Haven: Yale University Press, 1974), passim.

10. Cohn, *Pursuit of the Millennium*, p. 56.

According to Yonina Talmon, "Much of the deep dissatisfaction stems from incongruities and difficulties in the realm of *regulation of ends*" as a consequence of competing cultural systems. The encounter with a new system of values implies the inferiority of the old, especially when the new system is connected with a "more prestigious upper class or . . . a colonial ruling class. This causes much self-doubt and even self-hatred."[11]

This last point is absolutely central to understanding millennial beliefs. The actual cause of suffering and disorientation in various societies may be manifold: in Cohn's medieval studies it is nascent industrialism and urbanization; in Hobsbawm's studies of nineteenth and twentieth-century millenarian movements in Andalusia and Sicily it is the growth of capitalism; with the cargo cults in Melanesia it was the European colonialists and missionaries (who arrived, with their goods, in cargo ships). But the perceived cause is the inferiority of the local or indigenous culture and people. Whatever the traditional theodicy of a suffering and disoriented people may have been, suffering caused by the intrusion of an alien system of values and beliefs reduces it to one in which the intruding culture is deemed superior and the local culture inferior. When wealthy European traders went to the South Pacific, they were accompanied by fundamentalist missionaries who preached a message that clearly asserted the superiority of the Europeans. Jean Guiart reports that the missionaries were often endowed with godlike powers and that they themselves

> did not realize how they had oversimplified their faith. They were convinced that the natives of the Pacific area were in the main mere children who had to be given a simple choice between good and evil. Almost every aspect of the customary life was condemned as the work of the Devil. Their simple presentation laid great stress on the Apocalypse.[12]

There is a whole literature devoted to the psychology of people

11. Talmon, "Pursuit of the Millennium," pp. 414–15.

12. Jean Guiart, "The Millenarian Aspect of Conversion to Christianity in the South Pacific," in *Millennial Dreams in Action*, ed. Sylvia L. Thrupp (New York: Schocken, 1970), p. 127.

who not only suffer but also believe that they suffer because they are inferior, perhaps even diabolically corrupt. One outlet is self-hatred and self-abuse, and Frantz Fanon has given detailed clinical evidence of this syndrome in North Africa. Religious fantasies provide another outlet. But another consequence of this psychology of inferiority is millenarian revolution and that takes place by a process that I shall label "reversal." Those who are at the top, the privileged or superior class, are suddenly cast into the position of those who suffer (or should suffer), while the latter now see themselves as divinely appointed bearers of truth. The wealthy, the highly placed, even and especially the church, become the apostles of Satan, whereas those who felt inferior now number among the elect.

This kind of radical conversion is responsible for the remarkable way in which millenarian revolutions juxtapose images of good and evil. Cohn's study of medieval revolutionaries includes plates of the art these movements have produced; for example, Melchior Lorch's portrayal of the pope as antichrist, in which the Pope is given the bestial attributes of Satan and the papal cross becomes a phallic symbol.[13] In such an upside-down world it is not surprising to find two people using identical images and language, claiming identical loyalties, yet talking past each other as if they came from different worlds. Hobsbawm relates a dialogue between a judge and a brigand in southern Italy in the 1860s:

Judge Having this conviction, why did not you and your companions give yourselves up? You must have known that, being hated by the whole population, your life was every moment in danger? . . .

Brigand We were fighting for the faith.

Judge What do you mean by the faith?

Brigand The holy faith of our religion.

Judge But you surely know that our religion condemns the thefts, the setting fire to houses, the murders, the cruelties, and all the impious and barbarous misdeeds by which brigandage every day is marked, and which you yourself and your companions have perpetrated.

Brigand We were fighting for the faith, and we were blessed by the Pope. . . .

13. Cohn, *Pursuit of the Millennium*, plate 2.

> *Judge* . . . that in perpetrating such wickedness you should
> keep, as the witness, and I might even say, if the words were
> not impious, as the accomplice of your crimes, the blessed
> Virgin, by wearing, attached to your breast, that dirty figure
> of the Madonna del Carmine, is astonishing. It is enough to
> make me believe that your religion is more impious and
> wicked than the religion of the devils themselves, if the devils
> have any religion. Is not this the most infernal mockery that
> can be offered to God!
>
> *Brigand* I and my companions have the Virgin as our protec-
> tress.[14]

This is not a dispute over doctrine but a controversy arising from
two completely incompatible views of the locus of evil. Any attempt
to mediate the two views through philosophical or theological argument would be doomed to failure, since it is the assumption of each
antagonist that the other occupies his position falsely. A similar
point is articulated by the sixteenth-century German radical reformer
Thomas Müntzer, who refers to the "unmasking" of false belief. In a
pamphlet entitled *The Explicit Unmasking of the False Belief of the
Faithless World,* Müntzer charges that the princes and lords, the
rich and powerful, not only exploit the poor but deceive them:

> The powerful, self-willed unbelievers must be put down from
> their seats because they hinder the holy, genuine Christian faith
> in themselves and in the whole world, when it is trying to emerge
> in all its true, original force. . . . the great do everything in their
> power to keep the common people from perceiving the truth.[15]

Müntzer could well utilize the words of the Italian judge, but invert
the terms of their application and call the action of German princes
and lords "the most infernal mockery that can be offered to God."
When the German peasants rebelled against the princes and Martin
Luther sided with the princes, ". . . it is not surprising that Müntzer
for his part saw in Luther an eschatological figure, the Beast of the
Apocalypse and the Whore of Bablyon."[16]

14. Hobsbawm, *Primitive Rebels*, pp. 180–81.
15. Quoted by Cohn, *Pursuit of the Millennium*, pp. 241–42.
16. Ibid., p. 243.

The justice of the millenarian revolutionaries' cause, then, lies in the fact that the chosen of God find themselves face to face with the hosts of Satan himself. These forces have disguised themselves as the representatives of God's kingdom and have taken over the rule of the world. At a point of such high drama, where heaven and earth are at stake, the specific criteria that define a just cause (see chapter 2) are irrelevant. The legitimacy of the revolutionary cause is self-evident. Not only has real injury been done, it is the ultimate injury, for the very throne of Christ has been usurped—evil is at its very highest pitch. To ask whether all peaceful means of redressing the injury have been exhausted is tantamount to asking whether it is not yet possible to reach a compromise between the justice of God and the perfidy of Satan. The just war criteria simply do not fit the climactic war against the powers of evil.

The process by which the revolutionaries come to see their roles in this drama amounts to conversion.[17] What I have called a gestalt shift, Müntzer called "unmasking." But this process was not essentially an intellectual one. Most of Müntzer's pamphleteering had the clear purpose of moving the peasants to action. It is only in action, in striking out against the forces of evil, that the truth of the new perspective is proved and, conversely, that the participants prove that they are among the elect. Cohn quotes Müntzer's letter to his followers at Allstedt:

> I tell you, if you will not suffer for God's sake, then you must be the Devil's martyrs. So take care! Don't be so disheartened, supine, don't fawn upon the perverse visionaries, the godless scoundrels! Start and fight the Lord's fight! It's high time. Keep all your brethren to it, so that they don't mock the divine testimony, otherwise they must all be destroyed . . . Don't be moved to pity. . . .
>
> Throw their tower to the ground! So long as they are alive you will never shake off the fear of men. One can't speak to you about God so long as they are reigning over you. At them, at

17. This is hardly a new point with respect to radical social movements, but it has not been sufficiently noted in the literature on the ethics of revolution. Cf. Guiart, "Millenarian Aspect of Conversion"; McLaughlin, *Studies in Social Movements*, chap. 3.

them, while you have daylight! God goes ahead of you so follow, follow![18]

Satan's forces cannot be unmasked by mere rhetoric nor can one be counted among the elect by a passive "act of faith." Truth emerges only in the toppling of those who have power ("One can't speak to you about God so long as they are reigning over you"). There could not be a clearer statement of the unity of theory and practice. The reconfiguration of the view of evil and its concomitant social patterns takes place on the level of symbols and on the level of revolutionary activity simultaneously.

In this kind of dualistic revolution cause and means are not easily distinguished. The very process of determining "just" cause (the new perception of rulers as agents of Antichrist) emerges through the act of overthrowing the foe. Personal conversion and the radical transformation of society go hand in hand, or, to put it another way, the means by which society is to be transformed is modeled upon the transformation of the self—a radical, abrupt shift in the organizing patterns of the mind. Before turning to the question of means, however, several points of clarification on this conversion process are in order.

As already noted, all millenarian revolutionaries share the conviction that the cause of their suffering and of evil in general can be located in a specific group or institution. In the case of Müntzer and his followers, the locus of evil was the German princes and anyone who supported them. In Hobsbawm's studies, it is the representatives of the new values and institutions of industrialism and capitalism. In colonial situations, the colonizers are the most obvious candidates for identification with the work of Satan. But the locus of evil does not always have to be an intruding class or a group proclaiming their own superiority. The social-psychological literature on out-groups, scapegoats, social fantasies, and so on is immense and beyond the scope of my topic, but Cohn in particular has shown that in times of severe disorientation any number of out-groups have been candidates for the moral outrage of the millenarians, among them Jews, clergy, Moslems, and merchants.

That the moral outrage of millenarian revolutionaries can be

18. Cohn, *Pursuit of the Millennium*, pp. 247–48.

directed to a variety of objects indicates the complexity of the shift in symbol structure when a theodicy paradigm changes. Talmon calls the millenarian attitude toward the past ambivalent:

> The rejection of the present usually includes the near and often the more distant past as well. Millenarism usually has a strong anti-traditional component and preparation for the millennium has often entailed a ritualized overthrow of traditional norms. . . . Yet this strong anti-past orientation is often mitigated when the millennium is envisaged as a return of a mythical golden age. When the millennium is regarded as a paradise regained, those elements of tradition which are viewed as embedded in it, become also components of the new order.[19]

I have already noted that in all revolutions much of the past is retained, but rather than saying that millenarians are ambivalent toward the past it is more accurate to say that the past is reconstrued. What actually changes are the perceptions of the roles that groups play within a given symbol structure. So in the court interrogation I cited earlier, judge and brigand both claim the Virgin's support. Luther charges the peasants with rising up against the order of God, while Müntzer calls Luther the Beast of the Apocalypse. This reversal of roles involves a selective use of tradition, of course; Müntzer emphasizes the apocalyptic literature as well as the egalitarian elements in Christianity. But what counts is that revolutionary groups no longer accept their own suffering and position in society as legitimate. Nor do they accept the well-being and power of other groups as a sign of virtue or godliness. They reverse the pattern, but the truth of the reversal can emerge only in the actual battle against the usurpers of Christ's throne.

The Problem of Conduct: A Terrible Beauty Is Born

Two characteristics stand out in the actual conduct of millenarian revolutions: the participants are disorganized and politically naive, and they are moved by remarkable passion. The combination leads them to embark on a course certain of failure, if not outrightly suicidal.

19. Talmon, "Pursuit of the Millennium," pp. 406–07.

The reason for their disorganization is obvious: they are involved in the ultimate eradication of evil and fully expect divine intervention to win the battle.[20] Thomas Müntzer exhorts his followers, "If there are but three of you who, trusting in God, seek only his name and honor, you will not fear a hundred thousand."[21] Such words engender passion but not success.

It is a commonplace by now that one of the determining factors in successful revolutions is the capacity of the revolutionaries for discipline and organization, together with a fairly precise idea of how the transfer of power is to take place.[22] It is not easy to entertain a precise logic of the transfer of power from Satan to Christ.

On the other hand, it is easy to know what one ought to do in anticipation of the transfer: strike out against the powers of evil. So the revolutionaries strike out in a variety of ways, all of which partake of blasphemy and atrocity in the eyes of those whom they attack. They engage in brigandage and rob the rich,[23] they go on crusades against the Moslems, they torture Jews, they destroy religious art and buildings, they attack the superior forces of princes and lords.[24]

Although such activities surely attract perverse minds and feed a multitude of passions, it would be a mistake to attribute them generally to malice. Rather, they are demanded by the logic of the dualistic ethic. As Hobsbawm says about the burning of forty-three churches and convents in the town of Malaga in 1931,

> The conscientious anarchist did not merely wish to destroy the evil world—though he did not normally believe that this would in fact involve much burning or killing—but rejected it here and now. Everything that made the Andalusian of tradition was to be jettisoned. He would not pronounce the word God or have anything to do with religion, he opposed bullfights, he refused to

20. Cf. ibid., p. 247.
21. Quoted by Cohn, *Pursuit of the Millennium*, p. 247.
22. See Hobsbawm, *Primitive Rebels*, p. 58, and Michael Walzer, *The Revolution of the Saints* (New York: Atheneum, 1969), passim. Walzer is especially interested in the contributions of Calvinism to discipline and organization.
23. Hobsbawm, *Primitive Rebels*.
24. These are some of many activities reported in Cohn, *Pursuit of the Millennium*, passim.

drink or even to smoke, . . . he disapproved of sexual promiscuity though officially committed to free love. Indeed, at times of strike or revolution there is even evidence that he practised absolute chastity, though this was sometimes misinterpreted by outsiders. He was a revolutionary in the most total sense conceivable to Andalusian peasants, condemning *everything* about the past. He was, in fact, a millenarian.[25]

Yet the rejection of tradition, including religion, is never total. One of the old Andalusian anarchists quoted by Hobsbawm consciously or unconsciously invoked Jesus' apocalyptic words about the Jerusalem temple: "And I tell you—not one stone will be left on another stone—no, not a plant nor even a cabbage will grow there, so that there may be no more wickedness in the world."[26]

What organization millenarian revolutionaries do have derives from a charismatic or even messianic figure. Such leaders generally come from a social class different from that of the revolutionary group, and they are usually better educated—a feature common to almost all revolutions, millenarian or otherwise. Occasionally, self-appointed leaders and messiahs manipulate millenarian groups for their personal ends, but more often the identification of the leader with the plight of his followers is sincere. I am not interested here in the psychology of the leader but in his function in the revolutionary group. As Talmon puts it, the leader is the "mediator between the divine and the movement":

Sometimes these prophetic figures move from mere prophecy to become messianic incarnations of divine leadership, but more often than not the figure of the messiah and the figure of the leader remain distinct. Leaders act as precursors of the messiah and as his prophets by announcing the good tidings. They develop their special brand of millenarism by emphasizing millenarian elements in their traditional culture and by seizing upon millenarian elements in the cultures which impinge on them. They interpret the millennial traditions and vulgarize them, combining disparate elements and systematizing. They supply their

25. Hobsbawm, *Primitive Rebels*, pp. 83–84.
26. Ibid., p. 83.

followers with secondary exegesis when their hopes fail to materialize. They teach the new ritual and preach the new moral code. They organize their followers and lead them in preparation for the advent.[27]

Since Weber, the role of charismatic leaders in breaking with tradition has been a focus of scholarly attention. In millenarian movements the lack of organization and disciplined objectives is compensated for by the symbolic role of the messianic figure (or anticipated messianic figure), together with elation at being in on the beginning of a new creation. The contagious quality of the leader's apocalyptic message generates "an atmosphere of high exaltation [that] ... provides teams of men and women who will spread the joyful tidings wherever they can, for at millennial times ... everyone becomes a propagandist."[28]

In the last chapter I suggested that revolutions resemble a zero-sum game and that it is therefore impossible to apply the principle of proportionality to the waging of revolution. This is certainly true of millenarian revolutionaries. They are not defending something that is theirs or recovering something that has been taken from them. They are rather moving from a position of disorientation marked by feelings of inferiority and self-hatred to a position of being the chosen of God (or some functional equivalent). It is the headiness of this inversion and the moral passion that accompanies it, symbolized in the leadership of the prophet or messiah, that is the reward of revolutionary action. Müntzer talks not so much about defending the faith but about a faith that "is trying to emerge in all its true, original force." What counts is that people who were passive are now active, those who were lost are now saved, those who were disoriented by the world are now giving it direction. No matter that eventually these movements fail—in the moment of action something wonderfully new has happened, something that is a witness to God's power. Hobsbawm is surely correct in turning to the poetry of Easter to account for this change: "It is this consciousness of *utter* change, not as an aspiration but as a fact—at least a temporary fact—which informs Yeats' poem on the Easter Rising":

27. Talmon, "Pursuit of the Millennium," p. 412.
28. Hobsbawm, *Primitive Rebels*, p. 106.

> This other man I had dreamed
> A drunken vainglorious lout . . .
> Yet I number him in the song;
> He, too, has resigned his part
> In the casual comedy;
> He, too, has been changed in his turn,
> Transformed utterly:
> A terrible beauty is born.[29]

The Problem of Ends

In the most extreme cases, such as the cult of the Free Spirit, the terrible beauty born of revolutionary activity entails self-deification.[30] While the theme of deification is present in much revolutionary thought, the extreme cases throw into relief the tendency of the millenarian revolution to collapse the goal or end of revolution into the act of revolt. The breaking of taboos, the destruction of traditional religious artifacts, sexual licentiousness, and violence against the state are marks of the Spirit and constitute the freedom sought, whether it is in self-deification or exaltation.

This is not to say that millenarians have no vision of the future—on the contrary, a vision of the future is central to what it means to be a millenarian. They share with all revolutionaries a hope for justice which is almost always egalitarian. While some revolutionaries may hope for material possessions, Hobsbawm notes that "the preindustrial poor always conceive of the good society as a just sharing of austerity rather than a dream of riches for all."[31] But the fact remains that they have no technique for realizing this vision, no organizational strategy for guaranteeing equality, any more than they have an organizational strategy for achieving a transfer of power.

This vagueness about the future should not be considered analogous to the reluctance of Marxists to describe the conditions of their future society. It is rather rooted in the dualist theodicy: if suffering and injustice are the fruits of Satan's reign, then the defeat of Satan

29. Ibid., p. 61.
30. Cf. Cohn, *Pursuit of the Millennium*, chaps. 8 and 9.
31. Hobsbawm, *Primitive Rebels*, p. 82.

means the end of injustice and the inauguration of justice (and abundance, if that too is hoped for), but there is a pronounced indifference to the political and economic structures this would require.

Theological language helps to clarify the point. We have seen the close relationship between millenarian revolution and religious conversion. In the Christian tradition, conversion, the turning to God, is part of the doctrine of justification. Yet that turning does not constitute the eradication of evil, even within the individual convert himself. Especially in the Calvinist and Thomist traditions, evil and sin are continuing powers against which the convert must resolutely do battle. Evil is present in the social structure, but it is also present in the habits of the convert and even in the inclination of the will. What is required now is sanctification, the disciplined ordering of life to make it holy. It is precisely the concern for sanctification that is missing in the millenarian framework. Since evil is clearly located outside the believer, all energy is devoted to its eradication, not to structures that will control or order it. This point cannot be emphasized too much in studying revolution.

For the millenarian revolutionary, then, questions of just cause and just ends are collapsed into the one process of unmasking and defeating the forces of evil. The act of revolt itself counts as everything. The "terrible beauty" of that moment reveals the truth of what the revolutionary is doing and exalts him as never before. There is little or no concern for the structure of life "after the revolution."

FRANTZ FANON

Fanon's description and analysis of revolution in a colonial situation rests on two interpretive theodicies, Marxist and Manichaean. The latter is of most interest since it is Fanon's peculiar contribution to revolutionary thinking. His Manichaean theodicy gives focus to almost all of Fanon's writings on violence and to his most penetrating insights into racial and colonial conflict, which have fascinating parallels with the millenarian view of revolutionary violence.

By choosing to emphasize Fanon's Manichaean theodicy, I do not want to suggest that it plays a larger role in his writing than his Marxist interpretation of the colonial syndrome. The Marxist scheme permits Fanon in theory to give attention to postrevolutionary organization. He spent a great deal of effort in adapting Marxism to the Third World, in particular by substituting the peasant for the proletarian as the revolutionary subject, by suggesting modes of rural organization, and by taking into account the complexities of a colonized people who have to struggle for independence while at the same time participating in the modern international economy. And it may be argued that the role of violence in Fanon's thought, which stems from his Manichaean analysis, has been greatly exaggerated and even distorted by some of his less perceptive followers and critics.[32] Nevertheless, the role of violence and its Manichaean character are indisputably of central importance to Fanon, and even his most sympathetic critics agree that his program for a Marxist revolution in the Third World is the least satisfactory aspect of his work.[33] He had almost no knowledge of the peasants whom he extolled as the revolutionary class, and he was guilty of the European propensity to view not only all of Africa but the entire Third World as a single entity.[34]

Fanon's Manichaean theodicy has no ontological roots—it is an artifact of colonial and racial patterns of domination, which for him constitute the cause of revolution.

The Problem of Cause

We have seen the pattern of disorientation, domination, and self-hatred that frequently accompanies millenarian revolutions. Nowhere does that pattern establish itself more distinctly and antagonistically than in colonial situations. Fanon sets out to explore colonial domination through the interpretive paradigm of Hegel's master-slave relationship as it was reformulated by Marx and Sartre.[35]

Trained in psychiatry, Fanon's entrée to understanding the world

32. Irene Gendzier, *Frantz Fanon: A Critical Study* (New York: Pantheon, 1973), p. 198.

33. For example, ibid., p. 269; David Caute, *Frantz Fanon* (New York: Viking, 1970), pp. 79ff, 89ff.

34. Cf. Caute, *Frantz Fanon*, pp. 73, 99ff.

35. Fanon's only direct discussion of Hegel is in *Black Skin, White Masks* (New York: Grove Press, 1967), pp. 216–22. Sartre's influence is felt in the language and categories used by Fanon throughout his work but in this book in particular. A brief discussion of the influence of Hegel and Sartre on Fanon may be found in Gendzier, *Frantz Fanon*, pp. 22–35.

of colonial and racial conflict was medical. He was early struck by
two remarkable facts. The first was the disproportionately high rate
of violent crime and mental disorder in black populations living
under white regimes; the second was the kind of interpretation this
was given by European doctors and other whites. The rate of crime
and mental disorder was the occasion for some of the most appalling
"scientific" writing in the annals of Western medicine, which Fanon
documents with both irony and passion. At the extreme was the
kind of work dating from earlier in the century which concluded, in
the words of one psychiatrist, that "the native of North Africa,
whose superior and cortical activities are only slightly developed, is a
primitive creature whose life, essentially vegetative and instinctive, is
above all regulated by his diencephalon."[36] This is not to be supposed
an isolated point of view, nor one that was limited to the missionary
period of European colonialism. According to a 1954 article by a
doctor in the World Health Organization: "The African makes
very little use of his frontal lobes. All the particularities of African psychiatry can be put down to frontal laziness."[37] The same
expert, Fanon notes, makes a "lively comparison" by suggesting that
"the normal African is a 'lobotomized European.'"

Under these official scientific pronouncements lay views more
subtle, including the popular belief by whites that "Negroes never
commit suicide," with the clear implication that a white man who
had to endure what a black man did would choose death rather than
submit to such humiliation. Fanon himself notes that he wanted to
devote a chapter of *Black Skin, White Masks* to "the death wish
among Negroes":

> According to Durkheim, Jews never committed suicide. Now
> it is the Negroes. Very well: "The Detroit municipal hospital
> found that 16.6% of its suicide cases were Negroes, although
> the proportion of Negroes in the total population is only 7.6%.
> In Cincinnati, the number of Negro suicides is more than dou-
> ble that of whites; this may result in part from the amazing

36. Fanon, *The Wretched of the Earth,*, p. 300. The psychiatrist quoted is
a Professor A. Porot writing in 1935.
37. Ibid., p. 302. The work cited here is by a Dr. A. Carothers.

sexual disparity among Negro suicides: 358 women against 76 men."[38]

The actual practice of medicine in the colonial situation perpetuates and strengthens its "scientific" hypotheses. Since most doctors are representatives of the colonizers, the dichotomy that characterizes the entire colonial situation extends also to the doctor's office: "The colonized person who goes to see the doctor is always diffident. He answers in monosyllables, gives little in the way of explanation, and soon arouses the doctor's impatience."[39]

What Fanon does in the face of the medical practice under colonialism is to use a form of what I have called reversal or inversion, finding the solution to the problem in the terms of the problem itself. Modern medicine treats the native as lobotomized; he therefore acts accordingly. Cause and effect are reversed. I have oversimplified the process, of course; nevertheless, Fanon's technique is to unveil and trace the complex system of colonial relationships that led Aimé Césaire to write, "I am talking of millions of men who have been skillfully injected with fear, inferiority complexes, trepidation, servility, despair, abasement."[40]

In the realm of law it is not only the case that the French legal system disrupts the traditional structure of North African custom; it is also the case that a Frenchman would not have been convicted for the murder of an Algerian even though French laws forbade the killing of one human being by another.[41] Sexually, a black woman can only become fully human by loving a white man, and she must therefore deny her own person—she wears a white mask.[42] Culturally, educationally, intellectually, the elements of the colonial situation combine to form a mosaic in which blackness appears as

38. *Black Skin*, pp. 218-19 and 6. Fanon is quoting a study by Gabriel Deshaies.

39. *A Dying Colonialism* (New York: Grove Press, 1967), p. 126.

40. Aimé Césaire, quoted by Fanon at the beginning of *Black Skin*.

41. Cf. also the case study at the end of *The Wretched of the Earth* (pp. 270-72) in which two young Algerian boys have killed a French playmate. Asked why he had done it, one boy responded, "There are Algerians killed every day, aren't there? So why are only Algerians found in the prisons?"

42. *Black Skin*, chap. 2.

the source of all evil and whiteness as the mark of culture, virtue, and humanity itself: "Good-Evil, Beauty-Ugliness, White-Black: such are the characteristic pairings of the phenomenon that, making use of an expression of Dide and Guiraud, we shall call 'manicheism delirium.'"[43]

The behavioral consequences of these colonial patterns are the violent crimes and mental disorders that so fascinated European doctors. The more profound consequence is a psychological constellation in which the colonized peoples are filled with self-doubt, resentment, and self-hatred. Fanon interprets the whole in the language of Hegel's master-slave paradigm: "Man is motion toward the world and toward his life";[44] and following Hegel, "Man is human only to the extent to which he tries to impose his existence on another man in order to be recognized by him."[45] The master, to effect his own projects and to be recognized in them, requires the slave or servant both as a source of labor (an extension of the master's power) and as another consciousness which recognizes his achievement. The servant, in turn, is recognized by the master. Each is both the fulfillment and the limitation of the other. But the servant's achievement and recognition is derivative in a sense that the master's is not. It is the master who has the initiative, the master whose projects and dictates set the terms of reciprocity—as some of Hegel's disciples put it, the master is the thesis while the servant is the antithesis.

> The Negro is comparison. There is the first truth. He is comparison: That is, he is constantly preoccupied with self-evaluation and with the ego-ideal. Whenever he comes into contact with someone else, the question of value, of merit, arises. The Antilleans have no inherent values of their own, they are always contingent on the presence of the other. The question is always whether he is less intelligent than I, blacker than I, less respectable than I. Every position of one's own, every effort at

43. Ibid., p. 183.
44. Ibid., p. 41.
45. Ibid., p. 216. Fanon has just quoted from *The Phenomenology of Mind:* "Self-consciousness exists *in itself* and *for itself*, in that and by the fact that it exists for another self-consciousness; that is to say, it *is* only by being acknowledged or recognized."

security, is based on relations of dependence, with the diminution of the other. It is the wreckage of what surrounds me that provides the foundation for my virility.[46]

The "contradiction" between master and slave is repeated in a fabric of contradictions which consistently frustrates the servant in his quest for self-recognition. In the colonial situation the native is taught an ethic of possessions but denied the means to attain them; he feels at every turn the instruments of force—police, torture, guns—but is taught an ethic of nonviolence;[47] the entire culture proclaims that to be a man one must live after the manner of the colonizer, yet to be a colonizer requires the continued existence of the colonized, the native. The master, to maintain his position, must keep the slave's frustration from boiling over and does so by creating the illusion of fulfillment: "In the capitalist countries a multitude of moral teachers, counselors and 'bewilderers' separate the exploited from those in power."[48]

At this juncture, Fanon begins to distinguish the black native from other slaves. What had especially fascinated Hegel was the ironic way in which the slave, caught up in the work demanded by the master, achieves a form of independence through that work while the master remains dependent upon the slave to mediate his own self-fulfillment. This avenue is not open to the black native in the colonial world because of his color.

I hope I have shown that here the master differs basically from the master described by Hegel. For Hegel there is reciprocity; here the master laughs at the consciousness of the slave. What he wants from the slave is not recognition but work.

In the same way, the slave here is in no way identifiable with the slave who loses himself in the object and finds in his work the source of his liberation.

The Negro wants to be like the master.

Therefore he is less independent than the Hegelian slave.[49]

46. Ibid., p. 211.
47. *The Wretched of the Earth*, pp. 43 and 61.
48. Ibid., p. 38.
49. *Black Skin*, pp. 220–21, n. 8.

Fanon's point is that racial difference introduces a surd into the master-slave dialectic which disrupts the reciprocity. The fact that the native is black and his master white means that the work he must do has a horizon that is by nature beyond his reach: he can wear a white mask, but he cannot become white. Conversely, the white master has chosen not to see his black slave as an other who is significant for his own identity except by nondialectical negation: "The settler paints the native as a sort of quintessence of evil."[50] As such, the native does not require a moral "bewilderer" who assures him that he, too, has a place in God's plan. He is from the beginning condemned by the settler to eternal damnation—a point stressed in the French title, *Les damnés de la terre*. I take it that this is what lies behind Fanon's statement that "in most cases, the black man lacks the advantage of being able to accomplish this descent into a real hell."[51]

The issue may also be stated in terms of the masochism and sadism discussed in chapter 2. To the extent that any society has patterns of domination, those who are dominated (the masochists) find meaning in their derivative status. An external observer or radical sociologist may call them bewildered (Marx said they suffer from false consciousness), but from their point of view—if they have been adequately socialized—they have a place in the ultimate scheme of things. That is the function of a society's theodicy. The positions of both dominator and dominated are maintained by a larger constellation of meaning in which inequities are finally resolved. But racial domination gives meaning to the dominated only negatively, and he is maintained in that position by a kind of force very different from the "meaningful" shaping of existence by a nondualistic theodicy. Such an experience in this country moved Martin Luther King to write:

When you have seen vicious mobs lynch your mothers and fathers at will and drown your sisters and brothers at whim; when you have seen hate-filled policemen curse, kick and even

50. *The Wretched of the Earth*, p. 41.
51. *Black Skin*, p. 8. Gendzier, *Frantz Fanon*, p. 25, comments that Fanon had only "exaggerated a point rather than introduced a new one." I do not find her arguments persuasive.

kill your black brothers and sisters; when you see the vast majority of your twenty million Negro brothers smothering in an airtight cage of poverty in the midst of an affluent society; when you suddenly find your tongue twisted and your speech stammering as you seek to explain to your six-year-old daughter why she can't go to the public amusement park that has just been advertised on television, and see tears welling up in her eyes when she is told that Funtown is closed to colored children, and see ominous clouds of inferiority beginning to form in her little mental sky, and see her beginning to distort her personality by developing an unconscious bitterness toward white people; ... then you will understand why we can't wait.[52]

What maintains blacks in their position is not a larger meaning-structure but brute force; or what Fanon calls an "atmosphere of violence."[53] It is this atmosphere that compels the growth of inferiority, not simply the fact of domination, because in it the self-worth of the dominated is under constant attack.

Here it is helpful to return to the definition of violence given by Chalmers Johnson which I cited in chapter 2:

We may define violence as action that deliberately or unintentionally disorients the behavior of others. Violence is either behavior which is impossible for others to orient themselves to or behavior which is deliberately intended to prevent orientation and the development of stable expectations with regard to it.... Violence is "antisocial action."[54]

The difficulties earlier expressed with respect to this definition are now abundantly clear: it is possible for some people or groups within a social system to experience violence from the system itself; a point that Johnson does not address. Fanon and King have addressed themselves precisely to this issue. In a racist society it is impossible for the racially oppressed group to orient its behavior

52. Martin Luther King, *Why We Can't Wait* (New York: Harper & Row, 1963), pp. 83–84.
53. *The Wretched of the Earth*, p. 71.
54. *Revolutionary Change* (Boston: Little, Brown, 1966), p. 8.

in relation to others because the ideals and values the culture holds up to them are at the same time unattainable for them by virtue of their color. The force felt by a proletarian and the force felt by a white slave under a white master are plausibly structured by stable expectations. The only stable expectation in a racial conflict according to Fanon is that the black man will be treated like an animal, as if he were not part of human society; in other words, he is the object of "antisocial action."

In an atmosphere of violence, the native too acts violently, but his violence is directed toward himself (thus neurosis and psychosis) and toward other members of his group. In a situation where negritude or blackness is not dialectically derivative but an opposing principle, the black man sets about to destroy blackness:

> In Algeria, Algerian criminality takes place in practice inside a closed circle. The Algerians rob each other, cut each other up, and kill each other. In Algeria, the Algerian rarely attacks Frenchmen, and avoids brawls with the French.[55]

That is the Manichaean world of colonialism. In Fanon's mind there is no possibility of the native's finding in productive activity the key to his freedom, as Marx thought the proletarian could. The link between the black native and the colonial master is not labor but violence. Before the Marxist analysis can come into play, the black native must cease trying to be white, and he must cease trying to destroy his blackness. That is likely to happen, according to Fanon, only when violence is directed at the white master.

The Problem of Conduct

In the preface to *The Wretched of the Earth*, Jean-Paul Sartre says,

> [Fanon] shows clearly that this irrepressible violence is neither sound and fury, nor the resurrection of savage instincts, nor even the effect of resentment: it is man recreating himself. I think we understood this truth at one time, but we have forgotten it—that no gentleness can efface the marks of violence; only violence

55. *The Wretched of the Earth*, p. 305.

itself can destroy them. The native cures himself of colonial neurosis by thrusting out the settler through force of arms. When his rage boils over, he rediscovers his lost innocence and he comes to know his self in that he himself creates himself.[56]

Here, as with the millenarians, cause and ends are collapsed into means. For Fanon violence against the colonial regime carries with it the awakening of a self-consciousness that realizes both the injustice of the earlier mode of consciousness and the possibilities of the future. Violence is its own victory. But as Sartre depicts it here, the movement from subhuman to human mediated by violence is, from a theological perspective, more awesome an achievement than anything claimed by the millenarians. It is true that some extreme millenarians claimed self-deification, but the power that conferred deity was no less than God himself. Millenarian violence and "Free Spirit" lawlessness contributed to the process, but the miracle was wrought by God, while according to Sartre man is created by man. The violence of the native is given the metaphysical status of God's "Let there be. . . ."

Sartre's other writings assure us he has not spoken hastily here.[57] The question is whether he has represented Fanon accurately. On close examination, Fanon is much more cautious, but some aspects of the Sartrean position are present. To begin with Fanon speaks of violence in a general way, as if it were a single thing. Violence is the inversion of the native's relationship to the white colonizer:

He of whom *they* have never stopped saying that the only language he understands is that of force, decides to give utterance by force. In fact, as always, the settler has shown him the way he should take if he is to become free.[58]

56. Ibid., p. 21.

57. Cf. Paul Ramsey's article, "Sex and Sartre," in his *Nine Modern Moralists* (Englewood Cliffs, N.J.: Prentice-Hall, 1962), pp. 71–109. A summary and analysis of Sartre's views on violence may be found in R. D. Laing and D. G. Cooper, *Reason and Violence* (New York: Vintage, 1971) of which Sartre says in the foreword, "It is, I am happy to say, a very clear, very faithful account of my thought" (p. 6).

58. *The Wretched of the Earth*, p. 84.

In this passage Fanon's statement of the difference between colonial domination and Hegel's master-slave relationship becomes clearer. Violence or force (Fanon does not really distinguish between the two) seems to replace work or production as the mediating term between master and slave. Whereas in Marx the proletarian is given the means of his freedom in the productive skills he learns as a worker, in Fanon the native is given the key to his freedom in violence: "It so happens that for the colonized people this violence, because it constitutes their only work, invests their characters with positive and creative qualities."[59] Whereas for Marx the proletarian revolution entails the substitution of one mode of production for another, for Fanon the violence of decolonization "is quite simply the replacing of a certain species of men by another species of men. Without any period of transition, there is a total, complete, and absolute substitution."[60] Whereas for Marx violence is the midwife of history, for Fanon it is the birth itself (and the mother does not survive).

But then Fanon proceeds to distinguish among different functions of violence. In the first place, violence has a strategic role: it is a weapon, when carefully wielded, against which the colonizer is virtually helpless. "The truth is that there is no colonial power today which is capable of adopting the only form of contest which has a chance of succeeding [against violent uprising], namely, the prolonged establishment of large forces of occupation."[61] In this observation Fanon shows keen insight into the fragility of the colonial presence in the modern world. He knows that the European populations will not put up with the efforts and sacrifices of colonial wars to the extent that they did in the nineteenth century. And most critics agree that in spite of the shortcomings of Fanon's prescriptions for peasant organization, his perceptions of the limits of colonial power are accurate.

The second function of violence is to mark a symbolic break with the colonial world:

The group requires that each individual perform an irrevocable action. . . . You could be sure of a new recruit when he could no

59. Ibid., p. 93.
60. Ibid., p. 35.
61. Ibid., p. 74.

longer go back into the colonial system. This mechanism, it seems, had existed in Kenya among the Mau-Mau, who required that each member of the group should strike a blow at the victim. Each one was thus personally responsible for the death of that victim. . . . This assumed responsibility for violence allows both strayed and outlawed members of the group to come back again and to find their place once more, to become integrated. Violence is thus seen as comparable to a royal pardon. The colonized man finds his freedom in and through violence.[62]

This account of violence is especially noteworthy because it compares the act of violence with a rite of passage in religion, a movement from one group or one state of being into another, in which a person's past is cleansed in preparation for a new life.

The third function of violence is the one for which Fanon is best known: "At the level of individuals, violence is a cleansing force. It frees the native from his inferiority complex and from his despair and inaction; it makes him fearless and restores his self-respect."[63] Here, colonial violence is therapy, but it should not be misunderstood as a cure. Fanon's own case studies at the end of *The Wretched of the Earth* demonstrate in no uncertain detail that the perpetrators of violence, both colonizer and colonized, suffer from continued mental disorders even when the violence has been directed at members of the other group. Fanon makes no claim of *general* self-renovation,[64] and in this he is much more careful than Sartre. Colonial violence is of therapeutic value only with respect to the mental disorders of colonialism, and he specifies the characteristics of the latter clearly: inferiority complexes, despair, and inaction. That one who has overcome these complexes may yet suffer other effects of violence is reported by Fanon himself.

In fact, it is to Fanon's credit that the therapeutic claims he makes for violence are closely intertwined with the other functions I have discussed. He knows that no continued struggle against the colonial

62. Ibid., pp. 85–86.
63. Ibid., p. 94.
64. This interpretation counts against Caute's observation that "Fanon's own close involvement with and understanding of such cases makes his theory of renovating violence more difficult to understand." *Frantz Fanon*, p. 95.

power is possible without the partial renovation entailed in overcoming self-hatred and inaction. He also knows that this new perspective on the world, this shift in the Manichaean theodicy, is not possible with the continued presence of the settler; his Manichaeism requires the settler to be totally rejected as the first stage in the solution to the problem of evil. Moreover, Fanon knows that such shifts in the perception of evil and the perception of self are rarely if ever individual movements. With Marx, he has a social view of the self which sees an act of violence, committed individually, as entailing movement from one social group to another, or from isolation to social solidarity. As Caute puts it, "It is in the context of effective social action that violence is renovating."[65]

The Problem of Ends

When all is said and done, Fanon is nevertheless hardly more satisfactory than the millenarians in his statements about the ends of revolutionary violence. The most obvious end is the expulsion of the colonial power. I have already mentioned Fanon's insight that the modern colonial power is helpless in the face of persistent violence. although his projections about the role of the peasant class have not been borne out by actual African revolutions.[66] More importantly, to the extent he projects beyond the termination of colonial rule he begins to approach Sartre's goal of "the creation of man by man," as when he says, "Let us decide not to imitate Europe; let us combine our muscles and our brains in a new direction. Let us try to create the whole man, whom Europe has been incapable of bringing to triumphant birth."[67] This passage falls within the conclusion to *The Wretched of the Earth*, in which Fanon recounts with biting irony and anger Europe's crimes and hypocrisies in the name of "man." Nothing is said about how the creation of a new man is to be accomplished except by negation ("Let us decide not to imitate Europe") and the general exhortation that "we must invent and we must make

65. Ibid., p. 94. This remark makes the previous quote from Caute less intelligible.

66. Cf. Jack Woddis, *New Theories of Revolution* (New York: International Publishers, 1972), chap. 2 ("Fanon and Classes in Africa").

67. *The Wretched of the Earth*, p. 313.

discoveries."[68] But these notions have nothing to do with Fanon's "renovative" violence except insofar as the expulsion of the colonial power transforms inaction and self-hatred into action and inventiveness. But why should mere action and inventiveness produce men who are different from the Europeans, who were also supposedly active and inventive?

The answer surely lies in Fanon's adoption of Marxism and the Marxist confidence in the ability of the proletarian to create a society free from patterns of domination. As I suggested earlier, in Fanon two theodicies are at work, the Manichaean and the Marxist. The former is provisional—it depends totally on the exigencies of colonial violence and domination. Once they have been overcome, once the native has expelled the European and become confident of his ability to shape his own destiny, Marxist analysis takes over. But Fanon's Marxist analysis is very sketchily developed. His substitution of the Third World for the proletarian class overlooks all that Marx said about the unique qualifications of the proletariat for a revolutionary destiny and begs countless questions about what actually constitutes the Third World. Moreover, he makes statements that sound much more like European liberalism than like anything a Marxist would say:

The Third World does not mean to organize a great crusade of hunger against the whole of Europe. What it expects from those who for centuries have kept it in slavery is that they will help it to rehabilitate mankind, and make man victorious everywhere, once and for all. But it is clear that we are not so naive as to think that this will come about with the cooperation and the good will of the European governments. This huge task which consists of reintroducing mankind into the world, the whole of mankind, will be carried out with the indispensable help of the European peoples, who themselves must realize that in the past they have often joined the ranks of our common masters where colonial questions were concerned. To achieve this, the European peoples must first decide to wake up and shake themselves, use their brains,

68. Ibid., p. 315.

and stop playing the stupid game of the Sleeping Beauty.[69]

This is a curious mixture of Marxism and liberalism in its recognition that the Third World must look to "the people" and not the political establishment for help, but without any indication of how the necessary awakening is to take place. It confirms that the Manichaean analysis is purely provisional—there is no continuing rancor toward Europeans in general. Otherwise Fanon offers little guidance.

In short, Fanon is a keen observer and analyst of the transformations that take place when a violated people resort to violence to regain a sense of their own worth, but when he ventures beyond this to talk of a total transformation of man, the breaking away from everything that Europe has done, he becomes rhetorical and vague. He has no real sense of what will happen "after the revolution,"[70] a point upon which Marx himself is a better guide.

THE ETHICS OF VIOLENCE

Imagine that you are a white Peace Corps volunteer in, say, an African country that is still under colonial rule. There you encounter many of the mental disorders described so vividly by Fanon and come to share his and Sartre's conclusion that the people there have been dehumanized by the psychosocial structure of colonialism. At some point, you become closely acquainted with the situation of one of these "dehumanized" beings and, as a human being, you are convinced that he will never overcome his self-doubt and self-hatred until he commits an act of violence against the colonial structure. Apart from the question of his willingness to listen to you, can you commend such a course of action to him?

It is one thing to commend an act of violence to a friend who is struggling with the legitimacy of such an act, performed in self-defense or on behalf of others. In this instance both of you have reasonably congruent perceptions of the nature of the act. It is quite another thing to commend an act that you perceive as therapeutic to someone who may perceive it as the eradication of evil. While you

69. Ibid., p. 106.

70. Indeed, most postcolonial Arab nations have gone in non-Marxist directions and have tended to revive Arab and Moslem customs from the past. See Gendzier, *Frantz Fanon*, pp. 257–60.

may hope that eventually the other will come to view the act in less cosmological terms, that the therapy will work, you nevertheless assume the somewhat condescending position that the other is incapable of making the kinds of judgments that full human beings would make, that for him the act must have a meaning that it would not have if he were not dehumanized.

It is possible, of course, simply to urge a dehumanized person to defend himself or others by using violence against violence and to hope that this by itself will be therapeutic. But if this is done in good faith, it must also involve an attempt to help that person structure the violence as defensive violence, that is, to make one's own and the other's expectations congruent. To commend violence simply as therapy tends to perpetuate the very structure that made it necessary, namely, the assumption of the other's inferiority and one's own superiority. In the doctor-patient relationship, the doctor is clearly in the superior position and frequently knows better than the patient what is best for him, but to treat a whole group as ill or dehumanized and urge it toward action on that basis is part and parcel of the dehumanizing process itself. It does not create a bond between you and the other but forever establishes your separation. In the face of the kind of spontaneous violence that Fanon describes, the sympathetic observer can only stand by and describe, perhaps silently applaud. But in relation to that other, he must remain mute.

The dilemma is just as acute from the side of the one who commits violence. If he discovers that a spontaneous act of violence against an oppressor has a regenerating effect, he is limited in his capacity to talk about it. This is not to say that he cannot talk about it at all—he can describe his experience to others, and he is in a sense more able to empathize with others going through similar experiences than is the imaginary white Peace Corps volunteer. But to empathize and describe is not the same thing as commending a course of action to another. Such an act has the same ring of inauthenticity as would the behavior of a person who embarked on a course of violent action arguing that it was legitimate for him to do so because he was not yet fully human. The repeated use of it as a justification for violent acts would be precisely what Sartre means by *mauvaise foi*. The perpetrator's distance from his actions places him in company with the Peace Corps volunteer and removes him forever from the capacity for spontaneous violence.

In short, one can never commend therapeutic violence—or, to put it another way, therapeutic violence can never be justified. It is to Sartre's credit that he does not commend violence to the black Algerians; he instinctively knows the impossibility of this. But to the extent that the entire preface to *The Wretched of the Earth* stands as a justification of violence by the native against the European, Sartre is not completely free from a paternalistic attitude. Fanon's empathy with the black Algerian rings true simply by virtue of his color, and also by virtue of his close experience there. Sartre's empathy seems more an occasion for continuing his hostility toward his fellow Europeans and intellectuals.

An account of renovative violence more authentic than Sartre's, and against which Fanon may be measured, is to be found in Frederick Douglass's description of his passage from slavery to manhood in nineteenth-century America. Douglass had been sent by his master for a year of disciplining and training under Mr. Covey, a man with considerable reputation as a "nigger-breaker." There he received many beatings and suffered under the most inhumane labor and treatment. He longed to be free but did not have the will to do it nor knowledge of how it could be done: after one particularly cruel beating, his first instinct was to return to the very master who had sent him to Mr. Covey in the first place to ask for protection! Then one day Covey attacked him in the barn, and Douglass, lying on the floor, was moved to resist: "At this moment—from whence came the spirit I don't know—I resolved to fight." The fight lasted for nearly two hours, and although it ended with both men exhausted, Douglass knew he had won.

> This battle with Mr. Covey was the turning-point in my career as a slave. It rekindled the few expiring embers of freedom, and revived within me a sense of my manhood. It recalled the departed self-confidence, and inspired me again with a determination to be free. The gratification afforded by the triumph was a full compensation for whatever else might follow, even death itself. He only can understand the deep satisfaction which I experienced, who has himself repelled by force the bloody arm of slavery. I felt as I never felt before. It was a glorious resurrection, from the tomb of slavery, to the heaven of freedom. My long-crushed spirit rose, cowardice departed, bold defiance took

its place; and I now resolved that, however long I might remain a slave in form, the day had passed forever when I could be a slave in fact. I did not hesitate to let it be known of me, that the white man who expected to succeed in whipping, must also succeed in killing me.[71]

Much here supports what the dualists have to say about violence and its rejuvenating effect. The experience is tantamount to conversion and rebirth, and the reward is the gratification of the act itself. But close attention to the passage and its context reveals two important differences from the dualistic literature I have been examining.

In the first place, the Douglass account portrays the act of rebellion rather than its violent nature as the source of his resurrection. That the act of rebellion took violent form followed from Douglass's situation—here there is agreement with Fanon's point that the violence of the native is a function of the atmosphere of violence in which he must live. But Douglass does not dwell on the aspect of violence, nor does it entail the eradication of an enemy. This rebellion is an act of self-assertion, and once done it cannot be undone—a point that is recognized by both the rebel and the former master. Douglass is now irrevocably on his way to freedom. That this is not a quibbling over words is shown by the remarkable sensitivity and humanity with which Douglass describes his masters, including Covey. They are mean and cruel—he does not soften this in the least—and their remarkable religious hypocrisy is revealed in ironic detail. But the attention he gives to the details of their lives and persons, their foibles and fears, reveals a humanity he did not lose even in his misery. Furthermore, he is able to distinguish among better and worse slaveholders and better and worse whites. In short, he retains the capacity for moral judgment that we normally associate with what it means to be human.

This calls into question what is meant when it is claimed that a person is "dehumanized." It is one thing to say that he is treated as if he were not a human being; it is another to say that as a consequence he is deprived of the attributes of humanity. It is still something else to claim that *all* traits of humanity have been effaced. The

71. Frederick Douglass, *Narrative of the Life of Frederick Douglass* (New York: Doubleday, 1963), p. 74.

import of this may be clearer from the second point of difference between Douglass and the dualists. While the act of violence against Covey was the turning point, the resurrection, the event was not without preparation. Earlier Douglass had been told by a master that the ability to read and write would make him unfit as a slave and would mark the beginning of freedom. At that moment, he knew he would learn to read and write.[72] He engaged in small acts of rebellion, including embarrassing (for his master) refusals to start a hymn in a worship service.[73] He prayed for freedom. The point is that there were sources of strength at work in him which finally culminated in the barn fight. In fact, Douglass does not talk about becoming a man for the first time but of "rekindling the embers of freedom" and "reviving" his manhood.

The claim of dehumanization can only be made by an external observer, and that is done at great risk, for it focuses attention on the weakness or deficiencies of the "dehumanized" person rather than on his latent strengths. This is serious for ethics and for all attempts by social scientists to understand "marginal" peoples, since it hides the question, What attributes have enabled these people to survive such treatment?[74] Thus, as Fanon reports, the alleged low suicide rate among blacks and other minority groups is interpreted as a sign of deficiency rather than as a mark of the strength to survive in the face of suffering.

The impossibility of commending violence to another as therapy, the paradox of even claiming that another has been deprived of "humanity," reveals above all the abyss created between man and man in a dualistic revolutionary situation. To the extent that there is dehumanization (and there almost certainly is), it is a function not so much of moral or character deficiencies in the oppressed but of the collapse of moral community. Dehumanization applies as profoundly to the oppressor as to the oppressed (although the former may be held responsible for it), and especially to the relation (or lack of it) between them.

In this sense the spontaneous violence of Douglass, Fanon, and the

72. Ibid., p. 36.

73. Ibid., p. 64.

74. This question has inspired the work of Robert Coles; see, for example, *Children of Crisis* (Boston: Little, Brown, 1967).

millenarians is genuinely apocalyptic–it reveals man's inhumanity to man. Many writers who have used the term *apocalyptic* in connection with revolution have forgotten that it means *revelation* and use it to mean only *sudden* or *radical*. But the last two meanings are derivative. We can say that when an apocalyptic revolution takes place, or when we are faced with the rejuvenating violence of a Douglass or one of Fanon's patients, moral community has already been shattered by the theodicy of the system against which the violence is directed.

While the radical transition characterized by such apocalyptic violence has been characterized in different ways, there is general agreement that it is spontaneous, not accounted for by the circumstances that preceded it. When religious language is used, this spontaneity of action is called divine intervention, which cuts across the explanatory structures of reason and human institutions. It is similar to a conversion experience and is so described by those who have gone through it. I have also likened it to the gestalt shift that Thomas Kuhn claims is at the root of scientific revolutions. In any case, the radical transition is marked by a sense of novelty, of irreversibility, and of violation of the old. What is violated in revolutionary violence is the network of human relationships that bound the revolutionary before his break and the theodicy that legitimated them. Such a radical transition is, I have suggested, illegitimate from the standpoint of the old theodicy. And while an external observer may develop his own moral judgments about a revolutionary situation, he must recognize that they are not likely to be congruent with the interpretation placed on it by the revolutionary participant. The logic of a radical transition makes sense only within the context of a dialectic opposing an old and a new paradigm, which because they are incommensurate appear illegitimate to one another. The simplest version of this incommensurability in social and political revolution is the dualistic one, which the revolutionaries resolve simply by inverting the terms of the paradigm.

Having stressed the difficulties of developing a logic of justification external to the actual dialectic of paradigm opposition, it is helpful to compare cases of dualistic violence with violent phenomena in normal human society, in order to clarify some of the moral issues raised by revolution. While violence occurs with some regularity in the daily life of any society, some of it is considered only destructive and is consistently repressed. Other instances, ostensibly similar, are tolerated and even legitimated as having a constructive or rejuvenating effect. This variance requires a closer analysis of violence.

The term *violence* is systematically confused unless it is distinguished from the more general term *force*. A host of writers have made the point that violence is simply illegitimate force, a definition in which the term *illegitimate* has no significance apart from its negative relation to a given society's general conception of legitimacy and authority. The argument runs like this:[75] Power and authority are the most general and fundamental concepts of political life. Power is simply the ability to effect one's will and decisions. Authority is the right to do so. That right derives from a combination of formal and informal relationships with the people, ranging from charismatic leadership to legally defined limits and obligations. Within that set of relationships, coercion as force is actually present and considered legitimate provided it does not violate these limits. This coercion is of many sorts, including the threat of legal sanctions, their actual use, regulation, jailing, handcuffing, and use of pistols in certain "violent" situations.

Violence is the illegal or illegitimate use of similar force. For example, we distinguish between police force and police violence even though the particular effects may be identical. A policeman who shoots or clubs a man who is attacking someone else is normally not called violent, but he could be charged with violence if he attacked an unarmed, unthreatening man. At the 1968 Democratic convention in Chicago the action of the police was called a "riot" and "violent" precisely because it was arbitrary in its application of force. If the police use force against you independently of whether or not you break the law, it becomes violence rather than mere force. Similarly, a law or a set of institutions that discriminates against blacks is effectively violent if the decision to single out skin color is conceived to be an arbitrary decision (which it is under the legitimating principles of the U.S. Constitution). For someone who

---

75. The following argument is adopted from Robert Paul Wolff, "Violence and the Law," in *The Rule of Law*, ed. R. P. Wolff (New York: Simon & Schuster, 1971), pp. 54–72. Although I agree with the analysis that Wolff makes of the terms discussed here, I do not agree with the conclusions he draws. A similar analysis has been made by Reinhold Niebuhr in *Moral Man and Immoral Society* (New York: Scribner's, 1932).

believes that distinction based on skin color is not arbitrary but "in the nature of things," racially discriminatory laws are not violent.

It is for reasons like these that Reinhold Niebuhr has called the distinction between violent and nonviolent resistance imprecise, since they can have similar consequences:

> Gandhi's boycott of British cotton results in the undernourishment of children in Manchester, and the blockade of the Allies in war-time caused the death of German children. It is impossible to coerce a group without damaging both life and property and without imperilling the interests of the innocent with those of the guilty.[76]

Gandhi's boycott, though nonviolent in form, aimed at causing economic hardship. This indicates that even passive resistance to the law or to a given order is likely to be perceived as violent by the larger society or by legal authorities. But the distinction we make between violent and nonviolent resistance is still morally significant.

Nonviolent resistance is generally considered "more legitimate" because those who participate in it more clearly "surrender" their case to the adjudication of the system as a whole than do those who engage in violent resistance. Even though the effects of both may be similar, the ostensible passivity of the nonviolent resister symbolizes his intention to be loyal to the legitimating structure as a whole while resisting a portion of it that he considers unjust or "violent." The "violent" resister, the one who uses physical coercion to achieve a similar end, does not so clearly reveal his ultimate loyalty to the rule of law, even if he intends to. Thus, the decision to use nonviolence or violent resistance or civil disobedience is chiefly a question of strategy, and the strategic considerations must always include (but are not entirely limited by) the potential response of the larger society to what happens. Even a violent resister may structure his use of force in such a way as to make clear that it has limits and is discriminate.[77] Violence during trade-union strikes frequently goes

76. *Moral Man and Immoral Society*, p. 172.

77. This analysis clearly does not apply to someone who is nonviolent on principle. Such a person might engage in nonviolent resistance even when he does not wish to assent to the adjudication of the larger legal structure. But principled nonviolence almost always claims legitimacy from some structure or belief that transcends the legal order, even if it appeals to the law itself for protection.

unpunished, having become legitimated by its restriction to a process with specific goals, goals that include reconciliation with those against whom the violence is directed.

In short, force that would be perceived as violence by the larger society may acquire a potential legitimacy if it shows itself willing to submit to the adjudication of the larger legal and moral system. Although the outcome of adjudication depends on the case, a limited and discriminate use of force increases the chances that those responsible will receive fair consideration. Civil disobedience, passive resistance, and even some kinds of violent disobedience, insofar as they are self-limiting, seem to have this potential legitimacy.

I have already suggested that revolutionary violence occurs when there is no overarching legitimating structure accepted by both parties—or when the revolutionary calls into question the legitimating structure (especially its theodicy) of his oppressor. Dualistic revolutions especially point up the absence of such a legitimating structure. I have therefore designated revolutionary violence as an apocalyptic act rather than a moral act, the latter characterization being reserved for acts that can be justified or legitimated, at the very least by an appeal to the potential legitimacy I have just outlined.

Some have argued that moral judgments are possible with respect to the way revolutionaries choose to limit violence after the transition. It is a commonplace that revolutionaries are future-oriented, and as Reinhold Niebuhr has pointed out, the moral evaluation of a revolution depends upon whether the society established by the revolutionaries is more just than its predecessor. Likewise, A. F. C. Wallace has noted that revolutionaries are "teleological moralists" rather than "procedural moralists."[78] But to the extent that dualistic revolutions involve the eradication of the enemy, such an appeal to the future is weak indeed, even if the external observer finds reason to condemn the prerevolutionary structure.

Yet if one does not believe that a given revolution marks the advent of the Kingdom of God, there seems to be no alternative to evaluating the *effects* of such spontaneous acts of rage and violence. Hobsbawm notes that without the moral passion generated by the

78. Anthony F. C. Wallace, "Violence, Morality, and Revitalization," in Wolff, *Rule of Law*, pp. 98–114.

millenarian confidence that evil can be overcome, no revolution would succeed. Millenarian beliefs are

> probably a necessary social device for generating the superhuman efforts without which no major revolution is achieved. From the historian's point of view the transformations brought about by the French and Russian Revolutions are astonishing enough, but would the Jacobins have undertaken their task simply to exchange the France of the Abbé Prévost for the France of Balzac, the Bolsheviks to exchange the Russia of Tchehov for that of Mr. Khrushchev? Probably not. It was essential for them to believe that "the ultimate in human prosperity and liberty will appear after their victories." Obviously they will not, though the result of the revolution may nevertheless be very worth while.[79]

It must be remembered that such an evaluation is possible only by imposing a structure of meaning on the millenarian's activity which he might not himself accept. Hobsbawm's judgment of worthwhileness can be made only if one has already settled certain moral issues with respect to the direction of history and the process of modernization. The revolutions he discusses were certainly not worthwhile from the standpoint of those who paid in blood—and they number in the millions. Such a moral calculus is also muddied by the imprecision of the qualitative factors involved: how is life under the czars measured against life under the Party?

Part of the difficulty is that dualistic revolutions are not genuinely innovative solutions to the problem of evil. They simply invert the terms of a theodicy that has been imposed upon them. This theodicy structures force and violence by directing them at the perceived source of evil, the oppressors, the white colonizers, the hordes of Antichrist. Even if the revolutionaries should succeed in eliminating the perceived source of evil, they would have no theodicy on which to model life after the revolution. They would have to either return to a theodicy derived from a source within their own culture and history or turn to still another framework, such as Marxism, to organize their lives once the enemy had disappeared. In fact, there is likely to be no shortage of candidates for organizing life after the

---

79. *Primitive Rebels*, pp. 60–61. Reinhold Niebuhr made almost exactly this point in *Moral Man and Immoral Society*, p. 277.

revolution. Revolutions are much messier than dualistic theodicies admit, and those who undergo passionate conversion are likely to be manipulated by countless groups and leaders who do have visions of what the future should be like. That, after all, is what the period of terror is about. It would be convenient if Christians had a powerful vision of the future that would permit them to step in at this point and dispense with the terror. But a Christian perspective probably requires examining the prehistory of the revolutionary process. Unless one assumes that all moves from political passivity to political activity or from premodern to modern forms of political and economic organization must take the route of apocalyptic violence, the first question to be asked is how the conditions that occasioned such violence came to be. Even Marx does not make his revolution dependent upon the therapeutic violence of the dualists. It would be possible to document numerous instances of profound changes in the patterns of domination and participation in societies that do not entail apocalyptic violence (Japan, for example).

Therefore, the Christian probably has to begin with some move of humility and repentance akin to this passage from Jacques Ellul:

> Instead of listening to the fomenters of violence, Christians ought to repent for having been too late. For if the time comes when despair sees violence as the only possible way, it is because Christians were not what they should have been. *If violence is unleashed anywhere at all, the Christians are always to blame.*[80]

This seems a harsh sentiment to apply to situations where Christians have not been involved. But if one remembers that almost all of the instances of revolutionary dualism I have described have been influenced by Christian ideas, or by "Christian" European culture, then Ellul's point is not far off the mark. Apocalyptic violence does reveal the inhumanity of man to man. To the extent that Christians have participated in any fashion in the institutional arrangements that allowed that inhumanity, they bear responsibility for it. Apocalyptic violence may reveal the weakness of those who find that they

80. Jacques Ellul, *On Violence* (New York: Seabury, 1969), pp. 155-56. Ellul's strong insistence that Christians are to be blamed for all violence everywhere derives from certain of his Christological assumptions. See, for example, *The Ethics of Freedom* (Grand Rapids, Mich.: Eerdmans, 1976), chaps. 2 and 3.

must undergo it, but it reveals even more the weakness of those who imposed dualistic conditions to begin with. This leads to two further points.

First, apocalyptic violence is likely to receive its strongest impetus in the encounters between widely disparate cultural forms: between black and white, between European and other cultures, between modern and traditional economies. That encounter involves institutions—economic, political, cultural—that extend considerably beyond the institutional forms of religion but that historically are inextricably bound up with the churches, or with the lives of Christians. For this reason a Christian concern for the conditions that occasion apocalyptic violence must include those other intitutions, since the moral issues at stake have first and foremost to do with the broader social policies and institutions contributing to the dualistic syndrome.

Second, when confronted with the fact of dualistic violence there seems to be no immediate reason for the Christian to accept either a neo-Marxist judgment that it is a necessary step on the way to modernization or the dualist claim of a hiatus between the old and the new world. The calculus involved in the former judgment is, as I have already suggested, imprecise; it requires the most careful statement of moral premises and a thorough assessment of empirical data. The claim of hiatus has both empirical and theological import. In the next chapter I shall look at Marx's attempt to provide an empirical account of innovation in revolution while also accounting for continuity. Theologically it must be said that while the Christian has no difficulty with the claim of novelty in history, his tradition also makes a strong claim for continuity. This is the subject matter of the last chapter. Here it need only be said that the testimony of a Frederick Douglass needs to be taken seriously: the experience of a resurrection may be very real indeed, but the past that laid the groundwork for that resurrection cannot be discounted.

4

Karl Marx and the End of Theodicy

> That the History of the World, with all the changing
> scenes which its annals present, is this process of develop-
> ment and the realization of Spirit—this is the true *Theo-
> dicaea*, the justification of God in History. Only *this*
> insight can reconcile Spirit with the History of the World
> —viz., that what has happened, and is happening every
> day, is not only not "without God," but is essentially
> His Work.

Hegel, The Philosophy of History

Marx's inversion or transformation of Hegel via Feuerbach provides
the groundwork for a systematic treatment of the issues of revolution. It is not surprising that Marx found in Hegel a starting point for
his theory, since Hegel found in the French Revolution a challenge
that shaped much of his thought. As Herbert Marcuse puts it, Hegel's
thought can be called a "theory of the French Revolution": "In
Hegel's view, the decisive turn that history took with the French
Revolution was that man came to rely on his mind and dared to submit the given reality to the standards of reason."[1] When Hegel
declared at the end of *The Philosophy of History*, following a discussion of the Enlightenment and the French Revolution, that everything that had happened was God's work, he claimed an insight into
God's mind which was at the same time the most audacious formulation of theodicy ever made.

Marx says that Hegel's claim is too modest. When he states that
"for Germany, the critique of religion is essentially completed; and

---

1. Herbert Marcuse, *Reason and Revolution: Hegel and the Rise of Social
Theory* (Boston: Beacon, 1960), pp. 5–6. See also p. 3: "German idealism has
been called the theory of the French Revolution. . . . Despite their bitter
criticism of the terror, the German idealists unanimously welcomed the
revolution, calling it the dawn of a new era, and they all linked their basic
philosophical principles to the ideals that it advanced."

the critique of religion is the prerequisite of every critique,"[2] he suggests the method by which the very need for a theodicy may be overcome. According to Marx, the fact that Hegel still uses the language of theodicy indicates that the conditions requiring a theodicy have not yet been removed. He therefore sets about the critical and revolutionary task of changing those conditions.[3] Marx, then, is the first to see clearly the key relationship between theodicy and revolution, and he brings us full circle back to the subject of chapter 2.

In addition to this general interest in the problem of evil (which for Marx is also the problem of suffering), Marx's view of revolution coincides at critical points with issues raised by the dualists. With them, he argues that prior to *the* revolution evil is at its highest pitch, that the nature of this evil is such that only a revolution can overcome it, that the transformation involved is fundamental and marks the movement of men from one mode of consciousness to another as well as the beginning of a new era. He also agrees that to talk of justifying revolutionary action is to misconceive the revolutionary process.

Nevertheless, Marx does one thing the dualists were unable to do: he attempts to give an account of the break between the old and the new, and he integrates the radical conversion within a larger structure so that the old and the new are separated not by absolute contradiction but by dialectical contradiction. The vehicle of integration is the dialectical method which Hegel used to reconcile the progress of reason with the Dark Ages, the central problem of the Enlightenment; and it is Hegel's *List der Vernunft* that Marx takes up to solve the problem of evil. Whether he succeeds in doing so, whether he actually avoids positing a new theodicy, is the chief interest of this chapter.[4] Marx's own analysis of the Hegelian theodicy and

2. Marx, "A Contribution to the Critique of Hegel's *Philosophy of Right*," in *Critique of Hegel's Philosophy of Right*, trans. J. O'Malley (Cambridge: Cambridge University Press, 1970), p. 131.

3. Thus, "The abolition of religion as the illusory happiness of the people is a demand for their true happiness. The call to abandon illusions about their condition is the call to abandon a condition which requires illusions." Ibid.

4. It goes without saying that my discussion of Marx must be highly selective and must presuppose some knowledge of Marx by the reader. It is customary for the writer of a book on Marx to defend his work against charges of unoriginality and redundancy, given the massive corpus of secondary sources now available. The writer of a chapter on Marx is perhaps spared this ordeal since

the problem of evil is elucidated at some length in the first section. The second section deals with Marx's view of the revolutionary process and his notion of praxis. The third section examines the problems surrounding Marx's conception of society after the revolution. These first three sections correspond roughly to cause, conduct, and ends; the final section is a critique of issues posed in previous chapters in light of the discussion of Marx.

---

the justification may simply reside, as it does here, in the development of a larger argument or exposition. Nevertheless, given the labyrinthian character of Marxist scholarship, the remarkable diversity of Marxist political forms, the continued controversies over the more troublesome and key Marxist ideas (alienation, humanism, dialectic, classless society, the relation between substructure and superstructure, to name only a few), the debate about the "early" and "mature" Marx, not to mention the relationship between Marx and his disciples, it seems wise to make some prefatory remarks about the approach I have taken.

Since it is not my intent to give a full exposition of Marx, to resolve all the controversies about his theories, I will list here some important assumptions which will not be debated in the text. While each of them is contestable, I am convinced that they are sufficiently supported by reputable scholars to write as if they were persuasive—the footnotes will indicate which scholars I have followed most closely.

First, Marx is viewed as firmly within the Hegelian tradition. What criticisms he made of Hegel—including the famous Feuerbachian transformation—were made within the Hegelian framework. As Engels pointed out, Hegel could only be overthrown by Hegelians. See Shlomo Avineri, *The Social and Political Thought of Karl Marx* (Cambridge: Cambridge University Press, 1968), p. 13.

Second, while Marx's thought certainly develops, there is no discontinuity between the "young" and "mature" Marx, no shift from "humanism" to "economic materialism." At most, the later writings work out in the economic realm the positions and hypotheses developed in the earlier writings.

Third, Marx has been served badly by his disciples, but he is not the first figure to be so treated, and his own ambiguities must bear some of the blame.

Fourth, there is merit in dealing with Marx alone (rather than with later developments of Marxism) both because he deserves such attention and because later developments can hardly be understood or evaluated without understanding Marx himself.

For those who disagree with these starting points, or those who would like to see them fully debated, I draw attention to the dialogue between Socrates and Hegel, summoned up from the underworld by a relatively unsympathetic critic of Hegel:

THE PROBLEM OF EVIL IN MARX

Marx's analysis of the problem of evil and suffering in human life joins two accounts of the source of evil. His first account of evil and suffering is essentially an adaptation of Hegel's view of the unfolding dialectic of reason which in its cunning (*List*) apparently produces human suffering and self-alienation, but only for the purpose of a higher mode of human existence, a process that ultimately unfolds into human freedom. The second account of evil is derived from Feuerbach's inversion of Hegel, which is rooted in a much more broadly accepted nineteenth-century view that man's life is characterized fundamentally by conflict with nature. I shall argue that the second account is the more basic of the two. But first it is necessary to understand Marx's appropriation of Hegel's dialectic.

Hegel and the Master-Slave Encounter: Anthropogenesis through Conflict

It is not essential to enter into the debates about the nature and role of dialectic in Hegel's system as a whole, although I tend to agree with those who view it as relatively fluid and not always meaning the same thing.[5] Marx takes his cues almost entirely from the *Phenomenology*, and his language demonstrates that he is chiefly interested in section 4, which treats of self-consciousness in terms of the paradigm of lordship and bondsman or master and slave.[6] In the

---

Socrates: Shall we begin by being in complete disagreement or shall we agree about a thing we might call a presupposition?

Hegel: (Silent).

Socrates: What presupposition do you begin with?

Hegel: With none at all.

Socrates: Splendid! Then I suppose you do not begin at all?

Hegel: I do not begin, who have written twenty-one volumes?

This is a journal entry by Søren Kierkegaard, quoted by T. H. Croxall in an introductory essay to Kierkegaard's *Johannes Climacus* (Stanford: Stanford University Press, 1958), p. 61.

5. Cf., for example, Walter Kaufmann, *Hegel: A Reinterpretation* (Garden City, N.Y.: Doubleday Anchor, 1966), p. 156; J. N. Findlay, *The Philosophy of Hegel* (New York: Collier, 1962), chap. 3; Shlomo Avineri, *Hegel's Theory of the Modern State* (Cambridge: Cambridge University Press, 1972), p. 238.

6. See Hegel, *The Phenomenology of the Mind*, trans. J. B. Baillie (New York: Harper Torchbooks, 1967), pp. 214–67.

early manuscript entitled "Critique of the Hegelian Dialectic and Philosophy as a Whole," Marx describes the *Phenomenology* as "the true point of origin and the secret of the Hegelian philosophy"[7] and proceeds to analyze section 4 and the implications of Hegel's master-slave dialectic for his own view of the centrality of labor in human history. To understand Marx's reasoning, then, we must look more closely at the master-slave discussion.[8]

The section on self-consciousness contains several premises which serve as the backdrop for the master-slave encounter. Man's consciousness of himself distinguishes him from the animals, but this self-consciousness is incomplete and becomes genuine only in the outward movement toward another self-consciousness, that is through desire. Full human self-consciousness is therefore social—it is the consequence of the mutual recognition of human minds and thus of mind as a general category: "Self-consciousness attains its satisfaction only in another self-consciousness."[9]

From these general considerations Hegel moves to a specific account of a meeting between two selves (I shall use "self" to denote "self-consciousness"). In the first instance, says Hegel, one self wants recognition from the other without recognizing it as another self-consciousness, an ego. Since both selves start from this position (which Kaufmann calls "pride"[10]) the encounter takes the form of a

7. Marx, *The Economic and Philosophic Manuscripts of 1844*, ed. D. J. Struik (New York: International Publishers, 1964), p. 173. At the beginning of this manuscript Marx also mentions Hegel's *Logic*, but he devotes his discussion almost entirely to the section of the *Phenomenology* cited and especially to the role of labor in the emancipation of the slave. In fact, he suggests that the *Logic*, which deals with "pure speculative thought," is nothing more than an estranged abstraction which rests on a "double error" in Hegel's *Phenomenology* and which hides the "outstanding achievement" of the *Phenomenology*: the fundamental role of labor in human existence and consciousness. See pp. 174-77.

8. In this summary of Hegel's master-slave account I have relied on, in addition to the *Phenomenology*, Kaufmann, *Hegel*; Findlay, *Philosophy of Hegel*; and Alexandre Kojève, *Introduction to the Reading of Hegel* (New York: Basic Books, 1969). The latter is very much a Marxist interpretation and therefore plays down the extent to which "labor" in Hegel refers to the work of reason as well as the transformation of nature.

9. Hegel, *Phenomenology*, p. 226. The larger discussion is contained in pp. 218-27.

10. Kaufmann, *Hegel*, p. 137.

battle in which each attempts to establish the truth of its own consciousness through the negation of the other. Such assurance can come only in the willingness to risk death—to stop short of that risk is to have left open the possibility that one's own self-consciousness is not genuine but only the object of another's self-consciousness. This life-and-death struggle, however, puts obstacles in the way of the original intention of self-affirmation: "Through death, doubtless, there has arisen the certainty that both did stake their life, and held it lightly both in their own case and in the case of the other; but that is not for those who underwent this struggle." This ironic remark leads Hegel to observe that there must of necessity be two classes of people in the world: those who do indeed take the risk of death and emerge triumphant with their lives, and those who prefer an unrecognized or enslaved life to death. The former are the masters or lords, and the latter are bondsmen or slaves.[11] In other words, human mind discovers that biological life is essential for consciousness and a compromise is reached where both adversaries continue to live by adopting a superior-inferior relationship. Kojève puts it this way:

> It does the man of the Fight no good to kill his adversary. He must overcome him "dialectically." That is, he must leave him life and consciousness, and destroy only his autonomy. He must overcome the adversary only insofar as the adversary is opposed to him and acts against him. In other words, he must enslave him.[12]

The willingness of the slave to submit rather than force the issue to the point of death appears to establish a modus vivendi in which the master has genuine selfhood (what Hegel calls "consciousness for itself") and the slave has only dependent selfhood ("existence for another").

But now a series of ironic and dialectical reversals takes place. The master's self and life are not what they were before the life-and-death struggle, for his reaching beyond himself, his desire, is now mediated by the slave. In a curious way he becomes dependent upon the slave insofar as it is the slave who does his work for him, the slave who expresses the master's will. In this way, the slave becomes the

11. Hegel, *Phenomenology*, pp. 231–35.
12. Kojève, *Introduction to Hegel*, p. 15.

"truth" of the master.[13] Furthermore, the recognition sought in the slave is no longer satisfying, for the slave's recognition of the master is not autonomous but forced: the master "is recognized by someone whom he does not recognize."[14] Thus "lordship showed its essential nature to be the reverse of what it wants to be. . . ."[15] At the same time, the slave discovers that the work he must perform in service to the master becomes for him the equivalent of the master's desire or will, that is, he discovers the beginnings of autonomy and his own self-consciousness. This happens because, while the master's control over nature is achieved only through the mediation of the slave, the slave begins to exercise control over nature directly, through labor:

> In becoming master of Nature by work, then, the Slave frees himself from his own nature, from his own instinct that tied him to Nature and made him the Master's Slave. Therefore, by freeing the Slave from Nature, work frees him from himself as well, from his Slave's nature: it frees him from the Master. In the raw, natural, given World, the Slave is slave of the Master. In the technical world transformed by his work, he rules—or, at least, will one day rule—as absolute Master.[16]

In this reversal of roles, the master's desire finds satisfaction only in fleeting pleasures or continual risk on the battlefield. Neither is genuinely self-affirming. The slave, however, is formed and educated by his labor, which holds the key to his freedom,[17] and that freedom will be superior to the freedom the master gained through the slave since it is not mediated by another consciousness.

Now Hegel embarks on a further series of transitions as the slave experiences different modes of consciousness because of the discrepancy between his new consciousness and his actual position as a slave. The movement from stoicism to skepticism and finally to the unhappy consciousness makes a fascinating account, but since Marx

13. Hegel, *Phenomenology*, p. 237. Cf. Kojève, *Introduction to Hegel*, p. 47.

14. Kojève, *Introduction to Hegel*, p. 19.

15. Hegel, *Phenomenology*, p. 237.

16. Kojève, *Introduction to Hegel*, p. 23.

17. Hegel, *Phenomenology*, p. 238. Cf. Kojève, *Introduction to Hegel*, p. 24.

does not make a great deal of it, seizing rather upon the role of labor in effecting the slave's freedom together with the unhappy consciousness that accompanies the enslaved condition until the master is overthrown, I shall not deal with it further here. What is essential is that the master-slave relationship is the paradigm for Hegel's grand theodicy: as unfortunate as the slave's position may be, he would not have gained true freedom and true humanity had he not undergone the discipline and education of labor. This is the process by which consciousness itself, mind, emerges in human history:

> To be able to stop and understand himself, a man must be *satisfied*. And for this, of course, he must *cease* to be a Slave. But to be able to cease being a *Slave*, he must have *been* a Slave. And since there are Slaves only where there is a Master, Mastery, while itself an *impasse*, is "justified" as a *necessary* stage that leads to the absolute Science of Hegel. The Master appears only for the sake of engendering the Slave who "overcomes" (*aufhebt*) him as Master, while thereby "overcoming" himself as Slave. . . . The Master is only the "catalyst" of the History that will be realized, completed, and "revealed" by the Slave or the ex-Slave who has become citizen.[18]

It is in this fashion that Hegel is able to justify apparent reverses in history, as well as those periods when one civilization or one social class has dominated another. The moral objections that might be raised against these patterns of domination dissolve when the larger pattern of *die List der Vernunft* is perceived. To Kant's dictum that one should never treat another merely as a means, but as an end, Hegel replies, "What does that have to do with the Norman conquest of England?"[19] Such conquest is the stuff of history and the emergence of human autonomy—it could happen no other way.

Before turning to Marx's appropriation and criticism of this paradigm, several reflections are in order. The shifts and reversals that occur in the struggle between master and slave are of many different orders, all of which Hegel apparently considers as "dialectical

---

18. Kojève, *Introduction to Hegel*, p. 47.

19. Quoted by John C. Raines, "From Passive to Active Man," in *Marxism and Radical Religion*, ed. John C. Raines and Thomas Dean (Philadelphia: Temple University Press, 1970), p. 116.

movement." As Kaufmann notes, dialectic includes "the ironical reversal of the roles of master and servant," as well as "the instability of views and attitudes that, when adopted in earnest and pushed, change into other views and attitudes" (this latter is especially true of the movement from stoicism through skepticism to the unhappy consciousness).[20] At other places (especially the *Logic*), Hegel talks about the reversal of subject and predicate (utilizing here the vocabulary of syntax and grammar) and of the "objectification" of the self which takes on a life of its own. In all of this, the notion of dialectical contradiction is far from tight.

There have been many attempts to reconcile the various formulations of Hegel's dialectic and considerable disagreement about whether such reconciliation is possible.[21] Here we need only make two points. First, Marx picks up much of the diversity and richness of Hegel's terminology rather than attempting to simplify it. Second, there is one term that does offer a unifying focus, *Aufhebung* (verb, *aufheben*), which carries the dual meaning of abolition and transcendence, implying the preservation of key elements of that which is abolished. The slave does not merely negate what the master intends but surpasses him, actualizing what the master desired but which was beyond his reach, given the mediation of the slave. Master and slave were both required before the higher freedom could be realized. In thought, the articulation of one idea, thought through to its conclusion, leads the mind to see an alternative or even contradictory truth which would not have emerged without the original articulation; but on further reflection both ideas are found to be inadequate in themselves, yet in relation and transcended (*aufgehoben*) lead to a higher truth. Focusing on the term *Aufhebung* in no way resolves all the problems of dialectic but it does help prevent the looseness of Hegel's formulations from becoming, as it has in the writing of some, the basis for describing his position as one that characterizes the world simply as flux. The world is indeed in flux in Hegel's view, but that flux has a structure, as does the human comprehension of it, which Hegel attempts to penetrate with the notion of dialectical *Aufhebung*.

20. Kaufmann, *Hegel*, p. 156.
21. See, for example, Findlay, *Philosophy of Hegel*, chap. 3, especially sections 1 and 2; Marcuse, *Reason and Revolution*, pp. vii–xiv ("A Note on Dialectic").

It is also worth inquiring what status the master-slave paradigm has with respect to human relations in general. As widely admired as this section of the *Phenomenology* is, and as often as it has been used, it is not always clear whether Hegel intends the relationship to be a paradigm for only some human relationships or for all. Kaufmann calls the master-slave account a "skit,"[22] implying, perhaps, that it should not be elevated to the position of a paradigm for all human relationships. Sartre's "hell is other people" shows that for him the master-slave account is comprehensive: the "other" is the enemy.[23] We may perhaps judge that Hegel does not intend to go as far as Sartre, if for no other reason than that his discussion of the family demonstrates his conviction that in such a natural grouping, human selves relate without antagonism: the family is *the* ethical paradigm for Hegel. But the master-slave encounter has the function of explaining conflict, suffering, and evil as the way by which human consciousness is educated and progresses from the biological determinations of the family to the conscious universal life of the state.[24]

Marx accepts the antagonistic master-slave paradigm as a way of penetrating the conflicts of capitalist society and links it to still another dialectic, the struggle of man with nature:

> The outstanding achievement of Hegel's *Phenomenology* and of its final outcome, the dialectic of negativity as the moving and generating principle, is thus first that Hegel conceives the self-creation of man as a process, conceives objectification as loss of the object, as alienation and as transcendence of this alienation; that he thus grasps the essence of *labor* and comprehends objective man—true, because real man—as the outcome of man's *own labor*.[25]

In short, "Hegel conceives labor as man's act of *self-genesis*," but he

22. Kaufmann, *Hegel*, p. 136.

23. See ibid., p. 137. "Hell is other people" is from *No Exit*, but the philosophical position is spelled out most fully in *Being and Nothingness*. See also R. D. Laing and D. G. Cooper, *Reason and Violence* (New York: Vintage, 1971).

24. See Hegel, *Philosophy of Right*, trans. T. M. Knox (Oxford: Clarendon, 1957), pp. 105–21. For an excellent discussion of Hegel on the family, see Avineri, *Hegel's Theory of the Modern State*, pp. 132–34, 139–41.

25. Marx, *Manuscripts*, p. 177.

does this only in "the sphere of abstraction,"[26] that is to say, Hegel sees the laboring process as a working out or objectification of mind (*Geist*). In theological language, the labor process is God's unfolding in history. Hegel had a momentous insight but lost sight of its true significance by imagining that labor was a predicate of mind rather than mind being a predicate of labor. A penetrating and witty portrayal of Hegel's reversal is found in Marx's criticism of German idealism in *The German Ideology* (the first paragraph is a quote from a socialist article):

> "Man's struggle with nature is based upon the polar opposition of my particular existence to, and its interaction with, universal natural activity. When this struggle appears as conscious activity, it is termed labour."
>
> Surely, on the contrary, the idea of a "polar opposition" is based upon the observation of a struggle between man and nature? First of all, an abstraction is made from a fact; then it is declared that the fact is based upon the abstraction. That is how to proceed if you want to appear German, profound and speculative.
>
> For example: Fact: The cat eats the mouse.
>
> Reflection: Cat = nature, Mouse = nature; consumption of mouse by cat = consumption of nature by nature = self-consumption of nature.
>
> Philosophic presentation of the fact: The devouring of the mouse by the cat is based upon the self-consumption of nature.
>
> Having thus obscured man's struggle with nature, the writer goes on to obscure man's conscious activity in relation to nature; he conceives it as the manifestation of this mere abstraction from the real conflict. The profane word labour is finally smuggled in as the result of this process of mystification.[27]

What Marx intends to show is that the antagonisms between man and man, exemplified by the master-slave paradigm and actually present in the conflict between classes, is rooted in man's struggle with nature.

Marx's critical insight about Hegel is derived from Feuerbach, who

26. Ibid., p. 188.
27. Marx and Engels, *The German Ideology*, ed. R. Pascal (New York: International Publishers, 1963), pp. 114–15.

had early expressed a dissatisfaction with the abstract quality of Hegel's thought and with his attempt to reconcile thought and reality by positing the rationality of the phenomenal world (when understood in the light of dialectical reason).[28] According to Feuerbach, Hegel had inverted the world of man by suggesting that the natural world and man's experience of it through his senses are no more than manifestations of thought or mind. In reality, thought is a reflection or manifestation of the natural world:

> Philosophy is the science of reality in its truth and totality. But the sum total of reality is *nature* (nature in the most universal sense of the word). The most profound mysteries are hidden in the simplest natural things which the speculative philosopher, always aspiring to the beyond, tramples with his feet. The return to nature is the only source of salvation.[29]

Feuerbach denies that there is any "world behind the world," any *Vernunft* which, when its cunning is understood, makes sense of the natural world and becomes identical with it. What contradictions seem to appear between the natural world as it is and as it "ought" to be, what suffering and conflict man experiences in his social life, are consequences of the failure to recognize that the world of thought and culture are creations of material man rather than vice versa. All philosophy, therefore, must come to grips with man's sensible experience of the natural world and his reflections on nature. When it does this, it will discover that those realms once thought to have an independent reality, and in particular the realm of religion, are no more than alienated truths about man.

The technique that Feuerbach uses to criticize Hegel remains for the most part Hegelian. As Hans Frei has noted, from Hegel's *Logic*

---

28. Whether this is what Hegel actually did is much debated. Some writers have pointed out that Hegel is not nearly so abstract as sometimes charged, and that his theoretical formulations are always made with a close eye to empirical realities. Such attempts to rescue Hegel from his sharpest critics are fully documented in the lively debates contained in a volume entitled *Hegel's Political Philosophy*, ed. Walter Kaufmann (New York: Atheneum, 1970). Herbert Marcuse, *Reason and Revolution*, also argues that the very nature of dialectical thought demands close attention to empirical reality.

29. Ludwig Feuerbach, "Zur Kritik der Hegelschen Philosophie," quoted by Louis Dupré, *The Philosophical Foundations of Marxism* (New York: Harcourt, Brace and World, 1966), p. 73.

Feuerbach had learned that "all statements about a subject must also be statements about its predicate."[30]

> Now when it is shown that what the subject is lies entirely in the attributes of the subject; that is, that the predicate is the true subject; it is also proved that if the divine predicates are attributes of the human nature, the subject of those predicates is also of the human nature.[31]

In this neat dialectical reversal of Hegel, Feuerbach articulates the projection theory of religion. It is clear to him that every attribute predicated of God is also an attribute of man which man has projected outside of himself and posited as the divine. The cause of this projection is man's self-consciousness, that is, his capacity for self-transcendence, which in the first instance causes him to see his own powers, his own essence, as a reality which stands outside and against him: God. Hegel rightly understands this separation, this alienation of man from himself, as a necessary step in the development of true consciousness. But whereas Hegel sees concrete, natural man with his various historical moments of consciousness as an objectification and self-alienation of God, Feuerbach sees God as the self-alienation and objectification of man. True self-consciousness comes not in Hegel's abstract attempt to comprehend the identity of the ideal and the real but in "the race's discovery of the secret identity of God and man."[32] For Feuerbach, theology is anthropology in disguise.

Marx seizes on Feuerbach's transformation of Hegel's theology as a tool to criticize Hegel's political philosophy on its own grounds. In his *Critique of Hegel's "Philosophy of Right,"* Marx subjects paragraphs 261–313 of Hegel's work to a Feuerbachian transformation, showing that Hegel's political conclusions contradict his premises and conceptual schemes. Two examples will illustrate this and lay the groundwork for an examination of Marx's handling of the prob-

---

30. Hans Frei, "Feuerbach and Theology," *Journal of the American Academy of Religion* 35 (September 1967):250–56.

31. Ludwig Feuerbach, *The Essence of Christianity*, trans. George Eliot (New York: Harper Torchbooks, 1957), p. 25. Quoted by Frei, "Feuerbach and Theology," p. 252.

32. Frei, "Feuerbach and Theology," p. 252.

lem of evil: Hegel's delineation of the relationship between the state and civil society, and his views on property.

> The main achievement of Hegel's political philosophy was its attempt to construct the state as an entity abstracted from the social and historical forces which create and condition it in empirical reality. Hegel did this by depicting civil society as the clash of the social forces, to be transcended by the universality of the state. If this separation between civil society and the state could be shown to be fallacious, i.e. if it could be analytically proved that the objective arrangements of the state are just so many particular interests parading under the banner of the general and the universal, then philosophy would tumble down.[33]

Hegel recognized that in modern capitalist society (the term used to describe this social form is *bürgerliche Gesellschaft*—it is variously rendered "civil society" and "bourgeois society") the interests of individual men stand in mutual conflict. The pursuit of individual gain in economic life is essentially Hobbes's *bellum omnium contra omnes*.[34] But whereas Hobbes saw no solution other than a social contract which would establish an artificial identity of interests, Hegel claimed that in the state, which transcends the individual interests of civil society, there is a genuine identity of individual and corporate interests and therefore genuine human freedom. Thus he argues that "in contrast with the spheres of private rights and private welfare,"

> the state is the actuality of concrete freedom. But concrete freedom consists in this, that personal individuality and its particular interests not only achieve their complete development and gain explicit recognition for their right (as they do in the sphere of the family and civil society) but, for one thing, they also pass over of their own accord into the interest of the universal, and, for another thing, they know and will the universal; they even recognize it as their own substantive mind; they take it as their end and aim and are active in its pursuit. The result is that the

33. Avineri, *Marx*, p. 17. It was Avineri who first drew my attention to Marx's *Critique of Hegel's "Philosophy of Right"* in a seminar at Yale, and I am deeply indebted to him in the following discussion.

34. O'Malley, Introduction to Marx, *Critique of Hegel*, p. xlvii.

universal does not prevail or achieve completion except along with particular interests and through the co-operation of particular knowing and willing; and individuals likewise do not live as private persons for their own ends alone, but in the very act of willing these they will the universal in the light of the universal, and their activity is consciously aimed at none but the universal end. The principle of modern states has prodigious strength and depth because it allows the principle of subjectivity to progress to its culmination in the extreme of self-subsistent personal particularity, and yet at the same time brings it back to the substantive unity and so maintains this unity in the principle of subjectivity itself.[35]

Fine, says Marx. But whereas Hegel claimed that the rationality of the state thus constituted "enters upon its finite phase" by "sundering itself into the two ideal spheres of its concept, family and civil society,"[36] Marx argues that the state is an external necessity produced by the divisions and conflicts of modern life "in an unconscious and arbitrary way."[37] Hegel has the relationship backward, and the reason he has it backward is that he starts with the idea of the state rather than with the natural conditions of men that create the necessity for the state:

Had Hegel started with the real subjects as the bases of the state it would not have been necessary for him to let the state become subjectified in a mystical way. . . . Hegel makes the predicates, the object, independent, but independent as separated from their real independence, their subject. Subsequently, and because of this, the real subject appears to be the result; whereas one has to start from the real subject and examine its objectification.[38]

In this passage, Marx takes the language of Hegel's *Logic* and turns it against him by way of a Feuerbachian transformation. The Feuerbachian method is even more explicit a few pages later:

35. Hegel, *Philosophy of Right*, pp. 160–61.
36. Ibid., p. 162. The idea of the state so sunders itself, says Hegel, "in order to rise above its ideality and become explicit as infinite actual mind"; that is, the conflicts of civil society (and also its separation from the family) are moments in the realization of freedom.
37. Marx, *Critique of Hegel*, p. 7.
38. Ibid., pp. 23–24.

Hegel proceeds from the state and makes man into the subjectified state; democracy starts with man and makes the state objectified man. Just as it is not religion that creates man but man who creates religion, so it is not the constitution that creates the people but the people which creates the constitution. In a certain respect democracy is to all other forms of the state what Christianity is to all other religions. Christianity is the religion κατ᾽ ἐξοχὴν, the essence of religion, deified man under the form of a particular religion. In the same way democracy is the essence of every political constitution, socialized man under the form of a particular constitution of the state.[39]

The parallel between Christianity and democracy in a Feuerbachian context suggests that just as the historical appearance of Christianity "abolished the need for religion and was, consequently, self-destroying, so democracy as conceived by Marx poses the question whether it is not at the same time the apex and the transcendence (*Aufhebung*) of the political constitution, i.e. of the state."[40] I shall return to this point later. Here it is necessary only to point out that insofar as it is still necessary to posit a universal state, according to Marx, there are antagonistic conditions in society that have not been overcome.

In fact, once Marx has applied the Feuerbachian method to Hegel's argument, it is easy for him to show that Hegel fails to make empirical reality fit his universal claims for the state. Hegel tried to show that the representation of the particular interests of civil society through the mediating organ of the estates (*Stände*) assured the universal character of the state.[41] But according to Marx the economic character of the *Stände* (also the word for "classes") in civil society inevitably meant that its representatives did no more than further the interests of their own class. Furthermore, since Hegel made political representation dependent on private economic position (class), Marx claims that another curious inversion has taken place: "One is thus treated as a 'landowner,' a 'worker,' etc., rather than as a human being who happens to be owning

39. Ibid., p. 30.
40. Avineri, *Marx*, pp. 35–36.
41. See paragraphs 301 and 302 of Hegel, *Philosophy of Right*, pp. 195–97.

land or physically working. Again, the predicate becomes the subject."[42]

This last point permits Marx to turn to the issue of property. He points out that in some of the early paragraphs of *The Philosophy of Right* (65 and 66) Hegel argued that private property was subject to the free will of the owner, an extension of his consciousness, as it were, and as such inalienable. But, says Marx, in paragraphs 305 and 306 Hegel suggests that landed property, secured through primogeniture, guarantees the ethical superiority of the aristocratic class insofar as it frees the owner from a variety of pressures that might make him less than an ideal representative of the universal interest:

> This class is more particularly fitted for political position and significance in that its capital is independent alike of the state's capital, the uncertainty of business, the quest for profit, and any sort of fluctuation in possessions. It is likewise independent of favour, whether from the executive or the mob. It is even fortified against its own wilfulness, because those members of this class who are called to political life are not entitled, as other citizens are, either to dispose of their entire property at will, or to the assurance that it will pass to their children, whom they love equally, in similarly equal divisions. Hence their wealth becomes inalienable, entailed, and burdened by primogeniture.[43]

Marx passes over the remarkable naiveté of this passage and fastens instead on what appears as a subtle contradiction: whereas property first appears as an extension of the individual's consciousness, now property determines the political consciousness of its owner. Or as Avineri puts it, property "is transformed under Hegel's hands from an object of the will into a master. In saying that a person is determined by his class status one really says that man becomes a predicate of his property."[44] Once again subject and predicate are inverted, and once again the ironic shifts of the master-slave paradigm come to the fore. What is intended as the mode of freedom becomes instead the denial of freedom. Property, and with it class—defined by one's

42. Avineri, *Marx*, p. 27. Cf. Marx, *Critique of Hegel*, pp. 101ff.
43. Hegel, *Philosophy of Right*, p. 199.
44. Avineri, *Marx*, p. 27.

relation to property—turns out to determine a man's social and political status as well as his ethical life.

This almost purely philosophical critique of Hegel provides the foundation for Marx's analysis of the economic realities of capitalist society. What Feuerbach had permitted Marx to do was to show that Hegel's philosophy had cloaked or masked man's actual position in the world, man as a natural being who through his self-conscious struggle with the forces of nature produces the world of culture and ideas and thus also himself. Marx never doubts for a moment that the struggle of man with nature has been a process which in its unfolding is at the same time comprehended by man. In this he remains a true Hegelian, differing only in his starting point, in his insistence that man's labor is the basis for his consciousness and not the other way around: "Marx . . . always argues that the world is open to rational cognition because it is ultimately shaped by man himself and man can reach an adequate understanding of his historical activity."[45]

With respect to the issues of theodicy and the problem of evil, it also turns out that the master-slave paradigm, intended by Hegel as an explication of the dialectic of self-consciousness and thus as a justification of the evil entailed in the conflict, is a cloak for the struggle of man to gain mastery over nature. As indicated earlier, Marx claims that Hegel had almost seen this point when he located the self-creation or self-genesis of man in labor. But Hegel had inverted the subject and predicate by claiming that man's labor is a moment in the working out of the Idea. For Marx, all of the dominating patterns of history, from the first primitive division of labor[46] to the domination of the laboring class by the modern capitalist,

45. Ibid., p. 75. Cf. Nathan Rotenstreich, *Basic Problems of Marx's Philosophy* (Indianapolis: Bobbs-Merrill, 1965), p. 52.

46. The most primitive division of labor, according to Marx, is that between the sexes, followed closely by divisions and specialization owing to "natural pre-dispositions (e.g., physical strength), needs, accidents, etc., etc." Patterns of domination arose only with the distinction between "material and mental labor," which is the true division of labor. *German Ideology*, p. 20. That Marx does not consider the division of labor between the sexes to contain any natural basis for patterns of domination can be seen in his discussions in the early manuscripts of 1843–44, where he describes the relation between the sexes as the most natural *human* relationship. See *Manuscripts*, p. 134.

are simply moments or particular manifestations of man's struggle as a species to free himself from the domination of nature. The various historical forms of servitude or slavery are epiphenomena of man's attempt to master nature—they are what Marx designates the forms or relations of production.

Marx does not, of course, talk merely of subduing nature. In the *Economic and Philosophical Manuscripts* he says that "nature is man's *inorganic body* . . . with which he must remain in continuous interchange if he is not to die."[47] This symbiotic relationship is manifested historically in the dialectical interchange of natural and human needs.[48] But the emphasis Marx places on the importance of mastering nature in order for genuinely human needs to emerge gives it a central place in his argument on the possibilities of human freedom, an argument that is intended as a criticism of Hegel's theodicy. For once Marx has inverted the Hegelian relationship between labor and human consciousness, a possibility occurs which was not present in Hegel's formulation of the master-slave paradigm: if nature can be mastered, if man through his labor as a species can liberate himself from his subjection to nature, then the patterns of domination based on that subjection would also disappear. Hegel could achieve no more than a comprehension of the unfolding dialectics of domination and servitude, which he himself defined as a "true theodicy" for the unfolding of spirit in nature. In the Marxist framework it is possible to imagine the liberation of history from nature, which ipso facto means the end of domination and the very need for a theodicy.

Capitalism: Sovereignty over Nature and Individual Isolation

It is through his philosophical critique of Hegel, then, that Marx comes to see the possibility that history can be liberated from nature. His conviction that this possibility can be realized arises from his empirical analysis of the particular mode of man's relationship to nature in the present world, capitalism. It is not es-

47. *Manuscripts,* p. 112. Almost identical statements appear in the *Grundrisse* and in the opening pages of *Capital.*

48. See "The Meaning of Human Requirements," *Manuscripts,* pp. 147ff. See Bertell Ollman, *Alienation* (Cambridge: Cambridge University Press, 1971), part 2, for a discussion of "natural" and "species" (human) needs in Marx.

sential to my argument to trace Marx's analysis of the evolving modes of production from primitive human society to capitalism with their concomitant forms of alienation and class domination.[49] To complete the analysis of theodicy in Marx, as well as his view of the causes of revolution, it is however essential to understand his critique of modern economic life, capitalism (which he also calls "political economy").

For Marx capitalism marks the high point of the human endeavor to emancipate man from nature, although it fails to do so (hence, Hegel's inversion of the matter). The general thrust of Marx's argument is this: capitalism has secured the base for the liberation of man's history from nature by (1) developing the tools of production to such an extent that man is for the first time free from the controlling effects of scarcity; (2) applying these techniques universally to all sectors of mankind without respect to religious, cultural, and political boundaries, thereby creating a universal world history in place of the particular cultural histories of past centuries; (3) creating a set of values, founded in human reason, which, although not applied universally by the capitalist, nevertheless hold the secret of genuine human community. Conversely (dialectically), capitalism has created the greatest human misery ever known by (1) increasing alienation beyond what had ever been known under other modes of production; (2) ruthlessly destroying traditions, institutions, and beliefs which, however alienating they may have been,

---

49. Exactly what Marx thought about the movement from ancient modes of production to capitalism is not clear. He is often thought to have believed that there was a linear progression from the most primitive modes of production through the classical, feudal, and capitalist modes in which each is dialectically engendered by its predecessor. In fact, Marx's various writings do not offer such a clear-cut picture. The only dialectical movement he tries to account for is the breakdown of the feudal economy through the emergence of trade and a class of merchants, artisans, and petit bourgeois, which become the basis for capitalism, and the breakdown of capitalism through the emergence of the proletariat. With respect to primitive modes of production (based on the family and the tribe) and the classical mode of production (the classical city-state) Marx only shows that they become unstable. Hobsbawm has suggested that Marx has no linear development, that the breakdown of early modes of production can occur in several different ways. See E. J. Hobsbawm, Introduction to Marx, *Pre-Capitalist Economic Formations* (New York: International Publishers, 1964), pp. 1–65. I address these issues briefly in conjunction with Marx's views on "Oriental production" which is apparently not a chronological period and which he conceives as stagnant.

nevertheless provided a semblance of humanity for man prior to his maturity; (3) engendering one class of men, the proletariat, that suffers "universally," that is, retains no remnants of human community.

Each of the three dimensions of the misery of man under capitalism stands in dialectical tension with the three points sketching one of the achievements of capitalism, and each of the three pairs corresponds to the great struggle between the mastery of the capitalist and the slavery of the laborer. The struggle is resolved, as with Hegel's paradigm, by the educating and freeing effect of the laborer's work. The key to why this is the final stage of the struggle lies in the notion of universality together with dialectical *Aufhebung*. To understand this, I propose to examine each pair of elements in turn.

FREEDOM FROM SCARCITY AND RADICAL ALIENATION

"The most eloquent eulogy of capitalism was made by its greatest enemy," wrote Albert Camus of Marx.[50] That eulogy receives its most explicit form in the *Communist Manifesto*, where Marx and Engels claim that it is the bourgeoisie that has shown what man is capable of achieving:

> It has accomplished wonders far surpassing Egyptian pyramids, Roman aqueducts, and Gothic cathedrals; it has conducted expeditions that put in the shade all former exoduses of nations and crusades. . . .
>
> . . . The bourgeoisie, during its rule of scarce one hundred years, has created more massive and more colossal productive forces than have all preceding generations together. Subjection of nature's forces to man, machinery, application of chemistry to industry and agriculture, steam navigation, railways, electric telegraphs, clearing of whole continents for cultivation, canalization of rivers, whole populations conjured out of the ground— what earlier century had even a presentiment that such productive forces slumbered in the lap of social labor?[51]

It seems obvious to Marx that the full flowering of human creativity

50. Albert Camus, *The Rebel* (New York: Vintage, 1958), p. 192.
51. Marx, *The Communist Manifesto,* in Karl Marx and Friedrich Engels, *Basic Writings on Politics and Philosophy,* ed. Lewis Feuer (Garden City, N.Y.: Doubleday Anchor, 1959), pp. 10 and 12.

is possible only when man does not have to be preoccupied with labor, that is, with his metabolic relationship with nature.[52] In the past, the accumulation of wealth has permitted some individuals to give free play to their creative powers so that, as Marx puts it in *The Grundrisse,* "the highest development of productive forces" in a given period is united with "the richest development of the individual."[53] Capitalism has subdued nature to the extent that this development, once the attainment of a few, is now within the reach of all.

Unfortunately, the bourgeoisie's great achievements are accompanied by abysmal understanding. Instead of recognizing that the creation of individuality is a human creation, the culmination of an immense historical struggle to free mankind from the bondage

52. The notion that man's labor is a metabolism with nature was first developed by Marx in his early manuscripts. Nature is man's body, says Marx (*Manuscripts,* p. 112). Hannah Arendt, in *The Human Condition* (Garden City, N.Y.: Doubleday Anchor, 1959), argues that Marx's most critical weakness is his reduction of all human activity to labor. This overlooks the fact that in the *Manuscripts* Marx specifically differentiates human labor from animal metabolism by virtue of its creation of a world of objects and consequently culture (cf. *Manuscripts,* p. 113, and *German Ideology,* p. 7)—what Arendt says can only be the product of work (which she distinguishes from labor), of *homo faber.* Furthermore, she does not adequately grapple with Marx's claim that the progress of man from labor (the metabolic relation with nature) through work (the creation of permanent culture) creates conditions in which finally, after capitalism, men can interact with their fellowmen as peers—a condition which Arendt holds up as the highest ideal. Cf. the discussion of the "incomplete" character of human nature and the need to create a "second nature," culture, in Peter Berger, *The Sacred Canopy* (Garden City, N.Y.: Doubleday Anchor, 1969), p. 5.

53. Marx, *The Grundrisse,* ed. David McLellan (New York: Harper & Row, 1972), p. 120. *The Grundrisse* are notebook manuscripts which were to be the basis of a massive *Critique of Political Economy* of which the three volumes of *Das Kapital* constitute only the first of six parts. The work was never completed. That Marx is concerned at this late point in his writing with "the richest development of the individual" belies the view that in his later work he abandoned his early concern for human development. There is abundant evidence in the *Grundrisse* that all the categories and ideas of his writings of the 1840s were very much alive at the time he wrote *Das Kapital.* A full English edition of the *Grundrisse,* trans. Martin Nicholas (New York: Vintage, 1973) is also available. The McLellan edition is more accessible to the general reader and is therefore used here.

to nature, the bourgeoisie imagines that this individuality has existed from all time. The Marxist criticism of classical political economists like Ricardo, Smith, and Bentham is that, abstracting from the individualism of modern capitalism, they posit the original individuality and equality of men in a mythical state of nature and then make that a normative ideal, inverting subject and object (individuality as an "ideal" which stands over man) as well as the historical sequence. Moreover, the capitalist finds that even with his wealth he cannot really enjoy his creative faculties. In a small gem of irony, Marx again delineates the reversals of the master-slave paradigm, showing that, if the moral principles of political economy are taken seriously, the wealthy individual is a slave of his capital. The "moral science" of the bourgeoisie stipulates that

> the less you eat, drink and buy books; the less you go to the theater, the dance hall, the public house; the less you think, love, theorize, sing, paint, fence, etc., the more you *save*—the *greater* becomes your treasure which neither moths nor dust will devour—your *capital.* The less you *are,* the less you express your own life, the greater is your *alienated* life, the more you *have,* the greater is the store of your estranged being. Everything which the political economist takes from you in life and in humanity, he replaces for you in *money* and in *wealth*; and all the things which you cannot do, your money can do. It can eat and drink, go to the dance hall and the theater; it can travel, it can appropriate art, learning, the treasures of the past, political power—all this it *can* appropriate for you—it can buy all this for you: it is the true *endowment.* Yet being all this, it is *inclined* to do nothing but create itself, buy itself; for everything else is after all its servant.[54]

In this inverted world, a man is loved because he has money and collects art and goes to the theater (accompanying his money) because that is what people in his class do. This is at the heart of what Marx means by alienation, the complete acceptance of the identity imposed by property and class. It is also what Marx refers to as the "fetishism of commodities." The objects created by human labor not only define men but become the mode of intercourse among them:

54. *Manuscripts,* p. 150.

Every product is a bait with which to seduce away the other's very being, his money; every real and possible need is a weakness which will lead the fly to the glue-pot. General exploitation of communal human nature, just as every imperfection in man, is a bond with heaven—an avenue giving the priest access to his heart. . . .[55]

In sum, it may be said that while capitalism has provided the dialectical potential for freedom, for the exercise of man's creative powers, it has actually enslaved him. Capital, money, exploits human weaknesses rather than enhancing human powers.

THE UNIVERSAL THRUST OF CAPITALISM
AND THE DESTRUCTION OF HUMAN BONDS

The most specific way in which Marx understands capitalism to be universal in tendency is its capacity to cut across all the particular structures of human life, from family configurations to national and cultural groupings. When in the *Manifesto* Marx speaks of the bourgeoisie as a revolutionary class, he refers not only to its proved capacity to overthrow the aristocracy and landed interests remaining from feudalism (such as in the French Revolution) but, more important, to its subjection of all areas of human life to the principles of capitalist production, since "the bourgeoisie cannot exist without contantly revolutionizing the instruments of production, and thereby the relations of production, and with them the whole relations of society." In the beginning, this meant the destruction of "all feudal, patriarchal, idyllic relations" and the subjection of "the country to the rule of the towns." But the dynamic of capitalism pushes it to expand until "it compels all nations, on pain of extinction, to adopt the bourgeois mode of production." No cultural barriers can withstand this onslaught, so that even the most barbarian nations are drawn into civilization.[56]

This last point demonstrates that the principles of capitalist production include not merely techniques and instruments but an attitude toward nature that is at the heart of what Marx means by "civilization." In the *Grundrisse* the point is made more fully:

---

55. Ibid., p. 148.
56. *Manifesto*, pp. 9–11.

Capital first creates bourgeois society and the universal appropriation of nature and of social relationships themselves by the members of society. Hence the great *civilising influence of capital*, its production of a stage of society compared with which all earlier stages appear to be merely *local progress* and *idolatry of nature*. Nature becomes for the first time simply an object for mankind, purely a matter of utility; it ceases to be recognised as a power in its own right; and the theoretical knowledge of its independent laws appears only as a stratagem designed to subdue it to human requirements, whether as the object of consumption or as the means of production. Pursuing this tendency, capital has pushed beyond national boundaries and prejudices, beyond the deification of nature and the inherited, self-sufficient satisfaction of existing needs confined within well-defined bounds, and the reproduction of the traditional way of life. It is destructive of all this, and permanently revolutionary, tearing down all obstacles that impede the development of productive forces, the expansion of needs, the diversity of production and the exploitation and exchange of natural and intellectual forces.[57]

At no other point does Marx so clearly trace the multidimensional character of the capitalist world view and its impact on human life. All previous history had been particularistic, not simply because of the relative isolation of cultural traditions, but because within these traditions those who controlled the means of production did so only for the purpose of creating wealth, that is, for satisfying their existing needs. But capitalism is quite different:

We see here the universal tendency of capital which distinguishes it from all earlier stages of production. Although it is itself limited by its own nature, capital strives after the universal development of productive forces, and thus becomes the prerequisite for a new means of production. This means of production is founded not on the development of productive forces in order to reproduce a given condition and, at best, to extend it, but is one where free, uninhibited, progressive and universal development of productive forces itself forms the prerequisite of

57. *Grundrisse*, pp. 94–95 (first and last emphases added).

society and thus of its reproduction; where the only prerequisite is to proceed beyond the point of departure.[58]

We need only think here of the consistent emphasis on growth as the chief goal of modern corporate life. The managers of a corporation do this not to protect their land or to live more luxuriously within their castles, but for the purpose of continuously developing capital —that is what capitalism is about.

Across international lines, this has the most profound consequences. Prior to capitalism, conquerors occupied lands for the purpose of extracting wealth and natural resources and obtaining slave labor. Generally, they left the economic, political, and social institutions untouched (one of the greatest strengths of the Roman Empire had been its tolerance for local customs on every level). Capitalism, however, insists on *developing* a country, on molding it "after its own image."[59] In so doing, it has created a kind of interdependency among nations that did not exist under earlier empires, which appear superficially to have been more tightly knit. When the conquerors disappeared, the conquered nations could go on fairly much as before. Not so after the all-transforming hand of capitalism has gripped a nation. Marx draws a sharp contrast between precapitalist and capitalist modes of imperialism in "The British Rule in India" (he begins with a characterization by an Englishman of the old Dutch East India Company):

"The Dutch Company, actuated solely by the spirit of gain, . . . employed all the existing machinery of despotism to squeeze from the people their utmost mite of contribution, the last dregs of their labor, and thus aggravated evils of a capricious and semi-barbarous government by working it with all the practical ingenuity of politicians and all the monopolizing selfishness of traders."

All the civil wars, invasions, revolutions, conquests, famines, strangely complex, rapid, and destructive as the successive action of Hindustan may appear, did not go deeper than its surface. England has broken down the entire framework of Indian society, without any symptoms of reconstitution yet appearing. This loss of his old world, with no gain of a new one, imparts a

58. Ibid., p. 119.
59. *Manifesto*, p. 11.

particular kind of melancholy to the present misery of the Hindu, and separates Hindustan, ruled by Britain, from all its ancient traditions, and from the whole of its past history.[60]

The reason that capitalism transforms society on every level is that it constantly creates new needs, never being satisfied with natural needs or with the needs specified and circumscribed by a particular cultural configuration. It is this that Marx admires about capitalism, the implicit recognition that man is, as Berger puts it, an incomplete being without a fixed nature.[61] To be satisfied with fulfilling the needs of a particular culture or historical era, or to appeal to a "natural" image of man, is for Marx a form of idolatry of nature. On the other hand, once new needs are created, as Britain did in India, the cultural superstructure finds itself totally at odds with the new reality—the Indian cultural system entailed "a brutalizing worship of nature"[62] and as such was completely incompatible with the capitalist view that man is the sovereign of nature.

The new needs created by capitalism are not consumer needs, creature comforts, and the like (although these may follow). Rather, they are the more general and fundamental needs of man to express himself creatively, to move beyond the given world of nature and a culture rooted in nature worship, and to create a new and more complete second nature or culture rooted in human freedom and history. It is Marx's assumption that such creative possibilities were not present in what he calls Oriental culture, or in certain forms of ancient Western culture. But once man understands that he can be the master of nature and not the other way around, he can never be the same. Like Hegel's slave who through the work assigned him by his master discovers that he can control the world around him, can determine his own future, so also the Indian who has been uprooted from village life by the British settler discovers, however painfully,

---

60. "The British Rule in India," in Feuer, *Basic Writings*, pp. 475–76. This article was one of three on India written by Marx in 1853 for the *New York Daily Tribune*. He was responding to American socialists who decried British imperialism on moral grounds. For Marx such sentimentalism failed to see the genuinely revolutionary effect of Britain's empire. Cf. George Lichtheim, "Oriental Despotism," in *The Concept of Ideology* (New York: Vintage, 1967), pp. 63ff.

61. Berger, *Sacred Canopy*, p. 5.

62. Marx, "British Rule in India," p. 480.

that the world and nature and man have no permanent structure but are changed by man's activity. It is in this sense that India can never be the same after British rule has introduced India to *Weltgeschichte*. "Only where man consciously changes the world is there history."[63]

But this civilizing role of capitalism is played at great human cost and without the capitalists being fully conscious of what they are doing—England, Marx notes, "in causing a social revolution . . . was actuated only by the vilest interests."[64] The capitalist creates structural interdependency and the potential for the full development of human powers, but he does not create human interdependency, nor does capitalism actually develop human powers. Marx describes at length the way in which capitalism has improved the means of communication and transportation, while the increased specialization of advanced industry and its concentration in urban centers have made various segments of the economy as well as different nations more dependent on each other than had ever been the case under earlier modes of production. Furthermore, the capitalist finds that to expand his interests he must engage in practices which make him increasingly dependent on the structures of government and which involve more and more people in the capitalization process. Thus he requires government aid (including the outright gift of land under the "right of eminent domain") to build railroads and issues public stock offerings in order to capitalize projects otherwise beyond his reach.[65] Both of these policies tend to undermine capitalist premises and to create a kind of social interdependency. But the bond which holds people together in this mutual dependency is money. It is the supreme legitimater of contemporary forms of human interaction, and before it all other legitimations ineluctably fall.

The suffering consequent on the collapse of traditional legitimations is real, for however alienated men may have been under traditional cultural and religious forms they nevertheless provided a coherent world and a sense of human mutuality; Marx believed that under the Greek and Roman mode of production even slaves retained

63. Avineri, *Marx*, p. 166.

64. "British Rule in India," p. 480.

65. See Avineri, *Marx*, pp. 174ff., for an excellent discussion of Marx's views on stock companies and their role in transforming capitalism. Marx's chief discussion of stock companies is in *Capital*, especially vol. 3.

some sense of being part of the human enterprise. Religion, as the alienated form of man's consciousness and powers, at least represented residual human mutuality, though in a false form. Capitalism will have nothing to do with this. It tears apart nations, tribes, clans, and families and replaces these social organizations with nothing more than the organizing power of money and wage labor. In capitalist economics even the family, says Marx, is based "on capital, on private gain."[66]

The matter may be put most succinctly by using the terminology of personal identity. In past history man has answered the question, Who am I? with responses such as, I am an Englishman, a Watusi, a Christian, a MacGregor, or the like, all of which identify a person in relation to others. So also, our most natural terms, such as father, son, brother, sister, aunt, are relational terms which indicate the social character of human life. Even the slave or the serf, although in a position of bondage, is bondsman *to someone*, and that someone was understood to have an obligation to him—human reciprocity is present, even though unequally. But in the capitalist system with its emphasis on the priority of the individual the only bond among men is cash. The capitalist has only the obligation to pay for the labor time of the worker; once that contract is fulfilled, there is no continuing bond. In this sense, capitalism undermines all human bonds except the explicit bonds involved in contracts. While the resulting isolation of the individual creates a "sea of woes," Marx does not see this as a reason for moral anguish because previous human bonds were also a means for separating men from each other. To be a Christian is to exclude Jews; to be a member of a high Indian caste is to separate yourself from the lower castes. And to the extent that these group identities were conceived as natural or were "deified," they had a paralyzing effect on the human mind. Referring to the British destruction of traditional Indian society, Marx points out that

we must not forget that these idyllic village communities,

66. *Manifesto*, p. 24. The universalizing tendency of capitalism is the subject of Benjamin Nelson, *The Idea of Usury: From Tribal Brotherhood to Universal Otherhood*, 2d ed. (Chicago: University of Chicago Press, 1969). For a discussion of the disintegration of the family under capitalism, see Joseph A. Schumpeter, *Capitalism, Socialism and Democracy*, 3d ed. (New York: Harper & Row, 1962), pp. 157–63. This classic work was first published in 1942.

inoffensive though they may appear, had always been the solid foundation of Oriental despotism, that they restrained the human mind within the smallest possible compass, making it the unresisting tool of superstition, enslaving it beneath traditional rules, depriving it of all grandeur and historical energies.[67]

Capitalism, then, is the unwitting tool of history which by destroying all human bonds prepares the way for a world in which men conceive of themselves first as human beings and only secondarily as members of smaller social groups. Capitalism "demythologizes" human groupings.[68]

UNIVERSAL VALUES AND A "UNIVERSALLY EXCLUDED" CLASS

In spite of his scathing attacks on capitalism and civil society, including charges that the bourgeoisie were devoid of morality, Marx had no problem with bourgeois values per se. What he did believe was that they were not actualized. The reader searches in vain among Marx's writings for explicit discussions of ethics and values—he finds only that Marx takes most of the values of his time for granted while pointing out the dismal contradictions in the bourgeoisie's understanding and application of them. As George Lichtheim puts it, "The value system of the Enlightenment was part of [Marx's] mental baggage. He carried it about with him, and never dreamed of challenging it."[69] This is not to say that these values were to be based purely on reason, as in the Enlightenment. They had to be dialectically realized in the sensuous, productive activity of men.

It is essential here to bear in mind two points: first, Marx believes that in spite of its shortcomings capitalism is a necessary historical prerequisite for the full development of human powers. Second, capitalism is more than a technique of production; it includes a characteristic mode of social interaction as well as a full weltanschauung

67. "British Rule in India," p. 480.

68. Cf. Avineri, *Marx*, p. 162: "The whole world is thus divested of its myths. Under capitalism, men are brought to face the harsh realities of this world." Cf. also the second of Marx's "Theses on Feuerbach": "In practice man must prove the truth, that is, the reality and power, the this-sidedness [Diesseitigkeit] of his thinking" (Feuer, *Basic Writings*, p. 243).

69. George Lichtheim, "Reason and Revolution," in the *New York Review of Books*, April 11, 1968, p. 30. Lichtheim adds, "Nor is there any good reason why he should have."

with respect to nature, human values, and the like. The modes of consciousness that correspond to the capitalist mode of production are part and parcel of what capitalism is—in this Marx remains a truly dialectical thinker and not a simple-minded materialist. It follows, therefore, that Marx would also believe that the notions of the rights of man have genuine historical importance for man's autogenesis and that, had these notions not developed, human freedom would not be possible. Socialism does not have just an economic basis; it also has a conceptual basis, which is essentially the work of the Enlightenment. This means that there are times when Marx sounds as though he were fighting for little more than the universal acceptance and application of the American Declaration of Independence and the Bill of Rights. In fact, this is not far from the truth.

For example, in *The Civil War in France*, Marx enumerates the features of the Paris Commune of 1871 which, although he had doubts about its success, he believed was something of a model for communism. These features include universal suffrage; the disestablishment of the church; the transfer of military and police power from the state to the citizens (he wanted a citizens' army rather than a professional army); universal education free from either church or state control; and a judiciary system separated from the power of any ruling group ("Like the rest of public servants, magistrates and judges were to be elective, responsible, and revocable").[70]

Marx notes that the same aims had been proclaimed by the bourgeoisie when they wrested power from the aristocracy in 1830 (after abortively trying in 1789), but they were never more than ideals. In fact, the rights implicit in the proclamation applied only to the bourgeois class because they rested on a still more fundamental right in civil society, that of private property. For those who were connected to the larger society only by their labor power, that is, only by the capacity to sell their labor for cash in order to subsist, these proclamations of the rights of man meant nothing. Such persons were effectively excluded from political power and at the same time had

---

70. *The Civil War in France*, in Feuer, *Basic Writings*, p. 366. It is easy to forget from the standpoint of twentieth-century America that these features were almost unheard of in the nineteenth century except to some extent in America. Universal suffrage was not a reality even in America, and the other features have required consistent defense.

no protection from the power of the bourgeois state.[71] Avineri expresses it in this way: "Only a socialism that knows how abstract and empty are the Rights of Man in alienated society—and total alienation exists only in capitalist society—can try to evolve a social system to realize the content of these rights while abolishing their external form as just another expression of alienation."[72]

The exclusion of an immense group of men from the political realm by virtue of the system of capital and wage labor leads Marx to a fascinating discussion of what he calls the "universal suffering" of the proletariat. Capitalism is universal in its thrust, but it is only potentially universal in its actual consequences. The actualization of capitalism's potential lies in the proletarian class because of several features peculiar to it, chief among which is its universal suffering. This theme is first put forth in the 1844 essay, "A Contribution to the Critique of Hegel's *Philosophy of Right*," where Marx argues that the proletarian class is potentially a universal class because unlike any class before it, it has no property, no vested interest to protect when it revolts.[73] All other classes that have waged revolution have done so in order to protect a particular interest over against the vested interests of a decaying ruling class and have thus set themselves up as a ruling class in their own right. The proletarian class will not set itself over other classes because by definition it can have no property to protect. But as stated, this is hardly plausible, since there is no good reason why the proletariat should not simply try to replace the ruling class (to reverse positions with the master). Marx intends a great deal more by universal suffering than the mere absence of property. The possibility of emancipation resides

> in the formation of a class with radical chains, a class in civil society that is not of civil society, a class that is the dissolution of all classes, a sphere of society having a universal character because no particular wrong but unqualified wrong is perpetrated on it; a sphere that can claim no traditional title but only a human title; a sphere that does not stand partially opposed to

71. Cf. Marx's discussion of the liberties of the revolution of 1848 in *The Eighteenth Brumaire of Louis Bonaparte* (New York: International Publishers, 1963), pp. 29ff.

72. Avineri, *Marx*, p. 183.

73. *Critique of Hegel*, especially pp. 141ff.

the consequences, but totally opposed to the premises of the German political system; a sphere, finally, that cannot emancipate itself without emancipating itself from all the other spheres of society, thereby emancipating them; a sphere, in short, that is the complete loss of humanity. This dissolution of society existing as a particular class is the proletariat.[74]

To understand the dialectical points of this critical paragraph, it is necessary to recall the nature of Marx's critique of religion and the idea that traditional social structures and religion serve to give coherence to the world even though it is a false coherence. The full mutuality of human society is unavailable to the particularistic forms of past society since groups are divided from each other. Nevertheless, those same forms do provide for limited mutuality, and the religious beliefs of a society do provide, through their theodicy, a guarantee of the ultimate inclusion of a suffering class in "the family of God." The proletarian has none of this—he has no "traditional title" but only a cash relationship (which may be arbitrarily broken) to capitalist society.

The notion of "radical chains" is especially revealing. The serf on a medieval manor is limited, but the very notion of "serf" entails a relationship to another human being (the lord) who has reciprocal (although not equal) duties and rights. A slave in chains is horribly exploited, but he is nevertheless a slave to someone and his very chains symbolize that link to another. By saying that the proletarian has "radical chains" Marx seems to imply that his enslavement is more profound and yet paradoxically lacks the fundamental characteristics of the slave relationship. Cash is no chain at all (one might say that money chains one "from" rather than "to" another person) and yet the proletarian is completely dependent on cash; capitalist society gives him no alternative (a slave who does escape can go to work the land; a serf can travel to a free city, and so on). In other words, the proletariat does not actually participate in capitalist society. It is a class that is "not of civil society," that is, it is not really a class at all.

The proletariat is an amorphous horde of individuals who are caught up in a brutally competitive situation—literally Hobbes's *bellum omnium contra omnes*. Yet the picture is not complete, for

74. Ibid., pp. 141–42.

the proletariat is not totally amorphous in fact. Marx vacillates on this point, sometimes noting that the proletarian has no property, no family life, no national identity, no morality, no religion.[75] If this were actually the case, the proletarian would have no consciousness in the Marxist sense. But one of the most important points of Marxist theory is that the proletarian has a false consciousness. The problem is that some members of the proletariat have residual forms of consciousness which no longer adequately express their situation. This is true, for example, of large numbers of the bourgeoisie who slip into the proletarian condition, as well as of members of other classes which slowly disappear as capitalism polarizes the class situation. These people maintain the hopes, values, and ideals of their earlier status; they do not consider themselves proletarians but delude themselves into thinking that their situation is temporary.[76] The other proletarians have only religion to give coherence to their world, a religion that portrays them as members of a holy family even though they are excluded from the human family. Both of these forms of consciousness serve to prevent the proletarian from seeing his true condition.

Two important points follow from this. The first is that when Marx speaks of the increasing pauperization of the proletarian,[77] he is not referring simply to a worsening of his material conditions. Rather, he intends to refer to the impoverishment of all the proletarian's human relationships and to his completely unprotected situation in the capitalist system. Since radical individuality is a general characteristic of capitalism, many of the human institutions of the bourgeoisie (such as the family) have also been perverted. But in a free market system where individuals battle for personal advancement, the property owner has some protection: land or capital. And although Marx considers the necessity for protection from one's fellow man to be pathetic, it nevertheless affords survival. Without property, and in a society where human mutuality and reciprocal

75. For example, *Manifesto*, p. 18.

76. Cf. Dupré, *Philosophical Foundations*, p. 195. Dupré points out that these "losers" in the capitalist system direct their animis at the machinery of production, imagining that getting rid of modern productive methods would permit them to return to their prior way of life. The Luddites in England are the classic example.

77. See *Manifesto*, p. 19.

duties have been replaced by money, there is no safety, there is only "universal competition."[78] This point is critical for understanding the conditions that Marx deemed necessary for the proletarian revolution. He never suggests that they are created by poverty alone. Rather, it is a special kind of poverty that prepares the ground for revolution, "not naturally existing poverty but artificially produced poverty, not the mass of men mechanically oppressed by the weight of society but the mass of men resulting from society's, and especially the middle class', acute dissolution. . . ."[79] It is a loss of culture and a loss of humanity, not merely a loss of material sustenance, which constitutes the proletariat and which is dialectically present in the "acute dissolution" of the middle class.

The second implication is that when the proletarian loses either the residual consciousness of his former class status or his religious beliefs, his alienation becomes radical, and he succumbs to a state which modern sociologists call anomie. Now that in fact is not what Marx says. But if we are to make sense of many of his critical terms and phrases, such as "radical chains," "total loss of humanity," "acute dissolution of society," and the like, this would seem to be the interpretation required. Since the notion of radical alienation is so central to Marx's account of how the proletariat is to become the universal class and thereby the creator of a society without class domination, we need to look closely at the relationship of alienation, anomie, and universality.

Radical Marginality in Marx: Universality or Legerdemain?

Marx's account of the radical alienation and universality of the proletariat is essentially an account of a threshold status.[80] My dis-

78. *German Ideology*, p. 25.

79. *Critique of Hegel*, p. 142. Appreciation of Marx's views on this point would have saved a great deal of wasted scholarship on the question of whether the proletarian revolts when his situation is materially at its lowest point. Marx's emphasis is on the *structural* dissolution of modern civil society.

80. In chapter 3 I suggested that one of the functions of violence in Fanon's account was similar to a rite of passage, marking the move from one social status to another. It might be fruitful for research on revolutionary subjects to make use of work done in anthropology on such rites. Victor Turner, for example, notes that the attributes of people in a "threshold" or "liminal" state "are necessarily ambiguous, since this condition and these persons elude or slip through the network of classifications that normally locate states and

cussion is based on the interpretions already put forward together
with an adaptation of Peter Berger's understanding of estrangement,
alienation, and anomie. Berger provides a useful starting point for
placing Marx's understanding of alienation in perspective.[81]

ALIENATION, ESTRANGEMENT, AND ANOMIE

Following Hegel (and to some extent Marx), Berger states that

> the fundamental dialectic process of society consists of three
> moments, or steps. These are externalization, objectivation, and
> internalization. Only if these three moments are understood
> together can an empirically adequate view of society be main-
> tained. Externalization is the ongoing outpouring of human
> being into the world, both in the physical and the mental activity
> of men. Objectivation is the attainment by the products of this
> activity (again both physical and mental) of a reality that con-
> fronts its original producers as a facticity external to and other
> than themselves. Internalization is the reappropriation by men of
> this same reality, transforming it once again from structures of
> the objective world into structures of the subjective conscious-
> ness. It is through externalization that society is a human pro-
> duct. It is through objectivation that society becomes a reality
> *sui generis*. It is through internalization that man is a product of
> society.[82]

---

positions in cultural space. Liminal entities are neither here nor there; they are
betwixt and between the positions assigned and arrayed by law, custom, and
ceremonial. As such, their ambiguous and indeterminate attributes are expressed by a rich variety of symbols in the many societies that ritualize social
and cultural transitions. Thus, liminality is frequently likened to death, to
being in the womb, to invisibility, to darkness, to bisexuality, to the wilder-
ness, and to an eclipse of the sun or moon." *The Ritual Process* (Chicago:
Aldine, 1969), p. 95.

81. Complete development of Marx's view of alienation is beyond the scope
of this work. Several such studies have recently appeared, for example, István
Mészáros, *Marx's Theory of Alienation* (New York: Harper Torchbooks,
1972); Ollman, *Alienation*; and Richard Schacht, *Alienation* (Garden City,
N.Y.: Doubleday Anchor, 1971).

82. *Sacred Canopy*, p. 4. I have not altered Berger's proclivity toward
archaic and unusual spellings of technical terms, such as "objectivation" rather
than the more common "objectification" and "anomy" rather than "anomie."

This dialectical process is a continuing process, whether men are fully conscious of it or not. In fact, it may be said with some accuracy that historically few men are aware of the continually dialectical character of human society. The stability of any given social order depends upon forgetfulness, especially with respect to the moment of externalization. Because of forgetfulness, the objectified world seems to have existed for all time, "in the nature of things"; it becomes reified. Religion in particular serves to promote this forgetfulness since it frequently gives sacred legitimation to the existing order of culture. But although forgetfulness of man's creativity is historically the more common stance, there are also many examples of men who reject the objectified world and who accentuate the creative possibilities in man at the expense of the view of him as socially determined. This dual response to the objectified world of culture is possible because of the dialectical character of the process itself, and of the self participating in that process. At this point Berger's construction begins to differ from Marx's (but not so much from Hegel's).

While the consciousness of an individual is socialized in the process of internalization—in which the objective world of social structures and meanings becomes subjectivized—socialization is never total:

> Consciousness precedes socialization. What is more, it can never be *totally* socialized—if nothing else, the ongoing consciousness of one's own bodily processes ensures this. Socialization, then, is always partial. A *part* of consciousness is shaped by socialization into the form that becomes the individual's socially recognizable identity. As in all products of internalization, there is a dialectical tension between identity as socially (objectively) assigned and identity as subjectively appropriated. . . . the duplication of consciousness brought about by the internalization of the social world has the consequence of setting aside, congealing or estranging one part of consciousness as against the rest. Put differently, internalization entails self-objectivation. That is, a part of the self becomes objectivated, not just to others but to itself, as a set of representations of the social world—a "social self," which is and remains in a state of uneasy accommodation with the

non-social self-consciousness upon which it has been imposed.[83]

The tension here is between the active, outpouring self, the "I," and the socialized self, the "me." That tension produces two sets of "conversations," one between the self and significant others, the other within the self between the "I" and the "me." The external and the internal conversations and tensions they produce are the stuff of human life: they are the seedbed of creativity. But these conversations also entail the possibility "not only that the social world seems strange to the individual, but that he becomes strange to himself in certain aspects of his socialized self."

Now, as Berger notes, "*this* estrangement is given in the sociality of man, in other words, . . . it is anthropologically necessary." Given this estrangement, man may proceed in two ways,

> one, in which the strangeness of world and self can be reappropriated (*zurueckgeholt*) by the "recollection" that both world and self are products of one's own activity—the other, in which such reappropriation is no longer possible, and in which social world and socialized self confront the individual as inexorable facticities analogous to the facticities of nature. The latter process may be called alienation.[84]

Alienation, for Berger, "is the process whereby the dialectical relationship between the individual and his world is lost to consciousness." Insofar as this involves viewing the social-cultural world as similar to the world of nature, alienation is a form of false consciousness.

Berger then proceeds in some detail to demonstrate that alienation is the opposite of anomie. Whereas anomie is the subjective loss of structure (and therefore, multiplied by many subjects, the objective loss of structure in society), alienation is the unquestioning acceptance of structure. In fact, Berger points out, "such alienation can be a most effective barrier against anomy."[85]

My own gloss on Berger consists in the development of this latter

83. Ibid., pp. 83–84.
84. Ibid., p. 85.
85. Ibid., p. 94.

point. The conversation within the self which produces estrangement leads not just to the two possibilities mentioned by Berger—recollection and alienation—but also to a third, anomie. If alienation arises from forgetting the creative role of man in the dialectical process, anomie arises from the incapacity to accept major elements of the objectified world. Recollection is the creative use of cultural meanings. This may be schematized as follows:

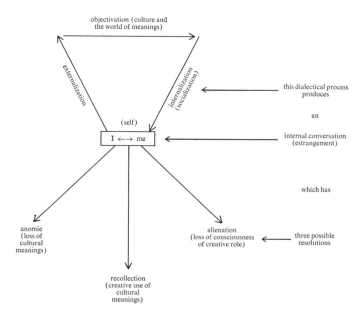

Accentuation of the socialized self tends toward alienation. Accentuation of the unsocialized self tends toward anomie. "Recollection" entails the acceptance of a portion of the socialized self which can become the basis for critical judgment about other portions of the objectified world and for creative outpouring into the world—that is, the continuing of the dialectical process.

Anomie can refer either to a state of subjective normlessness on the part of an individual or to objective normlessness in society.[86]

---

86. See also Robert Merton, *Social Theory and Social Structure*, enlarged edition (New York: Free Press, 1968), pp. 215-24. Emile Durkheim, of course, has written the classic texts on anomie, the normless state subsequent to the disintegration of collective moral life.

It is a relative term, since no society ever experiences complete absence of structure. The persistence of language alone would preclude that. Total subjective anomie therefore seems highly improbable, since it would seem to entail all loss of objectified structure, including language. Yet it exists as a theoretical type; it seems to be what Marx and perhaps other writers have meant when they talk about the "total negation of humanity," or of "radical marginality," and Marx's descriptions of the radical alienation of the proletarian tend to imply loss of structure or anomie.[87]

For Marx, alienation is historically a late development, the consequence of the historical (or prehistorical) development of man's powers. In Berger's construction, alienation is the first form of human existence, both individually and socially.

> All the evidence indicates that consciousness develops, both phylo- and ontogenetically, from an alienated state to what is, at best, a possibility of de-alienation. Both primitive and infantile consciousness apprehends the socio-cultural world in essentially alienated terms—as facticity, necessity, fate. Only much later in history or in the biography of individuals living in specific historical circumstances does the possibility of grasping the socio-cultural world as a human enterprise make its appearance. In other words, the apprehension of the socio-cultural world as an *opus alienum* everywhere precedes its apprehension as man's *opus proprium.*[88]

With these points in mind, we may return to Marx's view of alienation and "the complete loss of humanity" capitalist society entails. I propose to do this first by casting his arguments in terms of my discussions of theodicy in chapters 2 and 3 and then by looking more carefully at the dialectical character of "complete loss of humanity," or "radical alienation."

RADICAL ALIENATION AND THE DISSOLUTION OF THEODICY

Earlier I stated that by alienation Marx meant "the complete

---

87. The failure to distinguish among estrangement, alienation, and anomie is symptomatic of much contemporary social-scientific analysis. Berger is therefore refreshingly helpful. Schacht, *Alienation*, pp. 190–97, briefly distinguishes between alienation and anomie, and his entire work attempts to clarify the many different ways in which the word *alienation* has been used.

88. *Sacred Canopy*, p. 86.

acceptance of the identity imposed by property and class." He also often speaks, however, of man as being alienated from his labor, from the product of his labor, from nature, from his fellow man, or from himself. These notions all make alienation a form of separation, and as such they express an ineluctable condition of dialectical self-consciousness in the Hegelian mode of thought. That is to say, following Berger, it is in the very nature of human activity to pour oneself into the world and for that process to become objectified and thus appear "other" or strange. As already suggested, however, Marx does not carefully distinguish this general condition of man from that in which the objectified world becomes overwhelmingly determinative for man. When the latter happens, man forgets that the world of culture was initially his creation. Again the key is the master-slave paradigm: when the products of his activity, his "man-shaped" world, begin to appear to man as his master, then man is alienated "*from* his faculty of shaping his world."[89] Therefore, when man simply accepts as eternally valid the particular forms of political structure that he lives in, or the class designation he is born with, or accepts as in the nature of things the perquisites of private property, he is alienated from his capacity for self-creation.

To return to the two classes of capitalist society, both the bourgeoisie and the proletariat are alienated from their world-shaping capacities by the mediation of the class. In the case of the bourgeois, this means becoming a slave to one's property, to one's capital—a predicate of one's class. To be alienated in bourgeois fashion is to have accepted the bourgeois identity in the sense of being controlled by it. But to be a member of the proletarian class as Marx has described it is to be in a somewhat different situation, for the proletarian class has no form. What identity is held by a proletarian is either the residual identity of a former class situation or it is religion, which for Marx is the ultimate form of alienation. By implication (although I shall shortly want to qualify this point), this must mean that when the proletarian has religion stripped from him, he has no identity at all. This is to be in a situation of anomie, a situation without norm or structure, and it seems to be what Marx means when he says the proletariat is "the dissolution of all classes," a sphere that is "the complete loss of humanity." In fact, Marx is introducing here a

89. Avineri, *Marx*, p. 105 (emphasis added).

theory of radical marginality which at first appears similar to Fanon's native in a colonial situation. As Marcuse expresses it, "The proletariat is the negation not only of certain particular human potentialities, but also of man as such."[90]

That radical alienation turns out to be anomie, or radical marginality, may be made clearer by recalling chapter 2, wherein making use of Kuhn's theory of scientific revolutions I suggested that the breakdown of a theodicy was precipitated by the stresses of anomalous discoveries. The nature of anomaly in social and political revolutions (of Marxist interpretation) is now apparent: the proletariat discovers that *it is not actually included in the theodicy of the larger society*.

A nondualistic theodicy legitimates the unequal relationships within a society by explaining away suffering or promising a reversal of fortune in the future or in another life—or, in less rationally developed theodicies, by subsuming the good of individuals under a collective good.[91] In each of these cases, diverse though they may be in their construction, all the individuals in a society are given a place in an ultimate scheme of justice. This is not to say that certain persons are not potentially condemned or ultimately excluded, but the essential point and function of a nondualistic theodicy is to show that ultimate exclusion is not a function of the position occupied in this life. In contrast, the dualist theodicies examined in chapter 3 specified that the ultimate destinies of people *were* a function of group, racial, or class affiliation in this life. The Marxist view is a remarkably subtle melding of both kinds of theodicy while at the same time transcending both. The proletarian, to the extent that he has accepted the theodicy of the larger society (such as the otherworldly version of Christianity that promises him a reward in a life to come, a place in the Holy Family), is included in a larger scheme of justice. But as his position in society becomes more and more tenuous his theodicy is increasingly at odds with his situation.

Here it is critically important to remember that a theodicy is not merely an abstract belief-system imposed on a social reality, but

90. *Reason and Revolution*, p. 291. In spite of Marcuse's strong language here, he does not seem to recognize that radical alienation is no longer alienation but anomie.

91. See Berger, *Sacred Canopy*, pp. 60ff. The latter form of theodicy is the least rational; that is, it involves a psychological construction of the social personality that is pretheoretical.

includes social rituals, social bonds, clearly defined relations between superior and subordinate, and so on. The proletarian has lost all of these human connections. To use Berger's language of masochism and sadism, the proletarian is not even in a masochistic position, because masochism entails a continuing relationship to a superior (or superiors) from which meaning and even happiness may be derived. This point also sheds light on why the proletariat will not do what every revolutionary class before it has done, establish itself as a new ruling class over other classes. The proletariat, lacking a masochistic bond with the bourgeoisie, has no desire to become sadistic. As a class, it derives no meaning or happiness from its position and therefore would derive none from relegating others to a similar position. Similar reasoning led Max Weber to characterize capitalism as "masterless slavery."

The proletarian's relationship to the bourgeoisie is only one of cash and wage labor. Essentially, therefore, he has no continuing place, no human bonds, and is thus outside the actual structure of whatever theodicy the bourgeoisie may hold. Capitalist society, which may uphold some version of Christian theodicy, engenders (in spite of that theodicy) a functional dualism. It is not an actual dualism because no part of the theodicy specifies that the proletariat is an evil group. But it functions as a dualism because the proletariat is effectively excluded from the definition of what it means to be human, from the social bonds and social consciousness that make for at least partial humanity (in the Marxist framework complete humanity has not been present historically).

Here Marx's dialectical brilliance is at its best, for he shows that not only has the capitalist created a class of people who are excluded from humanity (and thus from sharing in the values and rights to which he subscribes); the capitalist has also a theodicy (if he still holds one) which no longer has any legitimating power—it does not apply to any existing inferior-superior relationships. The capitalist theodicy has no room for master-slave relationships among men, nor for a dualist view that a group is the representative of the dark and chaotic principle of life. It would be theoretically possible for an external observer to say that the proletarian is the "condemned of the earth," the dark principle of human life. But it is not possible for the bourgeois to do this historically, because his own theodicy does not permit this—it can evaluate the actions only of isolated individuals and therefore does not permit him to pass judgment on an entire group (or horde). He can say that a particular person is morally or spiritually defective, but if he said that of an entire group he would deny his own constitutive principles about the nature of man, that is, that only individuals can be judged.

Thus, ironically, and in true Hegelian fashion, the bourgeoisie does not have the conceptual tools to comprehend the situation of the proletarian. It can only mumble words about free opportunity for all, the democracy of God's kingdom, and so on. It is in this sense that Marx can say that the proletarian's marginality is a function of the "acute dissolution" of the bourgeois class: "When the proletariat announces the dissolution of the existing order of things it merely declares the secret of its own existence, for it *is* the *de facto* dissolution of this order of things."[92] The dissolution of the bourgeoisie is the dialectical opposite of its universal values.

With respect to the Christian theodicy, Marx (if he had addressed the issue) would argue something like this. The doctrine of Original Sin (in its Augustinian form) has a democratizing potential since it undercuts any claims to superiority on the basis of natural or traditional (customary) distinctions among men. Coupled with predestination, it is conceivable that this democratizing potential could be realized in practice, since the very notion of predestination entails that only God (and not nature or tradition) determines who is to be saved. In fact, Calvinists used predestination as a revolutionary doctrine, to undercut traditional social and political structures, as well as the sacral claims of the Roman church. But Calvinist predestination did not apply universally; rather, the elect were considered a relatively small group within a larger godless world. Ideally, the doctrine could still have revolutionary potential as long as it is never forgotten that there is no sure way to determine who is among the elect.[93] Any person or institution claiming eternal validity must be rejected. But historically (and for Marx history is everything) the opposite happened: the later Calvinists tended to equate material prosperity with election, or as Marx put it, "Locke supplanted Habbakuk."[94] In the first stage of this equation material prosperity

92. *Critique of Hegel*, p. 142.
93. A point which Calvin made over and over again but often forgotten by later Calvinists.
94. *Eighteenth Brumaire*, p. 17.

is merely a probable sign of election. But in dialectical fashion, material prosperity soon becomes not only the sign of election but is alleged to be its cause. An implicitly democratic Christian theodicy is inverted and perverted to legitimate economic and social inequity —the predicate becomes the subject.[95] However, as the dialectical process continues to unfold, so the theodicy, at first useful to the bourgeois Calvinist, applies less and less to his actual economic relations, both with other members of his class and with the proletariat, the excluded class. What originally gave structure to the people of God in the course of history has dissolved into atomistic bourgeois society.[96]

Here the portrayal of evil under capitalist society is complete. Capitalism has conquered nature, unleashing the full productive powers of man, and it has demythologized all previous human groupings which separated men from each other and which encompassed their minds within narrow horizons. In so doing, it has created the possibility of a human society liberated from the antagonisms evoked by scarcity of the goods required to satisfy the most basic human needs; and it has engendered a set of cultural potentialities which, if properly understood, would permit the full development of human creativity: man would consciously shape his own history (and thus his own being) rather than being shaped by nature.

At the same time, all these potentialities can remain only that so long as capitalism continues to exist, for capitalism produces the most alienated of all human societies in a double sense: the bourgeoisie has become a slave to a cultural product that is by definition

95. This view of the transformation of historical Calvinism is of course very similar to that of the Weberian school. Had Weber been acquainted with the full corpus of Marx's writings he might have seen the need for less "corrective" work.

96. This is in part the thesis of Michael Walzer, *The Revolution of the Saints* (New York: Atheneum, 1969). Although Marx himself seems not to have discussed Calvinism directly, Engels occasionally did, and some of his comments are similar to those I have made here. Nevertheless, Engels was guilty of relegating ideas to an almost purely reflexive role in society rather than seeing them in the dialectical fashion that Marx did; hence, he tends to see Calvinist ideas as mere reflections of the market system of capitalist society, rather than granting them the historical energy suggested by my hypothetical "Marxist" formulation. See Marx and Engels, *On Religion* (New York: Schocken, 1964), pp. 265–67 and 300ff.

impersonal, namely, capital (and Marx would add that the alienation is all the greater because of the contradiction between what the capitalist has achieved and his insistence that this human achievement is "in the nature of things"); and a class of people has been created whose enslavement is unlike any previous form of servitude— they are slaves without masters. The atomization of bourgeois society, the dissolution of human bonds and reciprocity, spills over into the proletarian class with a vengeance: the proletarian has not even the artificially created bourgeois state to maintain a semblance of human interaction. This class is marginal in a way that no other group in human history has been marginal: its members have no identity at all (they are a genuine mass), which means, ipso facto, that they can be embraced by no theodicy.

It follows from this that the proletarian is in a unique position historically. If he can strip away any residual illusions about his condition, he will discover a curious negative identity with all of humanity, that is, with men who do have identities, be they religious, cultural, or class. Furthermore, he is in what is for Marx the enviable position of being able to see that no historical identity has permanent validity—all identities are artifacts of the human struggle with nature. The proletarian is therefore the first man to face the natural world nakedly, without presuppositions, and Marx anticipates that this "negative humanity" of the proletariat will provide what he calls the material base for the emancipation of man.[97] It is necessary to look more closely at this notion of a "negative humanity" that lacks specific identity.

THE DIALECTICAL NOTION OF NEGATIVE HUMANITY

Up to this point I have spoken of the radical alienation of the proletariat as entailing a loss of norms and structure, a loss of identity, and even a loss of humanity. At the same time, it has been noted that Marx also says that the proletariat has a false consciousness, implying that as a class it does have at least a false identity. It was further suggested that the notion of total subjective anomie was implausible. Ultimately, I think this is a matter of conceptual confusion, but I will attempt to give the clearest account possible of Marx's dialectical intentions with respect to these difficulties.

97. *Critique of Hegel*, p. 142.

The stripping away of cultural and societal structures that form the proletariat does not culminate in a state of being where the proletarian has no identity whatsoever. If that were the case, there would be static states of being. But in the dialectical mode of thought all "states" are dynamic, being transformed constantly by the relations that define them or give them shape. Modes of production undergo internal transformation, as do their concomitant cultural forms. So also the proletarian must be continually undergoing transformation. Marx knows that to speak of a human being without any conscious identity at all is to speak of a human being without consciousness. In Hegel's master-slave paradigm, the slave finds in his condition of servitude, and especially in his forced labor, the key to his freedom. Marx's proletarian has less of a continuing tie to any master but he does have something; namely, his labor. He is not a completely unformed creature. Furthermore, he has language, and he has needs which have been shaped by capitalist society. All of these discipline the proletarian and form his thinking. Therefore, the statement that the proletarian is the first man to face the natural world nakedly, without presuppositions, needs careful qualification.

That qualification may best be made by contrasting the nakedness of the proletarian with the nakedness of primitive man, actual or imagined. Primitive man, emerging from nature and discovering through labor his potential creative powers, faced the world without language, without tools, without culture, without a history—his labor was the beginning of all of this. The proletarian resembles this man insofar as his particular history, his particular culture, his particular tools of production are alien to him and even stripped from him. But the resemblance ends here, for the proletarian has all of this human history to draw on. What is gone is the particularistic character of all these dimensions of existence, which he is now free to draw on in an emancipated state, that is, conscious that he is now creating history and shaping nature rather than the other way around. There is no returning to the original nakedness of man, and Marx resists (unlike Engels) the equation of communism with a primitive state of man.

We may say therefore that while the proletarian revolution (if it occurs) resembles the real or imagined emergence of human association at the beginning of history, it also utterly transcends it. The original emergence of man had the potential only for the creation of particular needs, particular histories, particular cultures. The proletarian has the potential for universal needs and relations, universal history, and universal culture. That such a transformation is now open to possibility is ineluctably dependent upon earlier forms of human history—the dialectical notion of *Aufhebung* prevents any claim of hiatus between past and present. And it is precisely this point that distinguishes Marx from the apocalyptic tradition, which, as we saw with the millenarians, claimed the creation of a new heaven and a new earth: there was hiatus rather than dialectical tension between the old and the new.

If the proletarian transformation is thus distinguished from pure apocalypticism, so also is the proletarian situation distinguished from the dehumanized state described by Fanon and Sartre. He may be stripped of the clothes of his culture, but forced to labor, he discovers the basis for reclothing himself through labor which he is able to see in its pristine form: the conscious shaping and mastering of the world. The capitalist has provided him with the tools for his own regeneration and the creation of new human needs. Therefore while radical alienation is for Marx the threat of anomie, the total lack of structure, that state never becomes reality because of the dialectical restructuring already present in the proletarians' condition. Marx calls attention to the weakness of the proletarian only for the purpose of demonstrating his potential but latent strength.

The assertion of dialectical restructuring does not of itself resolve the difficulties. The force of Marx's argument lies in large part in his capacity to show that the proletarian really is unclothed. If he remains clothed, he has something to fight for, he has a particularity that will prevent him from realizing his universal nature. Yet the dialectical frame of Marx's thinking makes it impossible for him to say that unclothed men actually exist. If the proletarian is to discover in his labor that he is a history-creating being and a social being, this is possible only because labor in the capitalist world is historically so far advanced in comparison to past forms of labor. But the superiority of capitalist labor is conceptual: as Marx never tires of saying, from the early manuscripts of 1843-44 to *Capital*, what distinguishes human labor from animal labor, what makes human labor historical, is that it involves consciousness.[98]

98. Cf. *Manuscripts*, p. 113; *Capital*, vol. 1 (London: J. M. Dent, 1933), p. 169.

There is simply no way that the proletarian may be said to have the capacity for advanced labor without also having consciousness. Therefore, what Marx must hold is this: the laborer's actual condition—that is, his relation to other men and to his labor, to nature—is one that approaches total disorganization, anomie. But he also has a false consciousness, in the form of religion and otherwise, which maintains a semblance of order. The latter must be overcome to discover the true condition of the proletariat, radical disorganization, loss of humanity. But in fact, there is no radical disorganization; instead there is labor, labor as structure, labor as discipline, labor as mastery of nature, labor as conscious creation of history. The question this evokes is whether Marx's description of a class that suffers universally is not a complete myth—or a remarkable piece of dialectical legerdemain.

In fact, the notion of man without presuppositions—granted, this is my formulation—of a genuinely universal man without any particularities seems implausible on the face of it. That notion first arises in Marx's thought because of his conviction that man's interaction with nature, in the form of labor, is the axis around which all other human activity rotates. Marx hopes to show this by stripping away the perverted forms of consciousness that have obscured the pivotal role of labor, but by his own premises such a procedure must be impossible, since there is no such thing as human creativity without consciousness, no axis without its peripheral apparatus. Hegel was not tempted to isolate labor as Marx does because he conceived of labor as the work of the mind, not merely interaction with nature.[99] Marx only yields to the temptation in those passages where he stresses that the proletarian is the negation of humanity, in terms which suggest that this entails a loss of humanity. In Hegel's master-slave encounter such a loss is never implied, even though the slave's humanity is derivative, mediated by the master (and eventually the master's humanity is mediated by the slave).

Marx tries to paint the proletarian as total negativity while at the same time making him the positive hope of the future. I would suggest that the notion of total negativity breaks the dialectical connection and makes a regeneration impossible.[100] To the extent that

99. See n. 8.

100. Marx's criticism of Proudhon actually follows similar lines: see discussion in text following.

regeneration is possible in Marx, it is rooted in the positive formation of man through labor and the transformation of his needs—and that must include consciousness. Nathan Rotenstreich, asking the question of what conditions would be necessary for man's "fundamental capacity" to be obliterated or even diminished, makes a similar point:

> In order to assign to history the force of prohibitive conditions, based on the pattern of what happens to an individual, one must first attribute to it the power to deprive humanity of the very capacity that created history. For, according to Marx himself, history would not have being, were it not for the creative power of consciousness.[101]

It is doubtful, then, that there is such a thing as a man without clothes, a man who carries no past with him. The historical proletarian will have clothes, whether they fit or not. What is needed is to persuade him to change his clothes, and Marx does not, it seems to me, offer a convincing argument that the change will be easier than it was for earlier groups, or that there is only one set of new clothes the proletarian will want to wear.

The ambiguity of Marx on the nature of the proletariat's negativity lies at the source of one of the critical debates in contemporary Marxism: when Marx said that the proletariat is potentially a universal class, did he mean "potentially" in the weak sense of a possibility which may or may not be realized, or did he mean it in the strong sense of something with a force or logic of its own? Both readings are possible. If you take seriously Marx's language of "engendering," then his notion of potentiality is close to the biological notion of inevitable growth and maturing. If potentiality is read weakly as "possibility," then a high degree of voluntarism is present. The history of capitalism in the one hundred years since Marx would suggest that the weaker reading is necessary (whatever Marx's own meaning), since capitalism has not produced a universal class but rather a form of cultural anomie, a proliferation of many groups and subgroups without an overarching universal structure. My discussion of revolutionary praxis will show that the ambiguity creates acute problems for human action.

101. Rotenstreich, *Basic Problems of Marx's Philosophy*, p. 141.

Marx cannot avoid the dilemma of all revolutionaries: it is impossible to talk about fundamental change in any area of human life without borrowing language from another area or field. One must either appeal to something beyond history as the millenarians did or utilize metaphors derived from historical experience. Whether Marx uses biological language or the language of human action (politics) or some other set of metaphors, he is in effect trying to extend Hegel's dialectic beyond the mere understanding of history to account for the transition to the active directing of history. Marx's notion of praxis is where these issues come to focus.[102]

REVOLUTIONARY PRAXIS

All of human history through capitalism shares one fundamental characteristic: what man actually accomplishes never coincides with what he intends. This may stand as a summary of the problem of evil in Marx, and it is the background against which his understanding of praxis must be seen. The Hegelian master-slave encounter is paradigmatic here: the cunning of reason adapts human intentions to its own purposes. For Hegel, man's freedom lies in the comprehension of this point, which is the task of philosophy. But for Hegel philosophical insight can come only at the culmination of history or of an era—it cannot anticipate. Hence, the famous Hegelian dictum, "The owl of Minerva spreads its wings only with the falling of the dusk."[103] While Marx accepts Hegel's characterization of historical

102. For a discussion of Marxist literature dealing with the problem of dialectical transition in Marx, see Louise Dupré, "Recent Literature of Marx and Marxism," *Journal of the History of Ideas* 25, no. 4 (October–December 1974):703–14.

103. *Philosophy of Right*, p. 13. The full paragraph is this: "One word more about giving instruction as to what the world ought to be. Philosophy in any case always comes on the scene too late to give it. As the thought of the world, it appears only when actuality is already there cut and dried after its process of formation has been completed. The teaching of the concept, which is also history's inescapable lesson, is that it is only when actuality is mature that the ideal first appears over against the real and that the ideal apprehends this same real world in its substance and builds it up for itself into the shape of an intellectual realm. When philosophy paints its grey in grey, then has a shape of life grown old. By philosophy's grey in grey it cannot be rejuvenated but only understood. The owl of Minerva spreads its wings only with the falling of the dusk."

understanding up to his time, he does not accept it as a permanent condition of man. The Feuerbachian transformation showed that the asymmetry between intention and accomplishment is part and parcel of the struggle with nature. The struggle with nature once won, intention and accomplishment coincide in human affairs.

But the Feuerbachian transformation itself is not sufficient—as a critical method it was a purgatory or "fiery stream" (*Feuer* plus *Bach*) through which the Hegelian dialectic had to go before human action could be recovered.[104] While Feuerbach had denied that there was a Hegelian "world behind the world," he did this by positing still another "world behind the world," namely, the world of a statically conceived natural or material man. The thrust of Marx's "Theses on Feuerbach" is that Feuerbach, like Hegel, is a reductionist. Human reality is historical activity, the conscious transformation of circumstances, the autogenesis of man, especially through social labor. Feuerbach misses this historical essence of human reality, as in his treatment of religion:

> Feuerbach resolves the religious essence into the *human* essence. But the human essence is no abstraction inherent in each single individual. In its reality it is the ensemble of the social relations.
>
> Feuerbach, who does not enter upon a criticism of this real essence, is consequently compelled:
>
> 1. To abstract from the historical process and to fix the religious sentiment [Gemüt] as something by itself, and to presuppose an abstract—*isolated*—human individual.
>
> 2. The human essence, therefore, can with him be comprehended only as "genus," as an internal, dumb generality which merely *naturally* unites the many individuals.[105]

Materialism and idealism are both to be rejected in favor of what Marx intends to be a genuinely historical view of man, expressed in the by now famous and overquoted eleventh thesis: "The philosophers have only *interpreted* the world, in various ways: the point, however, is to *change* it."

---

104. Cf. Rotenstreich, *Basic Problems of Marx's Philosophy*, p. 19.
105. Feuer, *Basic Writings*, pp. 244-45. (The passage is from the sixth thesis.)

Since man has in fact been changing the world and himself through-out history, unconscious of what he is actually doing, the point at issue is the conscious making of history which begins with the pro-letariat—and which marks the division between "prehistory" and "history proper."[106] I will attempt first to show what Marx intends by the phrase "revolutionary praxis" and then why his efforts to explain how man can consciously shape history flounder.

The Inapplicability of Moral Norms

Revolutionary praxis entails the extension of active participation in the affairs of men to groups that have historically been excluded from them in the sense of being able to play a decisive role. Only small groups of men have been actively involved in the shaping of history, while the great masses of men have labored to bring them the leisure necessary for such activity. But it also follows from Marx's dialectical analysis that those who have "made" history in the sense of being written about by the historians, those who are recorded as the heroes of history, are only in a superficial sense the makers of history. Granted, they have done the thinking, directed the wars, developed the creative powers of the human mind in art and literature, devised the political and legal systems. But all of this was predicated upon the labor of the classes who were unconsciously the real makers of history. The actual productive powers that made culture possible have never been reflected in the structure of con-sciousness of past cultures.

Once again we are confronted with the ironies of the master-slave paradigm. One of the first steps in the emanicpation of man is for those who have been the makers of history in the productive sense to recognize their true role, obscured by their exclusion from history books, from political participation, and from the artistic achievements of man. Therefore, revolutionary praxis is first of all a celebration of their accomplishments. Here Marx shares with the Romantics the great desire to let the dead voices of the past speak, to rewrite his-tory so that those who have no record in the historical archives, no

106. See Marx, "A Contribution to the Critique of Political Economy," ibid., p. 44: "This social formation [bourgeois society] constitutes, therefore, the closing chapter of the prehistoric stage of human society." Cf. Marcuse, *Reason and Revolution*, pp. 315–17.

monuments in the marketplace, are the new heroes of history. The folk, the common people, are resurrected.[107]

At the same time, the pretensions of the heroes of history are exposed, unmasked. They made genuine contributions, just as the capitalist has made contributions of momentous proportions, but never for the right reasons (that is, their achievements did not reflect their intentions), and what they did was in any case less than what man is capable of. Marx's characterization of past cultural achievements is that they are immature. He struggles with this point in the *Grundrisse*. An admirer of Greek art (who in the nineteenth century was not?), he must nevertheless find it inadequate. Much of this inadequacy is accounted for by the fact that classical art emerged from a social and economic milieu in which nature had still not been mastered except in the imagination: "All mythology masters and dominates and shapes the forces of nature in and through the imagination; hence it disappears as soon as man gains mastery over the forces of nature." It would be impossible, Marx suggests, for classical art to exist along side of modern technology: "Is Achilles possible side by side with powder and lead? Or is the *Iliad* at all compatible with the printing press and even printing machines?" [108] He recognizes that this does not explain why men still admire Greek art as a standard for all art, but the explanation is to be found in the growing maturity of mankind (as nature is mastered), which continues to admire the accomplishments of childhood even as they are transcended (*aufgehoben*):

> A man cannot become a child again unless he becomes childish. But does he not enjoy the artless ways of the child, and must he not strive to reproduce its truth on a higher plane? Is not the character of every epoch revived, perfectly true to nature, in the child's nature? Why should the childhood of human society, where it had obtained its most beautiful development, not exert an eternal charm as an age that will never return? There are

107. This is one of the points that utterly fascinated Georges Sorel. See his discussion of the anonymous stone carvers who made the cathedrals' sculptures, in *Reflections on Violence* (London: Collier-Macmillan, 1961), pp. 243–49. Marx differs from the Romantics in his belief that the resurrection of these dead voices could be salvific for the whole of mankind.

108. *Grundrisse*, p. 45.

ill-bred children and precocious children. Many of the ancient nations belong to the latter class. The Greeks were normal children. The charm their art has for us does not conflict with the primitive character of the social order from which it had sprung. It is rather the product of the latter, and is due rather to the fact that the immature social conditions under which the art arose and under which alone it could appear can never return.[109]

We may leave aside the question whether official proletarian art in modern communist states surpasses that of the ancient Greeks. Marx's contention, expressing a typical Romantic aesthetic, is that the art of the Greeks, like the productive advances of the capitalist (although Marx had nothing but scorn for the aesthetic achievements of capitalism), does not lose its value because it must be surpassed. Man matures, but he does not mature by condemning his childhood. It follows that the proletarian revolution does not represent a moral victory over capitalism, the righteous judgment of a morally superior class on its morally bankrupt opponent.[110] Granted, Marx never tires of pointing out the moral hypocrisy and bankruptcy of bourgeois society, and he seems at times genuinely horrified at the suffering that capitalism has produced. But he knows that his case is lost the moment the revolution is "justified" on moral grounds.[111] Two of his works in particular address this issue, *The Poverty of Philosophy* and the "Critique of the Gotha Program."

In the former, Marx discusses Proudhon's socialism and with wit and bite shows how Proudhon has utterly devastated the Hegelian dialectic by transforming it into moral categories:

> For him, M. Proudhon, every economic category has two sides—one good, the other bad. . . .

109. Ibid., pp. 45–46. One wonders further what accounts for precociousness among some of the ancients but not others.

110. Marx says at one point that history judges and the proletarian carries out the execution, but that is highly rhetorical and must be balanced against his more considered statements about revolution. Furthermore, he does not say that the *proletarian* makes the judgment. The role of executioner (dare we imagine a black hood?) is hardly one we would point to as an example of moral stature.

111. Not only is his case lost, says Marx, but also his soul! Thus at the end of the "Critique of the Gotha Program" he notes that in speaking out against the moralizing of the German socialists he has saved his soul: *"Dixi et salvavi animam meam."* Feuer, *Basic Writings*, p. 132.

The *good side* and the *bad side*, the *advantages* and the *drawbacks*, taken together form for M. Proudhon the *contradiction* in every economic category.

The problem to be solved: to keep the good side, while eliminating the bad.

Slavery is an economic category like any other. . . .

What would M. Proudhon do to save slavery? He would formulate the *problem* thus: preserve the good side of this economic category, eliminate the bad.

Hegel has no problems to formulate. He has only dialectics. M. Proudhon has nothing of Hegel's dialectics but the language. For him the dialectic movement is the dogmatic distinction between good and bad. . . .

. . . What constitutes dialectical movement is the coexistence of two contradictory sides, their conflict and their fusion into a new category. The very setting of the problem of eliminating the bad side cuts short the dialectical movement.[112]

For Marx, this cutting short of the dialectical movement is no mere philosophical problem. Rather, Proudhon's moralism is "stricken with sterility when it is a question of engendering a new category by dialectical birth-throes," that is, it is incapable of comprehending the emergence in history of new modes of human activity. The very positing of good and bad presupposes a neutral ground on which to make judgments. But that neutral ground always turns out to be a category derived from the previous state of affairs, and therefore there is no dialectical movement. Thus, Proudhon's most famous aphorism, "Property is theft," turns out to legitimate the institution of property: "'*Theft*,' as a forcible violation of property *presupposes property*."[113]

Marx issues similar warnings in connection with the use of moralizing language by German socialists in the 1875 Gotha Program, in which the socialists claimed that certain rights accrued to labor as

112. Marx, *The Poverty of Philosophy* (New York: International Publishers, 1963), pp. 111–13.

113. Marx to J. B. Schweitzer, in Marx and Engels, *Selected Works* (Moscow: Foreign Languages Publishing House, 1962), 1:392. As Marx says in this letter, he greatly admired Proudhon's first work, *What is Property?*, and was influenced by it, but Proudhon has "little . . . penetrated into the secrets of scientific dialectics." Cf. Avineri, *Marx*, p. 83.

"the source of all wealth and all culture" and called for "a fair distribution of the proceeds of labor." Marx objects to this appeal to a notion of "rights" and to a principle of distributive justice because in doing so the socialists keep the battle on bourgeois territory: "*equal right* here is still in principle—*bourgeois right*."

> What is "a fair distribution"?
>
> Do not the bourgeois assert that the present-day distribution is "fair"? And is it not, in fact, the only "fair" distribution on the basis of the present-day mode of production? Are economic relations regulated by legal conceptions or do not, on the contrary legal relations arise from economic ones? Have not also the socialist sectarians the most varied notions about "fair" distribution? [114]

In a society based on private property, rights will imply inequality. But even if private property were abolished, the notion of rights would still produce inequality:

> Right by its very nature can consist only in the application of an equal standard; but unequal individuals (and they would not be different individuals if they were not unequal) are measurable only by an equal standard in so far as they are brought under an equal point of view, are taken from one *definite* side only, for instance, in the present case, are regarded *only as workers*, and nothing more is seen of them, everything else being ignored. . . . To avoid all these defects, right instead of being equal would have to be unequal. [115]

Only when productive and social relations have been changed, only when those who have been following become leaders or active determiners of their own fate, can the appropriate distributional questions be worked out and justified. [116]

114. "Critique of the Gotha Program," Feuer, *Basic Writings*, pp. 115–16. See pp. 112ff. for the full argument.

115. Ibid., p. 119.

116. Cf. Robert Tucker, *The Marxian Revolutionary Idea* (New York: Norton, 1969), p. 46: "In short, the only applicable norm of what is right and just is the one inherent in the existing economic system. Each mode of production has its own mode of distribution and its own form of equity, and it is meaningless to pass judgment on it from some other point of view. Thus,

There are no moral grounds for adjudicating between an older form of society and a newer one that is emerging from the disintegration of the old. This disintegration of the old is caused by its incapacity to incorporate the new phenomena it generates, which it can treat only as anomalies. But this does not mean that there are no grounds for deciding which way to go or how to act. For Marx, the untenability of the old form of society is straightforward: it will collapse of its own weight. The embracing of the new is the reasonable thing to do.

But what is the new, how is it to be discerned, and by whom? In Kuhn's discussion of the discovery of new scientific paradigms, the process of discovery was rooted in the creative imagination disciplined by stubborn facts. The Marxist position has strong similarities, except that the creative imagination is not given as clear or decisive a role. It is expressed in a well-known passage from *The Poverty of Philosophy*:

> So long as the proletariat is not yet sufficiently developed to constitute itself as a class, and consequently so long as the struggle itself of the proletariat with the bourgeoisie has not yet assumed a political character, and the productive forces are not yet sufficiently developed in the bosom of the bourgeoisie itself to enable us to catch a glimpse of the material conditions necessary for the emancipation of the proletariat and for the formation of a new society, these theoreticians are merely utopians who, to meet the wants of the oppressed classes, improvise systems and go in search of a regenerating science. But in the measure that history moves forward, and with it the struggle of the proletariat assumes clearer outlines, they no longer need to seek science in their minds; they have only to take note of what is happening before their eyes and to become its mouthpiece. So long as they look for science and merely make systems, so long as they are at the beginning of the struggle, they see in poverty nothing but poverty, without seeing in it the revolutionary,

---

capitalism for Marx and Engels is evil but not inequitable." Tucker correctly sees that the Marxist revolution is not waged in the name of distributive justice, but his view of evil in Marx remains unreflective (he identifies it with exploitation) and undialectical.

subversive side, which will overthrow the old society. From this moment, science, which is a product of the historical movement, has associated itself consciously with it, has ceased to be doctrinaire and has become revolutionary.[117]

This passage has been a source of difficulty for many since in the second half Marx delivers one of his strongest statements on the self-unfolding character of the proletarian revolution, suggesting that the socialists have only to become the "mouthpiece" of a process that has got under way quite without them. But there is more here than meets the eye, just as there is more in poverty than meets the eyes of the utopian socialists. So long as socialists see in poverty only poverty, they can do no more than wring their hands in moral anguish and prescribe "more just" social orders. But the critical eye sees revolutionary potential in the apparent weakness of the proletariat. Proletarian poverty contains within itself the possibility of the *Aufhebung* of capitalism, that is, the universalization of capitalism's potential. What men must do is comprehend and grasp this potential and carry it through to its logical conclusion. This means grasping the structural dialectics of capitalism in its productive and cultural modes; and it means grasping the subversive and revolutionary implications of the very fact of proletarian existence.

Dialectical Surpassing of the Tendencies of Capitalism

Marx believed that the extension of the principles of capitalism involved capitalists in activities that undermined (Marx uses the word "contradicted") those same principles: for example, government involvement in the building of railroads and the development of stock companies to finance larger projects and guarantee growth. While capitalism espoused individual enterprise, it created instead structural interdependency. In the *Grundrisse* the point is made most sharply:

> The division of labour results in concentration, coordination, co-operation, the antagonism of private interests and class interests, competition, the centralisation of capital, monopolies and joint stock companies—so many contradictory forms of unity which in turn engenders all these contradictions. In the same

117. *Poverty of Philosophy*, pp. 125–26.

way private exchange creates world trade, private independence gives rise to complete dependence on the so-called world market, and the fragmented acts of exchange make a system of banks and credit necessary, whose accounts at least settle the balances of private exchange. National trade acquires a semblance of existence in the foreign exchange market—although the private interests within each nation divide them into as many nations as they possess full-grown individuals, and the interests of exporters and importers of the same nation are here opposed. No one would imagine that it was therefore possible to transform the foundations of internal and external trade by means of stock exchange reform. But within bourgeois society, which is founded on exchange value, relationships of commerce and production develop which are so many mines about to explode beneath them.[118]

From this, one would anticipate that Marx would advocate the extension of these contradictory (i.e., the interdependent) tendencies of capitalism as serving the interests of the proletariat, and in fact he does precisely that. For example, the concrete measures proposed in the *Manifesto* follow from the need "to increase the total of productive forces as rapidly as possible" and include features already present in advanced capitalist societies (and which we take for granted today), such as a graduated income tax, the creation of

---

118. *Grundrisse*, pp. 68–69. Avineri, *Marx*, pp. 174–84, has given an excellent, detailed discussion of Marx's views of stock companies as hidden "mines" which both extend and undermine capitalism.

The relevance of Marx's discussion to contemporary economic problems is striking. The transnational corporation, which was considered by its proponents to be the crowning achievement of capitalism and by its opponents as an ugly tool of imperialism, has recently been viewed with alarm by some economists as a means by which Third World nations could control the rich, industrialized economies. This has been most dramatically demonstrated with respect to the oil companies and other "extraction" industries but there is evidence that the web of interdependence created by transnational corporate operations is far too complex for simple judgments about their effects. Some surely are exploitative of the Third World, but some have been successfully harnessed by Third World governments to serve national needs. And all do have a profound effect on capital flow, balance of payments, the transfer of technology, and employment patterns, not to mention their effect on consumer patterns and indigenous social structure.

national banks, centralization of the means of communication and transportation in the hands of the state, and free education of all children in public schools.[119] There are many other passages where Marx anticipates developments that will undermine the basic principles of capitalism, including an extraordinary passage in *Capital* that foresees the separation of ownership and control in large corporations long before it was documented in this century by Berle and Means.[120]

Marx's intentions with respect to the political and cultural achievements of capitalism are not so clear. He takes too much for granted here, accepting, as I suggested earlier, the values of the Enlightenment and showing little sensitivity to their fragile nature. For Marx, like Tocqueville, the movement toward democracy in the sense of universal suffrage seemed a historical tendency that could not be checked. Furthermore, as Avineri has shown, universal suffrage was itself the *Aufhebung* of bourgeois society. The "democracies" of Marx's Europe had limited suffrage, and in *The Class Struggles in France* Marx tried to show that bourgeois society would do anything

119. Feuer, *Basic Writings*, pp. 28–29. Not all of the ten measures listed by Marx have in fact been instituted, but he himself says that different countries will require different programs. As Avineri notes, the "most amazing feature" of Marx's proposal "is that it does not include nationalization of industry as such." *Marx*, p. 206.

120. The passage is quoted at length by Avineri, *Marx*, p. 178, and concludes: "On the other hand, the stock company is a transition toward the conversion of all functions in the reproduction process which still remain linked with capitalist property, into mere functions of associated producers into social function . . . This is the abolition [*Aufhebung*] of the capitalist mode of production within the capitalist mode of production itself, and hence a self-dissolving contradiction, which *prima facie* represent a mere phase of transition to a new form of production. It manifests itself as such a contradiction in its effects. It establishes a monopoly in certain spheres and thereby requires state interference. It reproduces a new financial aristocracy, a new variety of parasites in the shape of promoters, speculators and simply nominal directors; a whole system of swindling and cheating by means of corporation promotion, stock issuance, and stock speculation. It is private production without the control of private property."

It is well to remember here that Hegel had thought that private property would assure virtue in public affairs. Marx seems to suggest that the separation of ownership and managerial functions removed all constraints from the managers with respect to public corruption.

it could, including the acceptance of a right-wing government (Louis Bonaparte), to prevent universal suffrage with its revolutionary implications.[121] Where democracies were in fact extending the vote to larger and larger populations, such as in England and in the United States, Marx even suggested that the proletarian revolution would take place at the ballot box, peacefully.[122] Here is strong evidence that violence was of little import in Marx's theory of revolution. What did count was the transformation of consciousness as men surpassed and abolished their former condition. The historical appearance of democracy in the sense of universal suffrage is the transcendence of all previous states precisely because through it men consciously shape the political process rather than acquiesce in political structures which they imagine to be in the "nature of things."[123]

Bourgeois democracy, for all of its shortcomings, produces internal economic and political tensions that will lead to its own *Aufhebung*. But the vehicle of that *Aufhebung* is the unique dialectical product of the bourgeoisie, the proletariat, whose existence is itself revolutionary.

The Growth of Association and Organization among the Proletariat

I left off discussion of the proletariat with the negative and positive dimensions of its alleged universality unconnected. When Marx deals specifically with the revolutionary praxis of the proletarian, his emphasis is on organization and education. Both are minimally necessary in the face of the anomic, mass character of the proletariat—that is, both are necessary in light of its negative universality. But it is clear that Marx does not have to call for worker organization as an external form to be imposed upon them. Worker association was an empirical fact of his time, called forth by the capitalist means of production. At first that association is fragmentary and relatively unorganized, chiefly defensive and without much direction.

121. Ibid., pp. 212-13.
122. This is suggested in his speech of September 18, 1872, to the Hague Conference of the International in Amsterdam. See ibid., p. 216.
123. Thus democracy stands to the state as Christianity stands to religion. Just as the latter with its doctrine of Incarnation carries within it the secret that God is man (Feuerbach), democracy, with its implication that there is no government except from the people, marks the end of politics as an immutable realm where some are dominated by others. See Marx, *Critique of Hegel*, p. 30.

As Marx suggests in the *Manifesto*, it is at first no more than the consequence of the increased concentration of workers in industrial centers and their being treated as a class by the bourgeoisie. Isolated and "without clothes" with respect to traditional ties and identities, their first collisions with the bourgeoisie are spontaneous revolts which achieve their ends, if at all, at great cost. But then, says Marx, "they found permanent associations in order to make provision beforehand for these occasional revolts."[124]

Even these more permanent associations are at first only means to private ends—they serve to keep up the wages of the individual workers. But they do not remain purely instrumental groupings, for the individuals within them soon discover that their solidarity is itself a need and an end:

> When communist *artisans* associate with one another, theory, propaganda, etc., is their first end. But at the same time, as a result of this association, they acquire a new need—the need for society—and what appears as a means becomes an end. In this practical process the most splendid results are to be observed whenever French socialist workers are seen together. Such things as smoking, drinking, eating, etc., are no longer means of contact or means that bring together. Company, association, and conversation, which again has society as its end, are enough for them; the brotherhood of man is no mere phrase with them, but a fact of life, and the nobility of man shines upon us from their work-hardened bodies.[125]

Two critical points must be made about the development of the proletarian. First, the solidarity that the individual proletarian discovers with his fellow workers is a solidarity which has its occasion in work and not in other human groupings such as clan, tribe, nation, village. Those, we have seen, were torn asunder and left behind through the revolutionizing movement of capitalism. Thus, in his work the proletarian discovers himself as a social being (Marx frequently uses the term "species being"). For the first time work is aligned with a recognition of the universal social nature of man, at least potentially. Granted, the work the proletarians do is not their

124. Feuer, *Basic Writings*, p. 16.
125. Marx, *Manuscripts*, pp. 154–55.

own, but their solidarity in relation to it, a solidarity born out of mutual suffering and dependence as well as the positive joys they find in association, at least creates the possibility for regaining their creative powers.

Secondly, as Avineri points out,

> The association of workers in their meetings and groups is by itself a most revolutionary act, for it changes both reality and the workers themselves. This association creates other-directedness and mutuality, it enables the worker to become again a *Gemeinwesen*.[126]

To be a *Gemeinwesen* is to be everything that the bourgeoisie is not—it marks a transition from a society based on atomistic individualism to a society based on mutuality (which obviously spells an end to any theodicy predicated upon the disposition of individual personalities). Furthermore, it marks a transition from passivity to activity, from a situation in which the worker is no more than a commodity in the labor market to a situation in which the workers together attempt actively to transform their condition. Once this occurs, capitalism can never be the same.

Up to this point Marx does little more than to describe what in fact is taking place within the capitalist system, and his analysis is the basis for the often quoted statement about revolutionary praxis in *The German Ideology*:

> Communism is for us not a stable state which is to be established, an *ideal* to which reality will have to adjust itself. We call communism the *real* movement which abolishes the present state of things. The conditions of this movement result from the premises now in existence.[127]

But Marx does not believe that association among the proletariat will of itself establish a transcendence of the existing order. On the contrary, the actions taken by the workers to further their position in society are likely to be precipitous and to advance under the wrong banners, such as the Gotha Program with its emphasis on equal rights. In fact, Marx is torn in his observations on the various

126. Avineri, *Marx*, p. 141.
127. *German Ideology*, p. 26.

worker movements of his time, applauding various movements (such as the Paris Commune) even when they fail, since each movement marks a genuine step forward and builds worker solidarity and confidence; yet he is constantly saying that "the time is not yet ripe" for the proletarian seizure of power.[128]

Education of the Proletariat: The Need for Shaping

What is to be done to avoid precipitous action and wrongheaded ideas? The answer lies in education and in the critical role of the intellectuals. Everywhere, Marx stresses the importance of worker education, and the last of the ten measures delineated in the *Manifesto* specifies that education is to be combined with industrial production.[129] This combination has concrete import: the workers must be acquainted with the full range of techniques if they are to make the productive process their own. But much more is at stake here than technical knowledge. Education must be linked to labor because the productive process is the source of man's self-creation, the possibility of his emancipation from nature. Education combined with labor is an important step in aligning intentions and consequences, in bringing together the various dimensions of human existence. Without this alignment, what the laborer accomplishes through his associations (such as higher wages) may be at odds with what is expected of him in his civic life (such as the necessity of slowing down a wage-price spiral, or of keeping goods priced below those of competitors from other countries). Marx's intention is to make the productive process the focal point of all human education, moral, political, and cultural.

It is interesting in this respect that Marx never considers abolishing child labor, because labor plays a critically formative role in the life and education of every individual. He was certainly in favor of doing away with child labor as it existed in his time. Measure ten in the *Manifesto* includes the statement, "Abolition of children's

128. Cf. Marx's letter to Ferdinand Nieuwenhuis, February 22, 1881: "According to my conviction, the critical conjunction of a new international workers' association does not yet exist; I therefore consider all labor congresses, particularly socialist congresses, insofar as they are not related directly to specific conditions in this or that nation, as useless, even harmful." *On Revolution*, ed. Saul K. Padover (New York: McGraw-Hill, 1971), p. 67.

129. Feuer, *Basic Writings*, p. 29.

factory labor *in its present form*" (emphasis added). And he supported all efforts aimed at shortening the working day.[130] But there was to be "equal liability of all to labor," including children, not for purposes of equity but to align man's thinking and culture with his most fundamental creative activity. Education is not something that is to permit one class of children to escape labor and necessity but rather a process in which man's social productive power is to be discovered as the basis for the development of human creativity. This combination of labor and education will produce, over time, a society in which no one develops his capacities at the expense of others:

> In a higher phase of communist society, after the enslaving subordination of the individual to the division of labor, and therewith also the antithesis between mental and physical labor, has vanished; after labor has become not only a means of life but life's prime want; after the productive forces have also increased with the all-around development of the individual, and all the springs of co-operative wealth flow more abundantly—only then can the narrow horizon of bourgeois right be crossed in its entirety and society inscribe on its banners: "From each according to his ability, to each according to his needs!"[131]

The final line of this passage has often been taken as Marx's moral prescription for the society of the future, but it is not that. It was a socialist slogan of the Gotha Program and Marx criticizes it as offering a moral norm without specifying the social transformations required for it to be a reality. It might become meaningful, but only after man had realigned labor and consciousness, recovering his *Gemeinwesen*.

But who is to do the educating? Marx certainly does not intend to leave this to the workers themselves, for they are, with few exceptions, uncultured and unsophisticated. Organization alone will not make up for the fact that they have been stripped of their cultural and historical sensibilities. In a revealing letter to Feuerbach, Marx notes how the proletariat differs in this respect from country to country:

---

130. See his discussion of "The Working Day" in *Capital* (Feuer, *Basic Writings*, pp. 147ff.).

131. "Critique of the Gotha Program," ibid., p. 119.

> You should be present at one of the meetings of French workers so that you could believe the youthful freshness and nobility prevailing among these toil-worn people. The English proletarian also makes enormous progress, but he lacks the cultural character of the French. I should not forget the theoretical achievements of the German labourer in Switzerland, London and Paris. But the German labourer is still too much a hand-worker [sc. he does not use his head].
>
> Anyway, it is among these "barbarians" of our civilised society that history is preparing the practical element for the emancipation of man.[132]

Marx is notoriously vague in his statements of the role of ideas and education in the proletarian revolution. But this kind of statement, together with the theoretical importance he gave to his own work, indicates that intellectuals had an important role to play in civilizing the proletarian elements. The proletarian, after all, had not only to grasp the significance of his individual labor and that of his immediate fellow workers but also to place this activity in the context of a coherent whole; *Capital* was intended to provide that whole for him. Furthermore, Marx makes it clear that members of other classes may take on a revolutionary consciousness "through the contemplation of the situation of [the proletarian] class."[133]

Quite apart from the weakness of Marx's discussion of the role of ideas and of the intellectual in the education of the proletariat, his own premises demand the transcendence of historical concepts of politics and culture, as well as the methods of production. Otherwise, men would be returned to a state more barbarous than the "immature" art of the Greeks. So the proletariat needs philosophy, not just any philosophy but a philosophy that comprehends its condition while at the same time reshaping it and lifting it above previous philosophical and cultural achievements. In discussing what is necessary for German emancipation, Marx says,

> Just as philosophy finds its material weapons in the proletariat,

---

132. Quoted by Avineri, *Marx*, pp. 140–41 (Avineri's parentheses).

133. *German Ideology*, p. 69. For a complete discussion of the role of intellectuals in the revolution, see Avineri, "Marx and the Intellectuals," in *Journal of the History of Ideas*, April–June, 1967, pp. 269–78.

so the proletariat finds its spiritual weapons in philosophy; and once the lightning of thought has struck deeply into this naive soil of the people the emancipation of the Germans into men will be accomplished.

Let us summarize:

The only practically possible emancipation of Germany is the emancipation based on the unique theory which holds that man is the supreme being for man. In Germany emancipation from the Middle Ages is possible only as the simultaneous emancipation from the partial victories over the Middle Ages. In Germany no form of bondage can be broken unless every form of bondage is broken. . . . Philosophy cannot be actualized without the abolition [*Aufhebung*] of the proletariat; the proletariat cannot be abolished without the actualization of philosophy.

When all the intrinsic conditions are fulfilled, the day of German resurrection will be announced by the crowing of the Gallic cock.[134]

"When all the intrinsic conditions are fulfilled": here we are brought back to the fundamental ambiguity in Marx's theory of the proletariat, for there is nothing in the analysis that Marx gives of revolutionary praxis to demonstrate that the proletarian transition from negative universality to positive universality, to emancipation as consciously self-creating men, will not be short-circuited. On the contrary, there is every likelihood it will be. The more anomic the proletarian is—the more he is the "negation of humanity"—the more shaping he will need from without. There is no guarantee that this will be done by minds of Marx's persuasion, or even by those who value the rights of man; it might just as easily be done by a Hitler. The less anomic the proletarian is—the more culture he has retained from his past—the more likely he is to maintain a particularistic view of the world. (So the more "cultured" character which Marx detected among the French workers may have a great deal to do with continuing French ideals of nationalism.) Marx hoped that the negative universality of the proletariat would make solidarity across cultural and national lines more likely, and the universalistic character of capitalist productive methods should further this. But the

134. Marx, *Critique of Hegel*, p. 142.

history of socialist movements has been a fragmented one, indicating that even the socialists cannot agree on the proper way to shape the proletariat. Such an empirical argument is not, of course, decisive against Marx, but it does render his account increasingly implausible.

Marx's view of the universal potentialities of capitalism and its internal contradictions really amounts to a theory of the exhaustion of the possibilities of one mode of human culture and activity and the concomitant creation of new possibilities. His conviction that these possibilities would be realized in universal fashion, that the emancipation of the proletariat would amount to the resurrection of man, is based in part on the Hegelian confidence in the growing maturity of man and in part on the belief that the struggle with nature has been won. The latter point entails irreversibility, that is, it does not seem possible to Marx that once man sees that he is his own maker, he will be prone to return to modes of life characteristic of past periods of history.

There are places where Marx clearly recognizes the limits that past forms of consciousness place on human possibilities:

> Men make their own history, but they do not make it just as they please; they do not make it under circumstances chosen by themselves, but under circumstances directly encountered, given and transmitted from the past. The tradition of all the dead generations weighs like a nightmare on the brain of the living. And just when they seem engaged in revolutionizing themselves and things, in creating something that has never yet existed, precisely in such periods of revolutionary crisis they anxiously conjure up the spirits of the past to their service and borrow from them names, battle cries and costumes in order to present the new scene of world history in this time-honored disguise and this borrowed language.[135]

But this criticism of the "farce" of the revolutions of 1848 and 1851 does not prevent Marx from insisting that the revolutionaries of the nineteenth century can and should throw off the nightmare and borrow their poetry from the future rather than the past.[136] To this

---

135. *Eighteenth Brumaire*, p. 15.
136. Ibid., p. 18. The "farce" refers to Marx's opening lines in the book: "Hegel remarks somewhere that all facts and personages of great importance in

extent, Marx seems to underestimate the persistence of prior modes of consciousness, the imaginative capacity of men to be quite contrary and even perverse, and the role contingency (for example, in the form of nuclear holocaust or mass starvation) might play in preventing the development of universal consciousness.

The failure of the proletarian to develop into a universal class (or the failure of capitalism to develop a genuine proletariat) is a persistent problem in Marxist theory. It has led many Marxists to look for a different universal class (how often it turns out to be the intellectuals—surely a smug self-delusion!) or to transform Marxism into a theory of cultural criticism. But quite apart from the historical inconvenience of the absence of a universal class, Marx's theory of revolutionary praxis still does not seem to give direction to human action.

The Problem of Action

Even if a universal class did exist, would Marx want capitalists to be moved by the plight of the proletariat, or by the plight of those who were being molded into proletarians, to the extent that they ceased to be capitalists? His answer must surely be no, because until capitalism has exhausted its resources, the "intrinsic conditions" for emancipation will not be fulfilled. The long passage cited earlier from *The Poverty of Philosophy* directly states that the formation of the proletariat depends entirely upon the continued development of productive forces as "history moves forward." Capitalism must develop all of its potentialities.[137]

At no point is this more clearly evident than in Marx's comments on the British colonization of India. In response to American socialists who had protested the British presence in India on moral grounds, he asserted that England's brutal transformation of India was essential in order to overcome the brutalizing worship of nature in traditional Indian culture and raise Indian consciousness to an understanding of man's role as master of nature—in short, to undercut traditional Indian culture and society in order to create one mass

---

world history occur, as it were, twice. He forgot to add: the first time as tragedy, the second as farce."

137. Avineri, *Marx*, pp. 181-84.

proletariat. If one takes this position seriously, then Camus is right in his observation that Marxism can be interpreted quietistically. Even Lenin wrote that "it is a reactionary way of thinking to try to find salvation in the working class in any other way than in the top-heavy development of capitalism."[138] It would appear that if imperialists stopped their activity in the Third World and if capitalists ceased extending the principles of capitalism, then the process of human transformation would be aborted. But should those who wish to give active direction to this process then volunteer to head up capitalist enterprises in the Third World?

Marx's answer would surely be that such a question is nonsense, that it raises abstract issues of the sort that are antithetical to praxis. Capitalism will take care of itself. What one should do is to look at the inner tendencies of capitalism and seize upon them in order to transform and transcend them. Such an answer asks for a continuing "critical theory" or even a "permanent revolution." But the plausibility of such approaches depends in part on whether it is possible to specify as clearly as Marx did the causes of human domination in advanced industrial societies. The complexity of industrial society and the absence of a universal class are further complicated by the fact that Marxist ideas are very much in the air now; they are part of our intellectual equipment, so that we are all Marxists in one sense or another. All segments of society have become self-conscious about what they are doing, not in the sense of the unity of intention and consequence but in the sense of second-guessing their own actions. These considerations have led some Marxists to argue that in modern society the "deprivations" of man are more "secret" than ever before and require even more sophisticated forms of critical analysis.[139] But this latter point only attests to the remarkable strength of ideas in human action.

If in fact the deprivations of modern man are more secret than Marx anticipated and if there is no clear universal class, then the Marxist view of human action leads us to conclude that there are

138. Camus, *The Rebel*, p. 206.

139. This is the view of many theorists associated with the Frankfurt school, such as Herbert Marcuse and Jürgen Habermas. Cf. Habermas, *Theory and Practice* (Boston: Beacon, 1973), pp. 195ff., and Marcuse, *One-Dimensional Man* (Boston: Beacon, 1964). Habermas, it should be noted, has pursued lines of thought which take him well beyond the Marxist framework.

two classes of men: (1) those who act blindly in history, including the bourgeoisie and various marginal groups, pursuing their projects without insight into the fate that must await them; and (2) those who have insight and take it upon themselves to read, interpret, and direct the course of history (human action) from a superior vantage point. Thus Marcuse, among others, combines Marxist and Freudian analysis into a therapeutic theory of social emancipation in which the intellectuals (but not all of them) are the therapists and the marginals (as well as the rest of society) are the patients.[140] Anyone who claims such insight into the ways of history and the deprivations of men is in a position analogous to those who claim that the oppressed must engage in violence to become fully human: they perpetuate their own superiority. And the division between intentions and consequences which according to Marx has plagued human action throughout history persists in the division of society into therapists and patients. I shall return to these issues at the end of this chapter.

THE GOAL OF REVOLUTION

Marx says very little about the future society because he knows that there is no historical precedent for it and because any attempt to establish its outlines in advance would be a violation of his notion of human praxis. However, it should be clear from the foregoing that human association after the proletarian revolution is not seen as a static state of being and that to the extent its future outlines can be anticipated they are to be found in the universalizing of present tendencies. For my purposes several general observations will suffice.

In the first place, the universalization of the present tendencies of bourgeois society means that all of mankind will consciously participate in the shaping of their own lives. The realms of politics, economics, art, law will not be conceived as permanent structures or orders of being but as artifacts of man's historical and social existence. Thus, Marx's theory is not dissimilar to (and is in part the origin of) contemporary theories of modernization and secularization.

---

140. According to Marcuse, the repressions of modern society are so subtle and so consuming that intolerance of certain ideas is essential in order to emancipate man. See his essay, "Repressive Tolerance," in Robert Paul Wolff et al., *A Critique of Pure Tolerance* (Boston: Beacon, 1969), and his 1968 "Postscript" in the same volume.

Men are to "remember" that the human world has been created by them and that it requires their continual efforts for sustenance and adaptability.

Second, patterns of domination based on the struggle with nature or on scarcity would disappear. This does not mean that everyone would be recompensed equally or that distinctions of rank and office would not be present. What it does mean can perhaps best be understood by contrast with certain characteristics of contemporary capitalist society. In the mid-seventies we have had a curious combination of recession and inflation in which one difficulty is that goods have become either scarcer or more expensive. In such a situation, society as a whole has to tighten its belt. Concretely, that has always meant that some people have to tighten their belts more than others—the question is, which ones? Forgetting for the moment those who are already living in poverty, the active debate usually is one between labor and those who are either white-collar workers, managers, or owners. The argument of the former is that everyone needs and has a right to a stable and adequate income. The argument of the latter is that the long-term health of the economy as a whole depends on continued capitalization and recapitalization (as well as on research and development), all of which would be seriously jeopardized if profits were cut or even limited. This last argument is almost always decisive among those who make decisions about belt tightening, perhaps with good reason. The question is, Why should one group of persons benefit immediately from a decision made for the long-range good of society while another group must sit and wait until the long-range plan has borne fruit? What Marx hoped for was a society in which the shock of tough, long-range decisions would be distributed across the lines of rank and office, and in which the decisions themselves would be made by all parties affected.

The more interesting question is whether Marx believed that old patterns of domination would continue, or new ones emerge, which were not based on scarcity. Since he believed that the future would not be static and that one of its features would be the continual creation of human needs extending far beyond "natural" needs— even as capitalism had already developed such needs—it is perhaps not contradicting the premises of his thought to imagine new patterns of domination emerging. However, he is essentially silent on this issue, demonstrating once again the extent to which the struggle with nature was decisive for him in creating human suffering and evil. It has been left to the neo-Marxists to place power relations and domination at the center of theoretical attention.[141]

Whether Marx was correct or not in his hope for the development of a universal class and the conquest of nature, he successfully articulated a theodicy that could serve as the basis for organizing human society and interpreting crisis and failure—the ultimate questions of life. Earlier I indicated that the decision to combine education with labor was based on the assumption that the conscious activity of man, the labor of the mind, must be rooted in and aligned with the labor that has freed history from nature. This combined with the fact that Marx saw in the workingmen's associations a model for the future (one that would still have to be transcended) meant that in the future society all forms of human organization, discipline, and education would grow out of labor, the fundamental universal activity of man. In short, Marx provided not only an interpretation of the passage of man from unwitting tool of history to conscious shaper of history, he also provided an organizational structure to nurture that passage and within which answers to organizational questions in other areas of life could be developed. Furthermore, when setbacks occurred, when the revolution was threatened, when socialist countries continued to have unresolved problems within or were threatened from without, an "ultimate" explanation was forthcoming: the struggle with nature was unfinished or older modes of man's relation to nature still persisted. On all these levels, the Marxist theory functions the way all previous theodicies have functioned: patterns of organization, including inequalities, are legitimated and the anomic situations in life are given a structure.

It is at this juncture that Marxism is successful in the sense of providing a revolutionary program, while the dualisms discussed in chapter 3 were not. It seems highly irrelevant whether or not Marx is able to specify precisely how the revolution is to take place—he makes it clear that different circumstances would require different measures.[142] What is relevant is that an organizational structure is

141. This has occupied the attention of the Frankfurt school of critical theory and especially the work of Jürgen Habermas and Rolf Dahrendorf. See Dahrendorf, *Class and Class Conflict in Industrial Society* (Stanford: Stanford University Press, 1959).

142. See *Manifesto*, p. 28.

provided that accounts for and gives direction to the anomic experiences of the proletarian class—and, as his own theory implies, the very organizing of these anomic experiences and of an anomic people is itself revolutionary. Any previous theodicy is irreversibly discredited.

It has often been argued that what made the Puritan revolutionaries in the seventeenth century successful was the power of Calvinist theology with its special emphasis on discipline and organization. That discipline found its focus in the Puritan families and local churches. Michael Walzer has shown that these organizational units became the basis for education, which the Puritans valued highly, and especially for training for political office.[143] They also provided for the molding of character to suit it for the high level of public participation Puritan life entailed. In all these cases, Puritanism provided an organization and an ethic that permitted men to deal with the anomic phenomena of seventeenth-century England, and at the same time it gave structure to the lives of "marginal" men.[144]

Two observations are pertinent here. The first is that there have been only two sets of revolutionary ideas that have succeeded in providing organizational principles together with an all-encompassing theodicy: Calvinism and Marxism. Calvinism organized life around the family and voluntary religious organizations from which educational and political institutions evolved, as well as a view of economics. At its core was a conviction that the fundamental struggle of man was internal and with God. Marxism organized life around the laboring activity of man, from which educational and political organization developed as well as the family and culture. At its core was a conviction that the fundamental struggle of man was with nature.

The second observation is a paraphrase of George Lichtheim: "The early Christians awaited the coming of the Savior, and what they got instead was the church. The French intellectuals expected the coming of the revolution, and what they got was the Communist party."[145] Analogously, the Puritans set out to establish the Kingdom of God and to create saints, but instead they established republican

143. Walzer, *Revolution of the Saints*, pp. 183–98; 219–24.
144. Ibid., p. 313.
145. Lichtheim, *The Concept of Ideology*, pp. 287–88.

commonwealths and created capitalists. The Marxists set out to establish the classless society and to create universal men; instead they established Marxist states and created bureaucrats.

RECAPITULATION AND ASSESSMENT

I have now focused the questions raised at the end of chapter 3 on two critical problems: the concept of marginal man and the directing of human action. The last problem includes the question of the relationship between the social theorist and marginal man.

The Concept of Marginality

Marginality is the social equivalent of Kuhn's scientific anomalies which violate the paradigm-induced expectations of a scientific community. In society, marginality is a threat to the legitimating theodicy. Anomic situations abound in human experience, but revolutionary potential develops when they are not isolated experiences but are of a kind that creates an anomic, marginal people. All of the revolutionary theories I have looked at have concepts of marginality. The question is whether marginality is a notion that can have any constant meaning.

The first point to be made is that marginality is a purely relational term: it can have no meaning in itself. Marx borrows Hegel's master-slave relationship to show how a particular form of domination goes through a series of internal transformations to produce a marginal people, a people who no longer fit the terms of the theodicy. In contrast, the marginals of a dualist revolution exist as the negative, dark, or evil principle in a dualist theodicy.

Marx clearly intends his special concept of marginality—negative universality—to be fundamental and irreducible, a marginality engendered without relation to a human master. But it is not at all clear that Marx has given an unambiguous conception of negative universality. The more he emphasizes the proletariat's total absence of structure (which is necessary if they are to be the true negation of humanity), the more difficult it is for him to account for their positive development as a universal class without excessive aid from another group such as the intellectuals. Obversely, the more able they are to develop spontaneously in a positive direction as a conscious group, the more likely they are to depend on residual forms of consciousness that by Marx's own assessment must be particularistic.

Marx's difficulty in elaborating a coherent account of negative universality is exacerbated by the fact that he gives two accounts of how this marginality develops. In the first the proletarian class is born in the "womb of capitalism" at the historical culmination of Western development. This essentially Hegelian account makes the proletarian heir, even though only dialectically and potentially, to the entire economic, political, and cultural achievement of the West, including Greek art, the rights of man, and the like. In the second account marginality is associated with the process by which capitalism expands internationally and undermines the traditional, nature-worshipping cultures of the non-European world. The anomic peoples thus created do not have benefit of the entire history of Western culture, since the capitalists would hardly succeed in transplanting all of it. Furthermore, Marx makes it clear in his observations on India that he expects no help from Indian culture itself, whose despotic political system makes the human mind "the unresisting tool of superstitution," and he describes "oriental" life as "undignified, stagnatory, and vegetative."[146] This view of the whole of the Asian continent, also borrowed wholesale from Hegel, has been a source of embarrassment and difficulty for many Marxists (and Hegelians) since it suggests that Marx has two philosophies of history: one to cover dynamic peoples, the other to cover peoples who are stagnant and require outside intervention in order to progress historically. In this respect Marx is as parochial about Europe as most nineteenth-century imperialists. There have been various attempts to interpret the problem of "Oriental despotism" in Marx,[147] but the main issue is that the anomic peoples created in the countries of what we now call the Third World cannot partake of the same kind of negativity as the proletarian class in Europe. In fact, Marx's negative characterization of "oriental" life would seem close to the kind of attitudes that create dualist marginality.

Marx does attempt to work out a dialectic for England's relationship to India, including the ironic reversal when England becomes dependent on India and finds that it costs more to administer than

146. "British Rule in India," p. 480.
147. See Lichtheim, "Oriental Despotism," in *The Concept of Ideology*, pp. 62–96; Shlomo Avineri, Introduction to Marx, *On Colonialism and Modernization* (Garden City, N.Y.: Doubleday Anchor, 1969); and E. J. Hobsbawm's Introduction to Marx, *Pre-Capitalist Economic Formations.*

the benefits warrant.[148] But this account has more to do with England's difficulties than with India's transformation. And Marx's own projection that the revolution will occur first in the advanced European countries such as France, England, and the United States indicates that for him the cultural sophistication is as necessary as economic development if a universal revolution is to take place. In his later writings he begins to entertain the possibility that the revolution will occur first in Russia or other "underdeveloped" countries, but this simply underscores the fact that he does not have a carefully worked out theory of negative marginality and the transition from it to universality. That Russia became a totalitarian state is not merely an inconvenience in socialist theory—it is a demonstration that the notions of the rights of man had never become part of Russian culture. There was no Enlightenment to transcend.

We may add to this the empirical observation that the reaction against imperialism in this century has rarely, if even, taken universal form. Much of it is best comprehended under Fanon's dualistic analysis. And the remarkable resurgence of nationalism probably reflects the fact that a "revolution of rising expectations" in a developing nation almost always turns out to be the rising expectations of a cultural elite. These modern cultural elites may be anomic and marginal in relation to the traditional culture, but their aspirations are likely to resemble bourgeois European aspirations (at least economically), linked frequently with attempts to revive certain portions of the past from their own culture.

If there is no clear picture of the development of universal marginality in Marx, it may be added that he did not foresee the development of other kinds of marginality in the modern world. Most notable is racial marginality which, whether it is found in colonial situations or not, frequently interprets its situation dualistically. Finally, there are the claims to marginality on the part of countless groups in this country (and possibly others), such as American Indians, Spanish Americans, and women. We have, in other words, not total subjective anomie but a kind of cultural anomie in which many groups, none universal, find no overarching structure of meaning. "Every revolutionary theory, under these circumstances, lacks

148. See Avineri, Introduction to Marx, *On Colonialism*, pp. 16–18.

those to whom it is addressed."[149] Most contemporary revolutionary movements show a crazy-quilt pattern of alleged marginal groups: revolutions make strange bedfellows. The probability that universality will be short-circuited seems very high.

It has been my argument that Marx's failure to account for a multiplicity of marginal forms is a consequence of his own hidden theodicy, his attempt to account for all of human domination in terms of the struggle for mastery over nature. If this argument is persuasive, then Marx has not succeeded in putting an end to theodicy. His dialectic of marginal and universal men, although an inversion of Hegel, still retains Hegel's propensity to subsume too much of the variety of human relationships under a single conceptual scheme. One could say that his account of the movement from negative to positive humanity is therefore still very much a "mystified" conceptual scheme, still very much a theodical paradigm.

None of this is to deny the power of Marx's conception. There is no more penetrating analysis of the internal transformations of productive modes and the ensuing incongruence (contradiction?) between the ideologies and the actual social relations that emerge from these transformations. The task facing social theorists is not to abandon these insights but to use them to construct a more complex and nuanced model of power relations in human society. In a sense, this is what social theory after Marx is about.

The Direction of Human Action

At the end of chapter 3 I argued that those who worked consciously within a dualist framework had either to content themselves with descriptions of the spontaneous rebirth of men who had been relegated to the negative pole of a dualist theodicy or enter into a therapeutic relationship with the marginal. The second course of action, even though it aims at the emancipation of the marginals, incurs the danger of maintaining them in an inferior status, since it implies that they are incapable of gaining insight into their own dilemma, and there is no guarantee that the outcome will be emancipatory. Marx's use of the Hegelian master-slave paradigm is an attempt to avoid the dualist dilemma, since the paradigm specifies that the slave's transformation and emergence

149. Habermas, *Theory and Practice,* p. 196.

into full self-consciousness are merely functions of his relationship to the master and the work required of him. Marx attempts to show that the proletarian builds on his own latent strength, a strength molded in the dialectical relationship with the capitalist mode of activity. But if my analysis has been correct, the idea of a complete negation of humanity cuts short this internal engendering of universality. At this point the question of how human action is to be directed reemerges, a question complicated by the account of plural marginality I have just given.

Even if Marx had succeeded in giving a single coherent account of marginality, it may be argued that the master-slave paradigm cannot provide a guide to action, either for those who are within the master-slave dialectic or for those who look at it from without. As G. A. Kelly has remarked, for Hegel the resolution of the master-slave encounter "can be only tragic or unbearably smug (one takes his pick) because history, the carrier of *Geist* and freedom, is also the perfect warrant for man's fate."[150] Hegel at least did not try to make his account a warrant for action one way or the other— philosophy only comprehends man's fate after it is sealed. But this puts the man of insight into the position of a spectator of history, and the spectator must secretly hope that all actors show up for the play even though the ending is ineluctable.

There is a remarkable scene in Goethe's *Faust* where the blind and dying Faust hears the spades of Mephistopheles' lemurs digging his own grave and imagines that his immense project to reclaim a portion of the sea is being carried out. Faust interprets the sound of the spades as a sign of progress toward brotherhood and the ideal society and thereupon says the fateful words, "Verweile doch, du bist so schön!" So Faust dies a happy death, and the abyss between the grave and the ideal society is further masked by Goethe's decision to save Faust's soul. Marx has no divine intervention to correct the grave. He also must hope that the masters have no insight into their historical activity, because there is no point in overseeing the digging of one's own grave. The work of the capitalist is tragic from his own perspective unless he has full confidence

150. George Armstrong Kelly, "Notes on Hegel's 'Lordship and Bondage,'" *Review of Metaphysics* 29, no. 4 (June 1966): 794–95.

in what he is doing. Marx must therefore depend upon the capitalist's retaining his illusions (or his smugness).

Marginal people fare little better. Their role in the play (if the play is to be at all interesting) appears to require the adoption of illusions, perhaps a dualist theodicy, in order to move the plot (history) forward. All of this tends to prove the correctness of Shaw's maxim, "The reasonable man adapts himself to the world: the unreasonable one persists in trying to adapt the world to himself. Therefore all progress depends on the unreasonable man."[151] But it was the Marxist hope that the revolution would be reasonable, that is, that the gap between intention and accomplishment would be overcome.

These dilemmas have led some Marxists to reintroduce normative appeals. Marcuse, for example, argues that "the ethics of revolution appeal to an historical calculus. Can the intended new society, the society intended by the revolution, offer better chances for progress in freedom than the existing society?"[152] He goes on to remark that

> the more calculable and the more controllable the technical apparatus of modern industrial society becomes, the more does the chance of human progress depend on the intellectual and moral qualities of the leaders, and on their willingness and ability to educate the controlled population and to make it recognize the possibility, nay, the necessity of pacification and humanization.[153]

We have here not only a normative appeal but a clear recognition that the leader and (or under the guidance of) the social theorist must make others recognize what is morally desirable and necessary. The revolutionary not only undergoes conversion—he is actively converted by another.

One might take Marxist theory in other directions. Lucien Goldmann has compared the Marxist confidence in history with Pascal's wager.[154] Jürgen Habermas and other social theorists have attempted

---

151. George Bernard Shaw, "Maxims for Revolutionists," in *Man and Superman* (London: Archibald Constable, 1907), p. 238.

152. Marcuse, "Ethics and Revolution," in Richard T. DeGeorge, ed., *Ethics and Society* (Garden City, N.Y.: Doubleday Anchor, 1966), p. 143.

153. Ibid., p. 147.

154. Lucien Goldmann, *The Hidden God* (London: Routledge, 1964).

a more nuanced reading of human domination. Habermas in particular has combined numerous strands of contemporary philosophical and social thought to distinguish among different cognitive interests: the technical, the practical, and the emancipatory; he has gone on to use Marx and Freud to develop a theory of social therapy in connection with the emancipatory interest.[155]

As challenging as these directions are, none of them changes the fact that the movement from marginality to universality in revolution presents intractable difficulties. By all accounts a movement toward universality is likely only if there is active intervention on the part of intellectuals and social theorists. If this is the case, and if there is a greak risk involved (Marcuse says that revolution always involves violence), then the moral questions have to do not as Marcuse says merely with means-end relations[156] but with the nature of the intervention and the insight claimed by those who want to impose their vision of the future on others. In every case, can they correctly interpret the sound of the busy spades?

155. In *Knowledge and Human Interests* and in *Theory and Practice*.
156. "Ethics and Revolution," p. 147.

5

The Dialectic of Hope and Evil:
Jürgen Moltmann

> Why did Hegel not become for the Protestant world
> something similar to what Thomas Aquinas was for
> Roman Catholicism?
>
> Karl Barth, *Protestant Theology*
> *in the Nineteenth Century*

From a theological point of view there are two ways of interpreting
the digging spades, of accounting for the transition from negative to
positive universality.[1] One is to stay within the Hegelian-Marxist
framework but to add an explicitly theological dimension: God's
promise provides the guarantee that the spades are not merely digging
graves. The other, more complex, involves a degree of agnosticism
about revolutionary transitions. This is the subject of the last
chapter.

The solution offered by a theological dialectic may be briefly
stated: marginality is given a theological meaning; the power for the
transition is found not in human work but in the work of God; and
the goal of revolution is the Kingdom of God. Within this framework
a number of movements including theologies of liberation, theologies
of hope, and theologies of revolution offer variations on the theme.
Some variations are close to the millenarian type. Others borrow
more from Hegel in order to account for both continuity and
novelty. But there is sufficient commonality among the variations to
permit a close analysis of one to illuminate the issues and problems
of the others.

I have chosen for this purpose the German theologian Jürgen

---

1. There are, of course, more than two responses if one chooses to ignore the
dialectical tradition altogether.

Moltmann, whose writing on the theme of Christian eschatology and hope has led him also to consider revolutionary action. The *also* is important: Moltmann is not first and foremost a writer on revolution. Furthermore, Moltmann's explicit writing on revolution is in many ways the least satisfactory aspect of his thought. Nevertheless, more than most recent theological writers on revolution he has self-consciously chosen to work within the Hegelian and Marxist tradition in his interpretation of Christian faith, and the consequence is an account of Christian practice connected to many of the themes of the preceding chapters. Moreover, Moltmann's theological approach is representative of much recent Christian writing on eschatology and revolution, and a critique of his position is broadly applicable to it.

Perhaps the most significant characteristic of what Moltmann calls the theology of hope is the use of Christian eschatology to reinterpret the relation of God to the world, of the eternal to the temporal. In particular, God's transcendence is understood in historical terms; that is, the divine is interpreted not as an eternal realm that stands over against time, but as a future goal that pulls the present toward it. To put it another way, history is movement toward the Kingdom of God, made possible by human hope.

> If we follow the biblical discourse about the "God of hope," we will have to give prominence to the *future as the mode of God's existence with us.* God is not present in the same way that the things in the world are at hand. God, like his kingdom, is coming and only as the coming one, as future, is he already present. He is already present in the way in which his future in promise and hope empowers the present. He is, however, not yet present in the manner of his eternal presence. Understood as the *coming one* and as the *power of the future*, God is experienced as the *ground of liberation*, and not as the enemy of freedom. He lifts man above the present palpable reality and liberates him from the systems of the existing world and contemporary society. As the power of the exodus, his promise causes men in hope to grow beyond themselves. For freedom consists in going beyond what is as such, even beyond what one is in himself, in order creatively to seize the new possibilities of the future. The "God of hope" was from the beginning a liberating God. The tran-

scendence of his future can be understood as the basis for the human transcending of every historical present. We should, therefore, not exchange Yahweh for Baal, but rather destroy the idols of domination, authority, superiority, law and order, to be able to find again the God of the exodus as the power of the future, as the strength of freedom and the source of the *novum.*[2]

This passage lays bare the interplay between theological language and the familiar Hegelian-Marxist themes of freedom and liberation, of the historical overcoming of previous limits, of the suppression of domination and authority. And it is the intertwining of these themes that leads Moltmann to suggest that Christian practice should be a liberating and even revolutionary praxis.

It will be useful to begin with a brief restatement of the key issues discussed in the preceding chapter. (1) A group of issues surrounds the related notions of *marginality* and *universality*. To the extent that marginality is understood as an occasion or even cause of revolution, it is important to specify how it comes into being. In particular, the theologian who borrows from Marx must account for Marx's own analysis of the dialectic of marginal and universal man in the self-generating struggle with nature. If other kinds of marginality are thought to exist, the status of these in relation to Marx's marginality, and to universality, must be clarified. (2) Another set of issues surrounds the problem of *action* or *revolutionary praxis*. One is the way in which marginals become nonmarginals or, a stronger claim, become universal. A connected issue concerns the role of those who are not marginal and who are not conscious of their roles in history (such as Marx's alienated bourgeoisie): what is their status and future? Finally, are there those, such as intellectuals or Christians, who fit into neither of these roles, and if so, what is their relation to the other two groups? (3) There is a third set of issues grouped around the relation between revolutionary action and the society of the future, or future institutions. In a theological context,

---

2. Jürgen Moltmann, "Introduction to the 'Theology of Hope'," in *The Experiment Hope* (Philadelphia: Fortress, 1975), pp. 50–51. Those interested in a full theological and philosophical background to Moltmann should see M. Douglas Meeks, *Origins of the Theology of Hope* (Philadelphia: Fortress, 1974). See also Christopher L. Morse, *The Logic of Promise in Moltmann's Theology* (Philadelphia: Fortress, 1979).

these issues find their parallel in the subject of the Kingdom of God and the relation it has to the world.

UNIVERSALITY, MARGINALITY, AND THE PROBLEM OF EVIL

Moltmann's most penetrating analysis of politics and revolution is to be found not in his explicit writings on revolution but in his theological writing on Christian identity and Christology. In these he resists the temptation to place the Christian above the dialectical fray of history, above the struggle between oppressor and oppressed, in the position of the critical intellectual or "neutral" therapist. Instead he argues that Christians are the universal class. The Christian's universality is rooted in his dialectical marginality, although this marginality is theologically construed. The decision to define the Christian in this manner serves notice that Moltmann intends his theology to be practical in nature. As Moltmann would put it, to be a Christian *is* to be political, to do Christian theology *is* to do political theology. His theology therefore must be subjected to the same scrutiny as was Marx's revolutionary praxis; that is, its test is in its practical manifestations.

Christians as Marginal and Universal

The idea that Christians constitute a universal class is implicit in Moltmann's first major work, *The Theology of Hope*. In discussing the freedom of man under the eschatological lordship of God, he tells us that "life under his lordship ... means the historic life of the nomad in breaking new ground and in obedient readiness to face the future—a life that is received in promise and is open to promise."[3] And again, the man of hope "becomes homeless with the homeless, for the sake of the home of reconciliation."[4] "Nomadic" and "homeless" life is at least a figurative expression for life without a particular identity, life without the historical place that normally shapes human existence. In the last chapter of the book, after discussing the various roles that society has assigned or "conceded" to the church,[5] Moltmann states that Christians must break through

3. Jürgen Moltmann, *The Theology of Hope* (London: SCM, 1967), pp. 216–17.
4. Ibid., p. 224.
5. These he designates as "religion as the cult of the new subjectivity," "religion as the cult of co-humanity," and "religion as the cult of the institution." Ibid., pp. 311–24.

the symbiosis implied in these roles. "If Christianity, according to the will of him in whom it believes and in whom it hopes, is to be different and to serve a different purpose, then it must address itself to no less a task than that of breaking out of these its socially fixed roles."[6]

> The Church lays claim to the whole of humanity in mission. This mission is not carried out within the horizon of expectation provided by the social roles which society concedes to the Church, but it takes place within its own peculiar horizon of the eschatological expectation of the coming kingdom of God, of the coming righteousness and the coming peace, of the coming freedom and dignity of man.[7]

In the language of Marxism, the socially conceded roles of the church are alienated roles, separating the church from its true vitality and creative power. But the church cannot rest in these roles. In its true eschatological hope, it "lays claim to the whole of humanity in mission," it is universal. As such, the church is an "Exodus Church," called out of all "continuing cities" in the service of a universal city to come. Christian hope

> will therefore endeavour to lead our modern institutions away from their own immanent tendency towards stabilization, will make them uncertain, historify them and open them to that elasticity which is demanded by openness towards the future for which it hopes. In practical opposition to things as they are, and in creative reshaping of them, Christian hope calls them in question and thus serves the things that are to come.[8]

These claims remain chiefly claims in *The Theology of Hope*, based on a biblical study of the theme of eschatology but without a thorough analysis of what this universality means in political and sociological terms. A warning is given, however, with an implicit promise of analysis to come: the attempt to detach oneself as an individual or a group from "conceded social roles" fails if it rests on either the hope of utopia (Marx) or on ironic reflection. The historical failure of the former has yielded in Europe to the latter, the

6. Ibid., p. 324.
7. Ibid., p. 327.
8. Ibid., p. 330.

reflective transcendence of inner subjectivity detached from the confusions of the social world. But such a move has the effect of turning "man into a 'man without attributes' in a 'world of attributes without man.'"[9]

> When, by means of reflection, subjectivity is withdrawn from its social reality, then it loses contact with the real conditions of society and robs these conditions of the very forces which it requires in order to give them shape and vindicate them to the future. . . . A thing is alive only when it contains contradiction in itself and is indeed the power of holding the contradiction within itself and enduring it.[10]

The last sentence is Hegel. It indicates that Moltmann, like Marx, wants to create a genuinely dialectical view of Christian identity while at the same time asserting its universality.

The full dialectical (and theological) analysis of Christian identity begins to take shape in various essays on political theology and Christian participation in politics.[11] In these the critical attitude that the Christian is to take in the face of "the immanent tendency of modern institutions towards stabilization" resides less in the hope of Christian faith and more in the humiliation and crucifixion of Jesus. Following Hegel again, Moltmann says,

> If the one profaned with crucifixion by the authority of the state is the Christ of God, then what is lowest in the political imagination is changed into what is highest. . . . If this crucified one becomes divine authority for the believers, the political-religious faith in authority ceases to hold sway over them. For

9. Ibid., pp. 336–37. Cf. Moltmann's chapter, "The Irony of the 'Man without Qualities,'" in his *Man* (Philadelphia: Fortress, 1974).

10. *Theology of Hope*, p. 337.

11. See especially "Political Theology," in *Theology Today* 28 (1971–72), pp. 6–23, and "The Cross and Civil Religion," in Jürgen Moltmann et al., *Religion and Political Society* (New York: Harper & Row, 1974), pp. 9–47. The latter is a translation of an article entitled "Theologisches Kritik der Politischen Religion," in J. B. Metz, Jürgen Moltmann, and Willi Oelmüller, *Kirche im Prozess der Aufklärung* (Munich: Chr. Kaiser, 1970). The English translation of the title is too narrow, since what is called "civil religion" in American circles is only part of what Moltmann means by "political theology."

them, the political forces are deprived of direct religious justification from above.[12]

It is evident that Christian identity, finding its locus in the crucified Christ, discovers ipso facto that it cannot be absorbed by the political institutions of a given historical moment. The crucifixion *is* a political event at its very core. Religious crimes at the time of Jesus were punished by stoning, whereas political crimes were punished by crucifixion.[13] Even though the Romans made a mistake in imagining that Jesus was a rebel against the Pax Romana, their response to him is rooted in the incapacity of any political religion, that is, the religious legitimation of any political order, to accept the challenge of the crucified Christ. The crucified Christ, as the source of the hope of God's future, undercuts the claims of any political order that can imagine the future only in terms of its own institutions. Rome's treatment of Jesus as a rebel becomes the dialectical confirmation that God's future is antithetical to any theodicy upon which the Roman order rested. Therefore, Christians who found their identity in the crucified Christ could not find a place in the structure of the political and social order of that time. From the standpoint of the Roman political religion they became "others," people who stood outside the Roman theodicy. As such, they joined dialectically all other groups who were oppressed by the Pax Romana, the poor, the slaves, all those considered "unlike" or "other."[14] Christianity's crucified God is a "stateless God."[15]

Moltmann's full position on the universality of Christian identity is worked out in *The Crucified God*. This book marks a shift in emphasis. In the *Theology of Hope* and many of the essays on revolution immediately following, Moltmann developed the eschatological theme in Christian faith as a source of hope and vision which

12. "Political Theology," p. 16. Cf. "The Cross and Civil Religion," pp. 34–35.

13. "Political Theology," p. 15. Cf. Moltmann, *The Crucified God* (New York: Harper & Row, 1974), pp. 136ff.

14. For Moltmann's discussion of "unlikeness" or "otherness," see "The Cross and Civil Religion," pp. 37, 43–44; "Political Theology," pp. 17–18, 21–22; and various passages in *The Crucified God* (for example, pp. 24–25), which is discussed in the text.

15. "The Cross and Civil Religion," p. 42.

moves men to liberating action. The themes of promise and fulfillment in both the Old and New Testaments, and especially in the resurrection of Christ, anticipate a future that cannot be projected from the tendencies or potentialities of the present.[16] The proleptic elements of the Gospel provide the historical energy to overcome the limitations implicit in every historical situation. In *The Crucified God* Moltmann seems motivated by two concerns. The first is the persistence of evil in spite of the many "liberating" movements which gave cause for optimism in the 1960s. He notes that Ernst Bloch, who had inspired much of his thinking, "too is becoming more and more disturbed by the problem of evil, and the failure of both philosophy and theology to give it conceptual form." The second concern is the problem of Christian identity that emerges from enthusiastic participation in political, revolutionary, and "humanizing" movements:

> The more theology and the church attempt to become relevant to the problems of the present day, the more deeply they are drawn into the crisis of their own Christian identity. The more they attempt to assert their identity in traditional dogmas, rights and moral notions, the more irrelevant and unbelievable they become. This double crisis can be more accurately described as the *identity-involvement dilemma.*[17]

Moltmann therefore holds out the promise that the problem of evil and the relationship between Christians and movements of liberation will be given detailed attention.

Crux probat omnia: Moltmann follows Luther in referring all questions of Christian identity to the cross of Christ. It is commonly understood in the church that the cross is a revelation of God. But what specifically is revealed in the cross? The crucified Christ was abandoned by God. Moltmann emphasizes that the distress Jesus suffered on the cross as well as before, and the various anguished statements attributed to him by the Evangelists, must be understood against the background of the Jewish notion of God's presence in

16. See "Resurrection as Hope," in *Religion, Revolution, and the Future* (New York: Scribner's, 1969), pp. 42–62. Cf. "Exegesis and the Eschatology of History," in *Hope and Planning* (New York: Harper & Row, 1971), pp. 56–98. Cf. also *Theology of Hope,* passim, but especially chaps. 2 and 3.

17. *The Crucified God*, pp. 5 and 7 (Moltmann's emphasis).

relation to life and death.[18] For the Jew, the presence of God *is* life. To be abandoned by God is to die. Hell is not something after death but is rather death in the condition of godforsakenness.[19] Given the emphasis in his ministry on the presence of God, as well as the messianic expectations of Judaism at that time, Jesus

> could not regard his being handed over to death on the cross as one accursed as a mere mishap, a human misunderstanding or a final trial, but was bound to experience it as rejection by the very God whom he had dared to call "My Father." When we look at his non-miraculous and helpless suffering and dying in the context of his preaching and his life, we understand how his misery cried out to heaven: it is the experience of abandonment by God in the knowledge that God is not distant but close; does not judge, but shows grace. And this, in full consciousness that God is close at hand in his grace, to be abandoned and delivered up to death as one rejected, is the torment of hell.[20]

How is it possible, then, that this abandoned Jesus should at the same time be proclaimed the Lord and the chosen one of God? This question would have no answer if theology were confined to a view of knowledge in which human reason comprehended the revelation of God by way of a fundamental affinity between reason and the *logos*, or being, of God. In this classical, fundamentally Greek understanding of religious knowledge (and all knowledge), "the process of knowing takes place under the guidance of analogy, and in these circumstances is always recognition."[21] But the principle of knowledge at work in the crucified Christ is dialectical rather than analogical. Quoting Schelling, Moltmann claims that "every being can be revealed only in its opposite. Love only in hatred, unity only in conflict."

Applied to Christian theology, this means that God is only

---

18. Ibid., pp. 146ff. Moltmann's stress on the abandonment of Jesus by God rests on a critical exegesis of the Gospels which lies beyond the scope of my essay. But see George Hunsinger, "The Crucified God and the Political Theology of Violence: A Critical Survey of Jürgen Moltmann's Recent Thought," pts. 1 and 2, *Heythrop Journal* 14 (1973): 266–79, 379–95.

19. Hunsinger, "The Crucified God," pp. 267–68.

20. Moltmann, *The Crucified God*, pp. 147–48.

21. Ibid., p. 26.

revealed as "God" in his opposite: godlessness and abandonment by God. In concrete terms, God is revealed in the cross of Christ who was abandoned by God. His grace is revealed in sinners. His righteousness is revealed in the unrighteous and in those without rights, and his gracious election in the damned. The epistemological principle of the theology of the cross can only be this dialectic principle: the deity of God is revealed in the paradox of the cross. This makes it easier to understand what Jesus did: it was not the devout, but the sinners, and not the righteous but the unrighteous who recognized him, because in them he revealed the divine righteousness of grace, and the kingdom. He revealed his identity amongst those who had lost their identity, amongst the lepers, sick, rejected and despised, and was recognized as the Son of Man amongst those who had been deprived of their humanity. And this makes it easier to understand Paul's theology of the cross in his doctrine of justification: in his revelation in the cross God justifies the godless, and always justifies them alone (E. Käseman). One must become godless oneself and abandon every kind of self-deification or likeness to God, in order to recognize the God who reveals himself in the crucified Christ. One must abandon every self-justification if one is to recognize the revelation of the righteousness of God amongst the unrighteous, to whom basically one belongs oneself.[22]

I have quoted this passage at length because it is the crux of Moltmann's approach to the question of identity and evil. Jesus is here pictured as the first completely "naked" man, that is, the first man whose identity is in no way shaped by the expectations, categories, or institutions of human history. His crucifixion by the political authorities shows him to be marginal like other outcasts, other oppressed people, but his universality derives from the fact that he is despised and abandoned not just by political religion but by God himself. He not only refuses to claim a human identity in terms of a given political and social order, but also to claim godliness for himself. It is this self-emptying, this *kenosis*, that constitutes the revelation of God.[23]

22. Ibid., p. 27.
23. The *kenotic* Christology of Philippians 2:7 is central to Moltmann's development of Christology. See especially chap. 6, "The Crucified God," ibid.

The God who is revealed in the crucified Christ is, then, a God who refuses to have dealings with any particular political and social institution, or with the religious forms devised by man. Man's political and social institutions are based on the principle "like seeks after like,"[24] and of necessity they exclude those who are not "like." To put it another way, "like seeks after like" is a dialectical principle, made possible only through an awareness of "otherness" or "strangeness." That the Christ is perceived by political institutions, in particular by the Pax Romana, to be an "other" is an indication that God himself is a stranger in the world, homeless among the institutions of man. But the same holds true for man's religious institutions: "If faith in the crucified Christ is in contradiction to all conceptions of the righteousness, beauty and morality of man, faith in the 'crucified God' is also a contradiction of everything men have ever conceived, desired and sought to be assured of by the term 'God.'"[25]

This last point, which is similar to themes developed by theologians such as Kierkegaard and Karl Barth, is extremely important. It implies that the revelation of God cannot be an answer to the religious longings of man, which means that the crucified Christ is not an answer to the problem of evil or human suffering in the usual sense of what men mean when put such a question. Moltmann does say time and again that the crucified Christ is the answer to the problem of theodicy, but this is precisely because theodicy is reconstrued in the crucifixion of Christ. That is to say, without the cross the problem of theodicy can only be posed by man in terms of the classical question, If God is good and all-powerful, why is there evil, why does man suffer? Working from that question with its presuppositions, the cross can only be viewed in terms of some form of satisfaction doctrine, where sacrifice is made before the judgment of a righteous and impassible God. But this reverses the order of knowledge: dialectically, the cross reveals that it is God himself who suffers on the cross and shares the abandonment and godforsakenness experienced by men.[26] God is therefore to be discovered in the suffering of the world:

24. Ibid., p. 26.
25. Ibid., p. 37.
26. This point leads Moltmann to the conclusion that the crucifixion must be an event within the Trinity, an event between God and God rather than an event between man and God. See ibid., pp. 235ff.

In Jesus' suffering God suffers; in his death, God himself tastes of damnation and death. . . . In the crucified one he withdraws from power and lordship and humiliates himself to the point of this death. . . . As happened in a hidden way in Job and in the Suffering Servant of Isaiah, God no longer stands before the forum of the human question of theodicy, but is himself incorporated into it, is at stake in it in a game in which the loser wins. The cross of the risen one, then, reveals who and where God is. . . . God is no longer the defendant in the human question of theodicy; rather, the answer is found in this question itself. The cross of Christ then becomes the 'Christian theodicy'—a self-justification of God in which judgment and damnation are taken up by God himself, so that man may live.[27]

The question that can be asked of God and the questions that can be asked of human identity can only arise out of the dialectic of cross and resurrection which "mutually interpret" each other. The cross without the resurrection would only be mute testimony to human suffering in history and of the inhumanity of man to man. The resurrection without the cross would be the source either of simplistic optimism or of hope for an otherworldly resurrection. That the resurrected Christ is the crucified Christ indicates that God participates in the hopelessness and suffering of history. That the crucified Christ is the resurrected Christ demonstrates that "freedom is born from his suffering; life from his death; the exaltation of the man of God from the self-humiliation of God."[28]

The question of Christian identity can now be put more precisely. Those who have faith in the crucified and risen Christ discover that they share in his self-emptying, unclothed condition. The future that they hope for (the City of God) is not rooted in the human capacity to devise political, economic, and social institutions for protection against the vicissitudes of history. Such institutions have real power for limiting the suffering of some, but always at the expense of "others."[29] They may hope to provide a continuing identity for man, but this hope for a lasting city is always predicated upon

27. *Hope and Planning*, p. 43.

28. Ibid., p. 44.

29. See *The Church in the Power of the Spirit* (New York: Harper & Row, 1977), p. 167.

keeping some people in positions of hopelessness while amounting to an act of self-justification on the part of the others. The future that Christians hope for is rooted in a God who creates the future *out of* suffering rather than by limiting suffering. The tendency of the cities of man is to handle suffering and evil by creating superstructures of roles, offices, morality, myths, and institutions, but these only "hold evil down" or sweep it under the rug. The future of these cities can be no more than an attempt to stay in the same place, to hold up, to extend existing structures in the face of continuing threat and suffering. The future of God and of the community of faith grows out of participation in suffering itself, out of becoming marginal with respect to life in the continuing cities of man. Because the community of faith in the crucified Christ finds its identity in self-emptying and in suffering rather than in the construction of particularistic edifices to "control" evil, the community of faith is universal.

This description of the universality of the community of faith may be summarized in the following way:

1. Moltmann's delineation of Christian universality seems to avoid one of the dilemmas of Marx's view of the universality of the proletarian class, namely, the problem of transition from negative to positive universality. In chapter 4 I tried to show that Marx derived this universality from the proletarian's radical marginality, which he variously characterized by phrases such as "complete negation of humanity" and "total loss of humanity," or by phrases suggesting the loss of all human attributes, especially social reciprocity. What was left was the proletarian's work, his creative capacities for transforming and mastering nature. But it turned out to be impossible to arrive at a notion of work that did not include precisely the attributes Marx claimed were lost in the radical alienation of the proletarian, and there seemed no way to move from a view of the complete negation of humanity (upon which the notion of universality critically depends) to a positive and universal view of human capacities. But for Moltmann, Christian universality is not merely negative. In dialectical fashion, it has its negativity both in relation to God (abandonment) and in relation to the roles and attributes of the world (rejection and oppression). At the same time, the abandonment and suffering of the crucifixion is interpreted by the resurrection—the negativity of the crucifixion does not stand alone

but is already comprehended and proleptically transcended by the resurrection. From the beginning the marginality and universality of the Christian is both negative and positive. Stripped of all worldly identities, the Christian finds at his center not his own work but the work of God in Christ.

2. The scientist works with a paradigm until the attempt to give that paradigm full empirical articulation occasions the discovery of anomaly. That anomaly is the source of creative tension from which a new paradigm may emerge (if the old paradigm cannot be adapted to comprehend the anomaly). The dualist does not actually discover anomaly—he finds himself on the bottom of a dualistic theodicy and simply inverts the terms, an immensely sensible if not very innovative move. The Marxist proletarian discovers anomaly in his own situation. What he is, his relationship to his own activity, to nature, and to others, cannot be handled by the bourgeois theodicy, a theodicy that in fact engendered the proletarian anomaly. It is this that makes the proletarian a revolutionary force with creative potential. The Christian discovers anomaly in godforsakenness. But that anomaly is not something discovered under or engendered by an old theodical paradigm but rather by a proleptic vision of the future. The suffering of the crucifixion and the universal man discovered in that suffering is not occasioned merely by political religion's rejection of Christ. Its unique significance lies in the meaning given to it by the resurrection and the coming of God. Put another way, the "anomaly" of the suffering Christ would not have been an anomaly had it not been for the new paradigm of history. Without the new paradigm, without the new theodicy, the suffering of Christ would not have been an anomaly at all, at least not in any unique revolutionary sense. The suffering of Jesus would only have been another case of a punishment justified by the Roman theodicy. It is in this sense that Moltmann can say,

We must try once again to read history eschatologically with a "reversed sense of time" and return from the future of Christ to his past. In terms of history and its sense of time, Jesus first died and was then raised. In eschatological terms the last becomes the first: he died as the risen Christ and was made flesh as the one who was to come. In historical terms Christ can be called the *anticipation* of the coming God on the basis of his resurrection from the dead. In eschatological terms, however, he must be called the *incarnation* of the coming God in our flesh and in his death on the cross.[30]

The doctrine of Incarnation means that something new has entered history which makes possible things that do not exist even potentially in the structure of human history. This *novum* creates anomalies that history itself could not have engendered.[31] The Christian is in a position different from that of the scientist: he has a new paradigm which solves the anomalies it illuminates or gives rise to, while the scientist has to look for a new paradigm as a consequence of discovering anomalies in relation to the old.

3. The universality of the cross and resurrection works itself out historically through a series of dialectical *Aufhebungen*. Christian universality first appears as marginal to the political religions of history, but it interacts with them and through a successive series of transformations extends itself. This idea itself is hardly new—theologians and others have frequently tried to trace the growth of universalism, of secularity, and of other characteristics related to "modernity" to Judeo-Christian roots.[32] According to Moltmann, however, this extension of Christian universality is revolutionary in its effects. In an essay entitled "The Revolution of Freedom,"[33] he locates five "revolutions for freedom" in Western history originating with Christ: (a) *The freedom of Christ*. In the person of Christ the

30. *The Crucified God*, p. 184. Cf. *Hope and Planning*, p. 42.

31. See "What Is 'New' in Christianity: The Category *Novum* in Christian Theology," in *Religion, Revolution, and the Future*, pp. 3–18. Moltmann develops his thinking in this essay in direct reference to Ernst Bloch, whose "principle of Hope" cannot rest on the intervention of the "new" in history.

32. The literature on what it means to be modern and how the characteristics of the modern developed is far too vast to cite here. The ideas of a secular society, pluralism, the growth of universal norms, Weber's "legal-rational" model, and a scientific world view all figure large in this literature. There is little agreement on what these ideas mean or how they relate to each other or whether they are desirable or undesirable. For a recent and very interesting study of some of these issues, see Peter Berger, Brigitte Berger, and Hansfried Kellner, *The Homeless Mind* (New York: Vintage, 1974).

33. "The Revolution of Freedom: Christians and Marxists Struggle for Freedom," *Religion, Revolution, and the Future*, pp. 63–82. The text following is a summary of pp. 71–76.

"idolatry of nature, of fate, and of political power" was broken by a
"life of free decisions." (b) *The freedom of the church.* The "great
revolution of the papacy and the church reform of Cluny in the
Middle Ages" marked the end of the identification of the Kingdom
of God with "the government of an anointed Christian Caesar."
(c) *The freedom of a Christian man.* In the Reformation insistence
on the priesthood and kingship of all believers, the "freedom of
being created in God's image was . . . maintained over against the
sinful supremacy of men over men." (d) *The freedom of the citizen.*
In the American and French revolutions, the freedom won by the
Christian man was extended to all citizens: the "free development
of the humane in every single person is the presupposition of the
humanization of society." (e) *The socialism of freedom.* In this
revolution the attempt is made to do away with the distinction
between "man" and "citizen" by liberating men from economic
slavery: "This represents a change from the society of *having* to a
society of authentic human *being.*"

In each of these revolutions the universal freedom of Christ is
extended while the limitations of the previous revolution are overcome:

> So far, no one of them has brought about the "realm of free-
> dom" itself, but each one has opened a new front in the struggle
> for freedom. None of these revolutions was as yet the "last
> battle," although every one set out under this apocalyptic sign,
> be it the struggle against Anti-Christ, against the beast coming
> out of the "bottomless pit" (Rev. 17:8), or against the class-
> enemy. Therefore, these movements have always corrected each
> other.[34]

There are, I think, insurmountable problems in this view of successive revolutions which I shall discuss shortly. Here, however, I
want to note that Moltmann seems to avoid one of the pitfalls of
much writing by contemporary radical Christians: the tendency to
equate the creative work of the church and of God solely with the
left-wing churches, with the dissident and sectarian movements in
Christianity, suggesting that all of the more institutionalized forms of

---

34. Ibid., p. 77.

the church are unfortunate aberrations. Such a view cannot be reconciled with the judgment of George Sabine that

> the rise of the Christian church, as a distinct institution entitled to govern the spiritual concerns of mankind in independence of the state, may not unreasonably be described as the most revolutionary event in the history of Western Europe, in respect both to politics and to political philosophy.[35]

Moltmann would surely agree with this judgment, adding only that both the revolution of the church *and* the anti-institutional revolutions created aberrations which also had to be overcome.

Marginality and Evil apart from the Crucifixion-Resurrection

Having given a description of Moltmann's view of Christian identity, it remains to look more closely at the relationship between Christian universality and marginality and other forms of marginality and suffering in the world.

First, Moltmann's explicit discussion of evil and suffering in the world apart from the Christian understanding of it is somewhat fragmentary and general, although there does seem to be some progression toward more specificity in *The Crucified God*. In the *Theology of Hope*, we are told that "the world and the people in it are in a fragmented and experimental state," and there is a discussion of guilt and death.[36] In general, the problem of man in the world is portrayed as self-estrangement in the alienating institutions of society. But these are all universal conditions and do not lead directly to the notion of marginality or "otherness" that Moltmann later develops. This development begins in the writings where the problem of evil and theodicy begin to play a role, and where his attention turns more to the suffering, crucified Christ.

Moltmann's starting point is the recognition that the problem of human suffering is still acute, perhaps more so than ever before. But the problem of evil is no longer a cosmological problem—rather, the human experience of evil today is political.[37] This is because science

---

35. George Sabine, *A History of Political Theory*, 3d ed. (New York: Holt, Rinehart and Winston, 1961), p. 180.

36. *Theology of Hope*, pp. 25 and 265–70.

37. *Religion, Revolution, and the Future*, pp. 99–100; cf. *Man*, p. 39, and Hunsinger, pp. 272–73.

and technology have enabled us to have more control over natural disasters and because "we experience reality as history and no longer as cosmos."[38] But the triumph over the tyranny of nature has itself created new problems which even intensify the experience of political evil and suffering, so that along with the benefits of technology we suffer from "images of apocalyptic terror."[39]

When Moltmann discusses the problem of political evil he has in mind the horrors of atrocities such as Auschwitz[40] and the tendency of all political, social, and economic structures to oppress certain classes of people, to be founded upon the distinction between "like" and "unlike." His analysis of this tendency is vaguely Marxist, and when he discusses revolution it is the liberation of these oppressed groups that he has in mind.

But the problem of evil cannot be limited to the oppression of certain groups by political religions. At the end of *The Crucified God* there is a chapter entitled "Ways towards the Psychological Libera-tion of Man" in which Moltmann notes the need to free men from "psychological compulsions" and suggests a "psychological herme-neutics of the word of the cross" as a means to escape the "vicious circle of sin, the law and death."[41] Calling for a "political herme-neutics of liberation," he lists five "vicious circles of death" which must be halted by the crucified God: "the vicious circle of poverty," "the vicious circle of force," "the vicious circle of racial and cultural alienation," "the vicious circle of the industrial pollution of nature," and "the vicious circle of senselessness and godforsakenness."[42]

It is not essential to examine each of these contexts of the experience of evil in detail. I have listed them here because they indicate that Moltmann's own examination of the problem of suffering and evil led him toward a complex view of it. In fact, he takes great pains to point out that human suffering changes from age to age, just as all of human culture changes and as the notion of health changes.[43] Just as "human life is complex and is lived at the

38. *Religion, Revolution, and the Future*, pp. 204–05.
39. *Man*, p. 28.
40. *Hope and Planning*, p. 33; *Religion, Revolution, and the Future*, p. 205.
41. *The Crucified God*, pp. 292–93.
42. Ibid., pp. 330–31.
43. See ibid., p. 314: "But health is a norm which changes with history and is conditioned by society."

same time in a number of spheres and dimensions,"[44] there are different forms of evil corresponding to each of them.

In spite of the complexity of evil, all forms of evil have one characteristic in common: they are the occasion for despair and for death. Despair, resignation, and hopelessness—the absence of hope is sin. It is at this point that the connection between the suffering of God and Christ and the suffering of the world is made. There is objective suffering in the world, but when that suffering is the occasion for despair, or for "*acedia, tristesse,* the cultivation and dandling manipulation of faded hopes,"[45] then it participates in sin. But hopelessness is revealed as sin only in the cross and resurrection of Christ, for there can be no sin, no absence of God, without the opposite, obedience to God in hope, no sense of the possibilities of God's future without the opposite, godforsakenness in suffering. Insofar as the cross of Christ reveals the godforsakenness of human existence, it also reveals "the historical solidarity of unredeemed being."[46] Insofar as the Christ of the cross is the risen Christ, the cross also opens the suffering of the present to the future, so that suffering becomes the occasion for hope and new creation.

It follows from this account of evil and sin that the Christian experience of suffering is qualitatively different from suffering outside the Christian framework. This is not only because Christian suffering is transmuted by the cross of Christ into the hope of God's future. It is also because those who suffer outside of the Christian hope do not really know what it is they suffer. They imagine that their suffering is unique, that it has a specific cause, that they are in some sense alone. They may even imagine that their suffering is in some fashion justified, that is, they comprehend their suffering and accept it in terms of some theodicy.[47] In all of this they do not feel solidarity with others who suffer, they do not experience their suffering as part of the groaning of "unredeemed creation." Such a view of suffering solidarity is possible only for those who are

44. Ibid., p. 292.
45. *Theology of Hope,* p. 24.
46. *Hope and Planning,* p. 41. Cf. p. 176.
47. It should be pointed out that to accept one's suffering as justified, to be resigned to one's lot and even to find meaning in it, is at the same time to see one's own position as different from that of others. A theodicy is of necessity particularistic.

dialectically related to hope, that is, for Christians. Conversely, whatever hope people outside the Christian dialectic do find, either in a political theodicy that justifies their suffering or in a revolutionary movement that hopes to overthrow a particular theodicy, can be only provisional hope. If it is not "taken up"[48] by the Christian dialectic, it results only in a new form of despair or in a new particularistic theodicy.

It follows further that Moltmann is not interested in specifying any one cause (or causes) for evil and suffering. The origin of evil cannot be fathomed by man, and neither theism nor atheism has solved the problem of theodicy.[49] The theologian can only say that "sin came into the world through sin" and "evil came into the world through evil." Evil is "the impossible possibility."[50] The language here is Barth's,[51] and Moltmann would agree with him that the nature of evil can only be known through its being overcome by God in Christ. The theologian and the Christian can describe the multiple experiences of evil in the world, but they can be understood only insofar as they are subsumed under the dialectic of the cross and resurrection.[52] This means that no claim to have understood the origin of evil outside of the cross can be taken seriously by Christians —and that, of course, includes the Marxist attempt to understand evil. It also means, as already mentioned, that under the dialectic of the crucified God, the problem of theodicy is transformed from the question, Why is there evil? to the question of the delay of the *parousia*.[53] If evil is understood to be "taken up by God himself," then the question of theodicy becomes, "Why only Jesus at first, and not the whole salvation of the world at a stroke?"[54]

48. Moltmann, *Hope and Planning*, p. 43.

49. Ibid., p. 33.

50. Quoted by Hunsinger, "The Crucified God," pp. 273-74, from "Die Teufelaustreibung, von Sinn und Unsinn einer Satanologie."

51. See Karl Barth, *Church Dogmatics*, vol. 2, pt. 2 (Edinburgh: T. & T. Clark, 1957), pp. 169ff.

52. Cf. ibid., p. 171: "It is also true that evil can only be the abyss of negation in order at once to be opposed and overcome by the Yes of divine predestination. . . . We will take evil seriously for what in its own way—but only in its own way—it is allowed to be on the basis of the eternal decree."

53. Moltmann, *Hope and Planning*, p. 44. Cf. *The Crucified God*, p. 184.

54. *The Crucified God*, p. 184. Moltmann's answer to this transformed question of theodicy seems to lie in the fact of the arousal of hope and the

Finally, it follows that Moltmann's "Christian" formulation of the theodicy question remains a theological formulation. That is, it does not have an immediate connection to the psychosocial dimension I have discussed in the preceding chapters. All experiences of evil, including such things as natural disasters, Auschwitz, war, political repression, inequalities of wealth, mental disorder, and personal failure are subsumed under the category of "the negative" and are to be incorporated "within the dialectic of the new creation."[55] Furthermore, all of these instances of human suffering are not decisively distinguished from suffering that is perceived as legitimate by its subjects. If we remember that it is part of the function of a theodicy to "justify" suffering, to enable people to comprehend inequality and some misery under a structure of meaning, then that suffering too, as part of a provisional or even "idolatrous" political and social order, participates in the negative that is to be overcome.[56] Further refinements in the description of social orders and their working out of social inequalities, such as the distinction between "traditional" and "modern" social structures, play little or no role in Moltmann's definition of the negative. The negative in general and all instances of negativity are to be incorporated into the dialectic of the crucified God. Moltmann's intention is to guard against the identification of any theodicy developed within a finite social and political system with the Christian order. The Christian order is future and transcends the provisional theodicies of this world. Also, he has apparently succeeded in "historifying" evil, that is, in showing that much of the human experience of evil is as socially and historically conditioned as the social and political systems men construct to "control" evil. He has avoided reducing human suffering to any one cause susceptible to any one theodical paradigm. The question that must be asked,

---

revelation that "God is for us." But if this is to be an adequate answer, it is only because the Hegelian dialectic is presupposed, so that what has happened could not have happened differently. I am open, however, to different suggestions on what Moltmann intends as the answer to his specifically "Christian" formulation of the theodicy question.

55. *Hope and Planning*, p. 49.

56. This is the term used by Moltmann to refer to political religions and to a variety of other attempts on the part of man to justify himself. See "Political Theology," pp. 17–20, and "The Cross and Civil Religion," pp. 33–41.

however, is at what cost. In particular, it is not clear that Moltmann has given a coherent account of the relation between the Christian dialectic of evil and redemption and the non-Christian's experience of evil. This deficiency shows up more emphatically in his discussion of what it is that Christians should do.

THE PROBLEM OF HUMAN ACTION

Moltmann's reflections on the dialectical meaning of the cross lead him to articulate two directives for Christian action: the Christian is to engage in dialectical criticism of all temporal institutions, and the Christian is to achieve critical solidarity with the oppressed of the world. The latter is possible only because the cross has "positive" content, that is, because the negativity discovered in the cross is not merely negativity; proleptically it is the content of God's future. It is also the source of Moltmann's interest in Christian participation in revolutionary movements and therefore warrants most of our attention. The first directive warrants less attention, not because it is insignificant in the development of Moltmann's thought but because it is a less original contribution on his part. In fact, the "critical" directive is almost identical with what Paul Tillich has called "the Protestant Principle"[57] and may be found in similar form in almost all major Protestant writers beginning with Luther (whom Moltmann uses frequently in the development of his theory).[58]

Dialectical Criticism

The critical task of Christians emerges directly from the identity they discover in the crucified God. Since the universality of Christian identity precludes full or permanent allegiance to any particular social, political, or economic form, Christianity is a "stateless religion," and no matter how close a society approaches the "ideal" (which can only be the Kingdom of God), the distinction between Christian existence and social existence must be maintained:

> True Christian existence can only be present in the best of all possible societies, or, in symbolic terms, can only "stand under

57. Paul Tillich, *The Protestant Era*, abridged ed. (Chicago: University of Chicago Press, 1957), pp. 161–81.

58. See, for example, Moltmann's discussion of Luther and the Second Commandment in relation to political idolatry in "The Cross and Civil Religion," pp. 35ff.

the cross," and its identity with the crucified Christian can be demonstrated only by a witnessing non-identification with the demands and interests of society. Thus even in the "classless society" Christians will be aliens and homeless. Where solidarity is achieved, this distinction must still be observed.[59]

The necessity of maintaining a distinct Christian identity involves Christians in criticism aimed in two directions: toward other "religious" structures and toward the historical forms of the church itself. The criticism of the religious structures of human history amounts to a critique of the idolatry and alienation of political religions. The basis of this critique is theological, rooted in Moltmann's analysis of the suffering of the cross: the theodicy of the cross undercuts the theodicies of history. But he also offers historical support for this position, arguing that in the history of Israel and of the church, God's people have in fact found themselves in a critical dialectic with respect to man's political religions. Israel's Exodus from Egypt was itself a desacralization of Egyptian political religion.[60] The Second Commandment is a direct assault on views of "cosmic holiness" and the political and religious institutions which were believed to be a medium, along with nature, linking gods and men: "The Second Commandment, then, protected and preserved for man his dominion over creation, for man alone is made in the image and likeness of God." The assault on political gods was continued by the Prophets, who "insisted that idols are the product of men's hands and, therefore, they cannot save their own creator."[61]

The Christian church, too, has had to wage a continual battle against the political idols of the Western world, beginning with the crucifixion of Jesus and the refusal of Christians to pay homage to the cult of Caesar, although "from the time of Constantine and the Christianization of Europe Christianity has taken over the role of the political religion of society."[62] In becoming the political religion of Europe, Christianity has transformed Europe (thus the five "revolutions of freedom"), but when Christianity has chiefly an integrating function in society, it loses its identity and ceases to be the church

59. *The Crucified God*, p. 17.
60. Hunsinger, "The Crucified God," pp. 383–84.
61. Moltmann, "The Cross and Civil Religion," p. 36.
62. *The Crucified God*, pp. 322ff. Cf. "The Cross and Civil Religion," p. 40, and "Political Theology," p. 10.

of the crucified one. Therefore, the church must also be consistently self-critical, to avoid being used by particular political forms as a political religion. (It should be pointed out that the fact that Christianity can be and has been used as a political religion is itself a negative proof that Christians cannot help but be political, but this is a point derived from the nature of political religions in general and not from the unique characteristics of Christian identity.)

Moltmann connects the critical task of the church with a discussion of Christology and the titles of Jesus:

> It is profoundly significant that the name of Jesus and his history remain fixed, as fixed as his death, whereas the titles of Christ which are a response to his openness are historically changeable with the passing of time, and in fact change history.
>
> Thus christology is essentially unconcluded and permanently in need of revision.[63]

The faith that confesses Christ, like the political structures formed by Christ, can never be closed or fixed. Since the Christ of faith is always interpreted by the crucified Jesus, so also all social and political forms, no matter how "Christian," are "resisted" by the cross.[64]

But a simple attempt to resist all misuses of the cross, or to engage in consistent self-criticism, is illusory. There is no neutral ground from which to make this kind of criticism, and in any case such a procedure is undialectical. Therefore, the dialectical criticism implied in the cross itself only makes sense, or takes hold, when it emerges from its other side, critical solidarity with the oppressed:

> The political theology of the cross has still deeper dimensions. It would be myopic to concentrate only on church-state relations with the hope of changing their relationship from one of mutual reinforcement to one of critical distance. The theology of the cross remains abstract if we only think about it in this context. According to its biblical traditions, the Church everywhere has to be with those for whom there is neither state nor status. The Christian faith founded on the cross must begin again to demythologize the state in which it lives. This will succeed

63. *The Crucified God*, pp. 106–07.
64. Ibid., chap. 2, "The Resistance of the Cross against Its Interpretations."

only if it concomitantly analyzes the religious situation of those who, according to the present order of things, have no status.[65]

Critical Solidarity with Marginals

The Christian's critical stance with respect to the political forms in which he lives becomes reality when he engages in creative love for the abandoned of the world:

> By alienating the believer from the compulsions and automatic assumptions of an alienated world, Christian identification with the crucified necessarily brings him into solidarity with the alienated of this world, with the dehumanized and the inhuman. But this solidarity becomes radical only if it imitates the identification of the crucified Christ with the abandoned, accepts the suffering of creative love, and is not led astray by its own dreams of omnipotence in an illusory future.[66]

In this passage, it is the Christian identification with the crucified which makes such solidarity necessary and makes it radical, that is, capable of liberating the alienated and oppressed. But Moltmann's account of who it is that Christians are to move toward in solidarity is confusing, and the notion of critical solidarity has little explicit content. It is not difficult to show that Moltmann's statements about the objects of Christian solidarity are apparently if not actually contradictory. In the preceding passage we are told that this solidarity is to be with the dehumanized and the inhuman; just before Moltmann had written that "Christian identification with the crucified Christ means solidarity with the sufferings of the poor and the misery both of the oppressed and the oppressors." Now, this is consistent with an expanded definition of suffering that includes all forms of alienation in society. As Marx would agree, the oppressors or ruling classes are also alienated and may be said to suffer from that alienation, although Moltmann does not accept the Marxist theodicy which yields a special role to the proletariat. Yet this expanded and general definition of alienation seems to contradict other statements of his that "the Church everywhere has to be with those for whom there is neither state nor status."[67] And Thesis 5 in

65. "The Cross and Civil Religion," pp. 41–42.
66. *The Crucified God*, p. 25.
67. See n. 65.

the essay "God in Revolution" does not seem to include solidarity with the suffering of oppressors: "The church is not a heavenly arbiter in the world's strifes. In the present struggles for freedom and justice, Christians must side with the humanity of the *oppressed*."[68]

In fact, a great deal of the force of Moltmann's discussion of the humiliation and suffering of Jesus resides in his argument that the crucified Christ, being an alien in the world (treated like an alien in the world) can only be understood by those who are also treated as "others," those who are poor, oppressed, and stripped of an identity. Two more passages from the same page of another essay again illustrate the problem:

> The Church exists, therefore, as a twofold brotherhood: those who are sent and those who are waiting. The former is the manifest and visible brotherhood of believers; the latter is the latent and hidden brotherhood of the poor. The former belongs to the resurrection, the latter, to the fellowship of the cross.

"Those who are waiting" are called "the poor," and we must assume, given the preponderance of similar statements elsewhere discussing the poor and the oppressed, that "the poor" is to be interpreted fairly straightforwardly. If so, then a large portion of mankind is left out of the "universal" church. But this is clearly not possible:

> This ecclesiology does not mean that the oppressed should become the oppressor. For the gospel reconciles all sinners. It must penetrate all social divisions and all political manifestations of self-justification made at the expense of another. Otherwise it remains abstract and ineffectual. Insofar as the gospel praises the poor as blessed and promises them the kingdom of God, it saves the rich also by revealing their real poverty. Unless the "subversive" character of the Bible as the "Bible of the poor" pervades eschatology, then the promise of a new and reconciled mankind receives no authentic witness.[69]

The most plausible reading of this would seem to be that Christians are to assert their solidarity with those who are poor in the eyes of the world and that by engaging in this "subversive" and "revolution-

68. *Religion, Revolution, and the Future*, p. 140 (emphasis added).
69. "The Cross and Civil Religion," p. 44.

ary" act they will bring those who are rich or who have status to realize that they, too, are poor when measured by the standard of the cross. The cross and resurrection, as the paradigm of God's future (and as the reconstrual of theodicy) reveals that the situation of the rich and those who have status is also an anomaly. In this fashion, they are included in the "latent and hidden brotherhood of the poor."

It is apparent from this reading that the Christian's solidarity with the oppressed does not liberate them from the oppressor in the way that Marx meant. Liberation in the Hegelian-Marxist scheme depends on a specific dialectic between master and slave. In Moltmann's Christian dialectic the potential for liberation does not reside in the internal transformations between oppressor and oppressed. The oppressor, too, is marginal in relation to God's future.

In fact, Moltmann clearly does not intend to suggest that the only dialectic of evil and suffering in the world is that between rich and poor, or between oppressor and oppressed. As I have already shown, he stresses the complexity of evil in the world, resisting the attempt to locate the source of evil in any one dialectic. Thus, the "vicious circles of death" specified at the end of *The Crucified God* demonstrate that there are innumerable planes and dimensions of human suffering and evil. I have referred to the vicious circles of poverty, force, racial and cultural alienation, industrial pollution of nature, and senselessness and godforsakenness;[70] to these Moltmann adds the vicious circles of sin, the law, and death, together with other psychological disorders,[71] and at other places he mentions natural disasters, tragic deaths, and the like. From this it is apparent that Christians will have many, many persons with whom to seek solidarity in suffering and that not all of these will coincide with the poor or with those who are oppressed by particular social, political, or economic structures. The more Moltmann seeks to take into account the complexity of the human experience of "unredeemed history," the more difficult it is to discover a direction for Christian solidarity except in the most general sense that Christians should align themselves with all suffering.

It nevertheless seems incontestable that Moltmann wishes to place

70. *The Crucified God*, pp. 329–35.
71. Ibid., p. 293.

the poor and the politically oppressed in a special position in relation to the suffering of the cross. There is no one citation to prove this—rather, it pervades all his writings and remains the most distinctive mark of his practical suggestions. The question is, Why this special place for those who "have no status," for the politically oppressed? One possible answer must be rejected at the outset. This is that political, social, and economic oppression is more "fundamental" than other kinds of suffering. To accept this would be to accept some version of the Marxist theodicy in which the struggle with nature is understood to be the key to human sufferings. Moltmann carefully resists all attempts to specify the origin of evil. If economic and political oppression is more important than other forms of suffering, it must be for reasons other than as some fundamental expression of the nature of man. (I shall return to this point later.)

There are two other possible answers, both supported by Moltmann's argumentation. The first is that the special place of political and economic suffering is derived from the content of the crucified Christ. It must be remembered that Moltmann insists that the cross is political from the beginning, since the revelation of God in the cross was understood by those who were suffering politically and economically rather than by those who were rich or who had status in the political religion of the time.[72] Even here, it may be asked whether the political dimension of the cross, which Moltmann has brilliantly laid open, exhausts its impact. If it does not—and Moltmann certainly does not claim that it does—it may further be asked how it is possible to decide whether the political dimension is the *decisive* dimension of the cross's impact. Moltmann's own statement of dialectical revelation is that "God is only revealed as 'God' in his opposite: godlessness and abandonment by God." The "opposite" here is general and means only that "grace is revealed in sinners."[73] There is no special warrant here for singling out political and economic sinners.

Furthermore, Moltmann's account of the "revolution of freedom" engendered by Christian freedom and the universality of the cross does not support a decisive role for the poor and oppressed.[74] The

72. An almost identical point is made by Karl Barth, *Church Dogmatics*, vol. 2, pt. 1 (Edinburgh: T & T. Clark, 1957), pp. 386ff.

73. *The Crucified God*, p. 27.

74. *Religion, Revolution, and the Future*, chap. 4.

second revolution of freedom was the freedom of the Christian church over against an "anointed Christian Caesar," but it does not seem possible to construe this as a consequence of Christian solidarity with the poor and oppressed. It can perhaps be construed as solidarity with a "negative" dialectically defined in relation to the sacral claims of a Christian Roman emperor, but then it would have to be argued that the focus of Christian solidarity changes in each historical epoch and the central role of the poor and the oppressed dissolves. Similar points would seem to hold with respect to the revolutions of the Christian man and of the citizen. Neither of these can be construed as arising out of political and economic oppression without seriously distorting history. Certainly, the principal actors in these "revolutions" felt themselves to be oppressed by other political and economic powers, and they were marginal in relation to the old orders. But the burghers of Geneva and the princes of Germany hardly fit the mold of Moltmann's "poor and oppressed"; they at least have little in common with the poor and oppressed with whom Jesus is supposed to have found a natural solidarity. Only the left-wing of the Reformation would seem to provide an example of Christian solidarity with the poor and oppressed, but Müntzer and others like him are curiously absent from Moltmann's account of the "revolution of freedom." In fact, Luther's "revolution of the Christian man" was at the expense of Müntzer's peasants.

This leads directly to the second possible answer to the question about the central role of the politically and economically oppressed. This is that the notion of political and economic oppression changes historically and is dialectically conditioned. It could then be argued that the decisive role of the poor and oppressed in liberating men from the vicious circles of death in the contemporary world is a function of historical forces presently at work. And Marx's work and his influence support the judgment that political and economic oppression constitute the chief forms of contemporary suffering. Accordingly, it would be a mistake to imagine that poor share-croppers in Alabama or poor sugarcane cutters in Brazil any more resemble the poor with whom Jesus associated than the Genevan burghers and German princes did. This dialectical view of the poor is probably what Moltmann intends, and I think it is fair to conclude that his view is a combination of both of the answers I have given.

However, this combination does not in fact yield a consistent view. On the one hand, Moltmann depends on a descriptive analysis of what has taken place historically, making use of Marx to show the dialectic of political and economic oppression in the modern world. On the other hand, he offers a view of oppression and marginality derived dialectically from his analysis of the cross which has no clear link to the descriptive analysis. At times the specifically Christian analysis of marginality and oppression is used to transform all other portrayals of evil and marginality, but at other times the Christian analysis seems to be used as a principle of selection, preferring the Marxist point of view over others, for example.

It seems necessary to recall that Marx wanted both to comprehend the revolutionary potential of the proletariat's marginality and to realize that potential in revolutionary practice. The substance of his analysis was dependent on a historical view of domination and suffering that made it possible to overcome theodicy by establishing the universality of the proletariat. Moltmann does not intend to overcome theodicy but to reconstrue it—which means that he does not have a genuinely dialectical view of theory and practice.

This point may be outlined more sharply by returning to the analogy with scientific revolution. Earlier I contrasted the positions of Moltmann's Christian and the scientist. The scientist must look for a new paradigm to comprehend the anomalies produced by the old; the Christian begins with a new paradigm which is not only capable of incorporating the anomalies produced by other paradigms; he is in possession of this paradigm before the old paradigms have failed. Pushed a step further, the Christian is like a historically dis-embodied scientist who goes around showing the shortcomings of everyone else's paradigms even before those paradigms have engendered their own anomalies. In the dialectical tradition the "new" comes out of the throes of dialectic itself; in Moltmann, the "new" is derived from eschatology—it cannot be anticipated from past history alone.

Moltmann's response here must be that the future has become past through promises and the proleptic event in Christ:

> Out of the mere negation of negative elements no definition of positive reality emerges. For that reason eschatology cannot be developed only as negative theology. The negation of negative elements must have its basis in a hidden anticipation of positive

reality, otherwise the negation would not be experienced and criticized as such. It is in the experience of divine promissory history, ever striving for fulfillment, that biblical eschatology anchors the negation of negative elements.[75]

But while this point may hold for those who live within the history of God's promise, it does nothing to alter the fact that for those who live outside that history the Christian paradigm appears as an *ought* in contrast to their *is*. For them, the Christian hope does not grow out of a practice and transformation derived from their own suffering and marginality.

In part we have here a repetition of the difficulty Hegel and Marx had in relating their account of the dynamic, dialectical history of the West to what they characterized as the stagnant and despotic East. But Moltmann's account has the further difficulty that the Christian theodicy always reconstrues even competing Western theodicies, so that the Christian always has a superior hermeneutical vantage point from which to derive practice.

If this analysis is correct, then it is not surprising that, as I will show, Moltmann approaches concrete revolutions not as a dialectical partisan (as his stated position and language would suggest) but as one who wishes to select among revolutions, to distinguish the good from the bad; in short, that he engages in traditional moral analysis.

Solidarity and Revolution

If it is the case that the content Moltmann gives to the term "solidarity" is vague and general, similar criticism may be directed at others among his ethical directives.[76] Words such as liberation, humanization, democratization, emancipation, all of which recur often in his writings, do not of themselves offer much concrete assistance. As Marx is supposed to have quipped, no one is against freedom. Moltmann has answered this criticism by remarking that no one can do everything, and that his inattention to the details of ethics arose partly from the hope that someone else would do this task.[77] Nevertheless, the tradition he works in prides itself on the

---

75. Moltmann, "Creation and Redemption," in *Creation, Christ and Culture,* ed. Richard W. A. McKinney (Edinburgh: T. & T. Clark, 1976), p. 129.

76. See, for example, Hunsinger, "The Crucified God," p. 393.

77. Moltmann, *Umkehr zur Zukunft* (Munich: Chr. Kaiser, 1970), p. 13.

close relationship between theory and practice. His own insistence on the capacity of Christians to offer "concrete Utopian" thinking[78] and his strong assertions that the verification of Christian theology is not a matter of orthodoxy but of "orthopraxy"[79] indicate that a critique of his thinking must begin with an analysis of his critical and practical theory.

The practice most pertinent here is of course revolution. In the writings in which he specifically addresses the question of violent political and social revolutions, Moltmann prepares the ground by noting that Christians too often raise the issue of violence in the abstract without looking at the concrete situation in which violence arises.[80] Christian love demands that we look at the possibilities and actualities of a given situation when we put the question of the just and unjust use of violence. Thus in Thesis 6 of the essay "God in Revolution" Moltmann says,

> The problem of violence and nonviolence is an illusory problem. There is only the question of the justified and unjustified use of force and the question of whether the means are proportionate to the ends.[81]

Here Moltmann introduces the principle of proportionality from "just war" theory and suggests that violence is just if it is not disproportionate to the ends.[82] But he also introduces the principles of just cause, just means, and just ends in evaluating revolutionary violence:

> The use of revolutionary violence must be justified by the humane goals of the revolution and the existing power structures unmasked in their inhumanity as "naked violence." Otherwise, revolutionary violence cannot be made meaningful or appropriate. Unless every possible means is put to use, the revolutionary future is not worth committing oneself to, but if disproportionate

78. *Man*, p. 42.
79. *The Crucified God*, p. 11.
80. "Gewalt und Liebe," in *Umkehr zur Zukunft*, p. 45.
81. *Religion, Revolution, and the Future*, p. 143.
82. For an outline and discussion of the just war principles, see the end of chapter 2.

means are employed, then the goals of the revolution are
betrayed.[83]

Violence can easily betray the humane goals of a revolution and
thereby merely repeat the "naked violence" of the original oppressor
(just ends and means). But violence may be the only means available
to the oppressed when faced with naked violence (just cause).
Christian love must be sensitive to the *structural* character of contemporary oppressive violence.

The distinction between just and unjust violence is made more
specific in Moltmann's discussion of the World Council of Churches'
decision to support liberation movements in South Africa. Some
German churches expressed the concern that money sent to the
liberation movements might be used to purchase guns for counter-
violence. Moltmann notes that the German Christian reactions reveal
"a confused attitude toward power in the German traditions as well
as a Christian repression complex as regards resistance against
tyranny."[84] In particular, he rejects the idea that the principle of
nonviolence can be effective in the political realm:

> The concept of nonviolence belongs to the eschatological
> remembrance of faith in Jesus. The hoped-for kingdom of God is
> the kingdom of brotherhood without violence and in this sense
> "anarchy" (Berdyaev). This explains the Christian's deep horror
> of violence already in the present. He does not want to be master
> of any slaves or the slave of any master and will do his best to
> create and extend spheres of communication that are free of
> domination. He will also give preference to nonviolent methods
> in political disputes. In the domain of politics, however, it is a
> question of power, distribution of power, and participation in the
> exercise of power.[85]

The Christian must therefore "settle the exact meaning of the words
violence, power, and domination." Moltmann proceeds to do this
by defining power as "the means by which we can obtain

---

83. *Religion, Revolution, and the Future*, p. 143.
84. "Racism and the Right to Resist," in *The Experiment Hope* (Philadelphia: Fortress, 1975), p. 132.
85. Ibid., pp. 136–37.

something by force."[86] He does not actually offer definitions of violence or domination. Instead he suggests that "justified 'violence' can be called power," and shows that violence is justified when it is used by Christians to resist tyranny. Further, Moltmann agrees with Dietrich Bonhoeffer that responsible action entails "the readiness to incur guilt." Violent action even in love involves guilt, but the attempt to maintain personal innocence leads to "more irredeemable guilt."[87]

These passages offer Moltmann's closest analysis of revolutionary violence, and they are most revealing. In the first place, it is clear that Moltmann's analysis of actual revolutions is one that puts the Christian outside the dialectical process and that he interprets revolution in terms of the traditional Christian statements on the just war and the right to resist tyranny (see the distinction between two kinds of revolution in chapter 1). This recourse to just war principles opens him to the charge of inconsistency. George Hunsinger, for example, has suggested that Moltmann's discussion of revolutionary violence "stands in contradiction to his theology of the crucified God." He argues that Moltmann carries on his discussion of political violence "with scarcely a reference to the cross except for the one principle that 'love must be ready to become guilty in order to save.'" Yet the guilt accepted by Jesus on the cross is clearly not the guilt of violence.

For the decisive mark of Christian suffering, as seen in the crucified God, is that it is voluntary and that it willingly takes suffering upon itself at all costs rather than inflict suffering upon others. On the cross the violence of injustice is overcome by the suffering of love; the injustice of man succumbs to the suffering of God. The very love that finds the suffering of others intolerable is the love that accepts suffering rather than inflicting it, in the hope that suffering will become redemptive.[88]

This argument finds support in Moltmann's insistence that those who suffer should not be molded by the strategy of their opponents but should find a creative response to violent social structures. In such

86. Ibid., p. 137.
87. Ibid., pp. 142–43.
88. Hunsinger, "The Crucified God," p. 393.

passages the notion that redemption comes through opposites or contradictions implies a dialectic of means, contrasting force and violence with the suffering love of the cross.

Such a view of dialectic should drive Moltmann toward a strategy of nonviolent resistance of a very active sort like Martin Luther King's—or to use Hunsinger's list, the nonviolence of César Chávez, Albert Luthuli, Helder Câmara, A. J. Muste, and Mohandas Gandhi.[89] If this were clearly Moltmann's position, then his dialectic would be a kind of moral dialectic in which the bad is opposed by the good, somewhat analogous to the moral dialectic that Marx found and rejected in Proudhon. He would also have inserted into the dialectic the doctrine of the two kingdoms, where the Kingdom of God is the domain of love and the Kingdom of the World is the domain of force. At no point is this theme more present than in passages where Moltmann suggests that Christians ought, in order to prevent the idolatrous and legalistic tendencies of revolution, to "laugh and sing and dance," even as Jesus celebrated with the outcasts "the heavenly banquet of the righteous," "in full view of the enemies."[90]

But as the use of just war principles indicates, it is not clear that this dialectic of means is Moltmann's position. He does not carefully distinguish idolatrous political forms from political forms in general, and there are times when he seems to think that all political forms are idolatrous. It is then that he emphasizes a dialectic of means. At other times his wanting the Christian to take sides clearly entails the use of force and violence, but in this case the "guilt" of the Christian is not so much the guilt of violence as the guilt of not being able to guarantee the outcome of the revolution, of not being able to assure that what comes after the revolution is not also idolatrous.

The source of his ambiguity is manifest if we look at another implication of his analysis of power. Power is equated with force, and Moltmann makes it clear that in the eschatological kingdom there is no power. Politics, on the other hand, is the arena of power, and the Christian must incur guilt in order to be effective in politics. This is a highly unfortunate definition of power (deriving in part from the fact that the German word for political power,

89. Ibid., p. 394.
90. *Religion, Revolution, and the Future*, pp. 145–46.

Macht, carries the connotation of domination), preventing the use of the term for a host of political actions that do not involve force. Furthermore, by connecting power in this way with politics, he implies that there is a guilt that is unique to political involvement. It follows directly that all political power is antithetical to the Kingdom of Christ.

Sheldon Wolin has noted that Calvinists have had a profound impact on politics because for Calvin "political and religious thought tended to form a continuous realm of discourse."[91] Moltmann's essays on "The Ethic of Calvinism" and on human rights,[92] together with his many essays on political theology, indicate that he wants to create such a continuous realm of discourse, but he does not achieve it in practice. He wants the church to be political, but his descriptions of how it might function politically are dialectically derivative, that is, the church is said to be political because it cannot be subsumed under the political religion of its time—it stands as a "contradiction" to the political. Precisely because the cross takes up with those who are excluded by the political, it is the negation of the political. And the directive that Christians should "laugh and sing and dance" during a revolution is an abandonment of political discourse. In short, there is opposition not merely to a particular kind of politics—the idolatrous—but to the essence of politics, power.

It is possible that Moltmann's difficulties here are not of his own making but are rooted in the adoption of dialectical language (even though I have argued that he does not have a genuinely dialectical theory of praxis). It has often been argued that once dialectic is moved from the realm of discourse and applied to history and politics, it becomes excessively ambiguous and presents intractable difficulties. Although Marx's dialectic does not entail a dialectic of means, it is not clear that he has avoided a view that assumes the overcoming of politics. We might go so far as to say that Luther's doctrine of the two kingdoms simply reappears in Hegel's dialectic. The continuity provided by the dialectic does not mean a continuous realm of discourse between the political and the religious but an overcoming of the political by the religious.

91. Sheldon Wolin, *Politics and Vision* (Boston: Little, Brown, 1960), p. 179.
92. In *The Experiment Hope*.

The Cross and Revolution

If dialectical language creates some of Moltmann's difficulties, the ground for choosing that language is his theology of the cross. The centrality of the cross and resurrection in Moltmann's theology, and the way in which he develops his thinking about the cross, gives it a decidedly Christocentric character in the tradition of Luther and Barth. It is not possible here to go into the intricacies of his Christology, his "dynamic" view of the Trinity, or his notion of the cross as an "intertrinitarian" event.[93] From the standpoint of ethics, however, it is critical that his Christocentric approach places great emphasis on the "breaks" rather than the continuities of history.

Again and again, Moltmann contrasts his view of the cross and of ethics with theologies of ordinances, natural law theories, and all attempts to link Christian theology with what he characterizes as the Greek way of thinking. Here is a representative passage:

> It is relatively unimportant whether a theology of ordinances develops from a doctrine of ordinances of creation or from a christological foundation. The concept of order which is both presupposed and sought for is, as such, rooted in the Greek structure of thought and logically always leads to unhistorical, naturalistic conceptions. The New Testament offers no metaphysical doctrine of ordinances. . . . It does, however, offer a historically dated reality which is to be appropriated anew in every generation. A theological departure from the question of stable hypotheses of order in the world and in history thus seems to be necessary and a search for pointers towards surrenders to the relativities of history to be desirable.[94]

As Moltmann himself recognizes, his view seems to place him in company with "individualistic decisionism," in which "between the God who commands and the man who is called there can only be a sporadic point of confrontation, a tangent-like contact, which has no effect, and the field on which this confrontation takes place."[95] He also admits that "A 'philosophy of the cross' can easily lead to

93. Moltmann works this out in *The Crucified God*, especially pp. 200–90.

94. *Hope and Planning*, p. 112. Cf. *Theology of Hope*, pp. 259ff.

95. *Hope and Planning*, pp. 118–20.

Gnostic speculations."[96] He attempts to counter these dangers by offering "a historical ethic of hope":

> One only does justice to the disclosure of reality as history sketched out above if one designs an *ethic of moral process* and if Christian ethics understands itself (like Schleiermacher's moral doctrine) as a *science of history*. . . .
>
> Similarly, one could say that the giving of oneself to the historical *novum* of the moment is part of the ethical process. At the same time, however, a part of this process is the opening up of the horizon of the future and the observation of the past, from which the present is determined. The synthesis between the instant and the moment is found in the present of the future. The ethical decision is always related to the instant and yet still points beyond it in hope, in self-surrender to and belief in a certain future. If, however, the future is not to be made unreal as empty openness for the arbitrary character of every new plan, one must talk about a concrete future. Only in terms of a concrete future do ethical instants acquire continuity, does history become a process within the context of its events. Definite hopes arouse definite remembrances. The past is preserved in the present by remembering when the present reaches out beyond itself into the future through hoping. Traditions are alive when hopes are aroused. When he gives up his future, man also loses his past and, therefore, his historicity and his history.[97]

This passage indicates that Moltmann wants an ethic that will not disrupt the continuities of history, just as he wants a continuous realm of discourse between religion and politics. But immediately afterward he again shows that for him the "contradiction" of the cross is not a dialectical contradiction with the historical past in general but only with the Christian past or with the past reconfigured from a privileged hermeneutical vantage point:

> One can then go on to say that covenant and commandment are always given in history to particular men and groups (through election and calling), men and groups which, through the historical covenant and its promise, are *ripped out of their previous*

96. *The Crucified God*, p. 218.
97. *Hope and Planning*, pp. 122–23 (Moltmann's emphasis).

attachment to home, nation, habit, etc. and are placed in a new historical process, namely, in the history of the promise.[98]

If the past is reconfigured by the prolepsis of God's promises for the future, and if that future means being ripped out of previous attachments (read historical processes) and placed in a new historical process, then the past has little integrity of its own.[99]

This becomes decisive for the doctrine of creation. At first glance, Moltmann's view of the work of Christ seems perilously close to Marcion's (whom he in fact credits with pointing sharply to the category *novum* in Christian faith).[100] But Moltmann avoids Marcion's heresy by his Trinitarian position that it is the God of creation who suffers on the cross. The next move is critical: the cross of Christ is not merely redemptive—it is also creative. "The crucified Christ must be thought of as the origin of creation and the embodiment of the eschatology of being.... The event of the resurrection of the crucified Christ makes it necessary to think of the annihilation of the world and the creation of every being from nothing."[101] In other words, God's redemptive activity and his creative activity are one and the same, with this qualification: the paradigm for God's relationship to the world is the cross. Creation proceeds through redemption. This means that the Fall, which in Christian theology has generally been understood as an aberration, a resistance on the part of man to God's intention in creating him,

98. Ibid. (emphasis added).

99. Cf. Hans Frei, Review of *Theology of Hope*, *Union Seminary Quarterly Review* 23, no. 3 (Spring 1968): 267–72, who makes exactly this point. The relative significance given to the past is one thing that distinguishes Moltmann from Wolfhart Pannenberg. Moltmann tends to emphasize the contradiction between historical reality and eschatological hope. Pannenberg's interest has moved toward "the history of the transmission of traditions." See E. Frank Tupper, *The Theology of Wolfhart Pannenberg* (Philadelphia: Westminster, 1973), p. 258.

100. *Religion, Revolution, and the Future*, pp. 13–15: "When the universal church excluded Marcion as a heretic, it lost for itself the category of the new." Marcion had posited two gods: a god of creation and justice (in the Old Testament) and a god of redemption and love (in the New Testament and especially in the writings of Paul).

101. *The Crucified God*, pp. 217–18. Cf. "Creation and Redemption," p. 128 and passim.

plays little or no role in Moltmann's theology. Just as the cross is an "intertrinitarian event," so also is the creation an intertrinitarian event, and so also is evil.

> With the Christian message of the cross of Christ, something new and strange has entered the metaphysical world. For this faith must understand the deity of God from the event of the suffering and death of the Son of God and thus bring about a fundamental change in the orders of being of metaphysical thought and the value tables of religious feeling. It must think of the suffering of Christ as the power of God and the death of Christ as God's potentiality.[102]

This is Hegel's view of the creation of the world, of evil as the self-alienation of God, and of redemption as the *Aufhebung* of this self-alienation: "If one describes the life of God within the Trinity as the 'history of God' (Hegel), this history of God contains within itself the whole abyss of godforsakenness, absolute death and the non-God."[103] (Incidentally, this Hegelian view of God's relationship to the world raises the question of whether Moltmann has avoided the Gnostic elements of Marcion by substituting the Gnosticism of Valentinus).[104]

For ethics, this means that the paradigm for the moral act is the cross. Put more strongly, but not less accurately, the paradigm for every moral act is revolution, a breaking with and transcendence of the whole structure of the past. The apparent close relationship between Moltmann's theology and revolution is not that he has provided a genuinely dialectical view of revolution or even a moral justification for revolution but that his theology and his ethics are based on a paradigm of the cross and resurrection understood as revolutionary transcendence of the past.

In short, Moltmann is drawn to revolutionary language because his theology of the cross leads him to the position that it is God's way with the world that there should be revolutions.[105] This theological-

102. Ibid., p. 215.

103. Ibid., p. 246.

104. See Hans Jonas, *The Gnostic Religion* (Boston: Beacon, 1958), chap. 8 and pp. 236–37, for a comparison of types of Gnosticism.

105. Hegel is supposed to have said, "Es ist der Gang Gottes in der Welt, dass der Staat ist." I have paraphrased Walter Kaufmann's translation of this: "It is

Marxist inversion of Hegel causes him to emphasize the breaks in history, to call upon Christians to criticize the existing order and embrace the negative. If the paradigm for the moral act is the cross, it follows that Christians must always stand in "dialectical" contradiction to the institutions of the world. Furthermore, it means that institutions and policies will always be built by others or by "the world." That at least is the implication of most of Moltmann's practical directives. One gets the sense that Christian ethics does not build but criticizes—or at best, building takes place through criticism, just as creation takes place through *re*creation or redemption.

THE CHURCH AND THE KINGDOM OF GOD

I shall expedite the discussion here by momentarily purging it of dialectical language and returning to the language Kuhn applies to scientific revolutions. The revolutionary process in science may be divided into five stages: (1) normal science, conducted under the guidance of a particular paradigm; (2) the discovery of anomalies as a consequence of applying the paradigm to a wider range of phenomena; (3) a period of crisis or disorder as the paradigm proves increasingly unable to comprehend the anomalies; (4) the articulation of a new, competing paradigm—this competition is the "battle" part of the revolution; (5) resolution, the choice between paradigms.

A full theory of revolution must account for all these stages. The dialectical revolutionary tends to concentrate on 2 and 3, that is, on the anomalies and the crisis. In chapter 4 I tried to show the difficulties involved in deriving a concept of practice from the structure of the crisis itself. Moltmann's theology seemed to have the advantage of being able to structure the revolutionary transition through the work of God in Christ, the prolepsis of the Kingdom of God. Even though I have argued that this revolutionary transition is not dialectically related to the past in a Hegelian-Marxist sense, the idea that the Christian already has a paradigm that anticipates all possible negativities and anomalies has a certain fascination. If

---

the way of God with the world that there should be the state." See his Introduction to *Hegel's Political Philosophy* (New York: Atherton, 1970), p. 4. This sentence, connected with section 258 of Hegel's *Philosophy of Right*, has been the subject of much scholarly controversy since an early English translation rendered it as "The State is the march of God through the world."

Moltmann could provide an ecclesiology that yielded principles for organizing human life, Christians might in a sense be called "revolutionary" by others.[106]

But Moltmann's writing on the church is disappointing on this score. In his early works his references to the church concentrated on the movement toward the oppressed. When he did describe the life of Christians together, he used the language of spontaneity, play, song, and dance: "I would expect from Christians, who believe in God's presence in the midst of revolution, that they would laugh and sing and dance as the first to be liberated in creation."[107]

> Marxism speaks of the transformation of work into free spontaneity. This is the transition from the "kingdom of necessity" into the "kingdom of freedom." This idea has a long history and is also alive in Christianity. Here it means the liberation from the law of works by faith, which brings forth the free fruits of love. . . . What does faith mean other than already here and now in the midst of the kingdom of poverty and necessity to begin realizing the future of freedom, love, and play? Where this spirit of freedom reigns, of freedom not only from masters and exploiters, but also freedom of man from himself, where this spirit of festivity and laughing becomes infectious, there the revolution within the revolution can take place, the deliverance of revolution from the alienating forms which it assumes in the struggle.[108]

Christian liberation certainly includes aesthetic qualities, and it may include play. It is possible that these qualities could, even in times of crisis, be infectious for others. But play is not an ordering paradigm, at least not for politics or the church. And it has nothing to do with historical revolutions.

What is missing here is a sense of the need for discipline and

106. See *Religion, Revolution, and the Future*, p. 137: "Radical Christianity will have a revolutionary *effect*, but a revolutionary program would be just the way to neutralize it. The title 'revolutionary' must, if at all, be given from outside; one cannot claim it for himself."

107. Ibid., p. 146.

108. Ibid., p. 147. See also Moltmann's *Theology of Play* (New York: Harper & Row, 1972), where he works out these themes in more detail and in particular develops the theme of the creation as God's play.

organization, a need that would seem especially acute in a church that according to Moltmann is to include "unlikes" rather than "likes." The influence of Luther is again suspected. Unlike Calvin, who saw the life of faith as needing constant forming and discipline under the instruction of the law, Luther emphasized the dramatic change in the act of justification itself. Sanctification, the forming of life according to the Spirit, is collapsed into justification. Upon justification the Christian is free in his love for his neighbor and free from the works of the law: "The law says: 'Do this!', and it never is done. Grace says: 'Believe in this one!', and forthwith everything is done."[109] The *forthwith* is the problem. For Moltmann, "Hope in this one!" is the gloss on Luther. Since the major dialectic is between the "kingdom of necessity" and the "kingdom of freedom," sanctification is collapsed not into justification but into glorification, the free spontaneity of the eschatological community.

The absence of attention to church organization is not surprising in light of Moltmann's definition of power which he equates with force. He calls his most recent major work, *The Church in the Power of the Spirit*, a "messianic ecclesiology," and begins by sounding themes from the earlier work: We live in a time of crisis, and the Christian should respond to this crisis in "free solidarity and critical fellowship."[110] Moltmann also tells us that the "political task of Christianity is not merely to live in an already existing political order, but actually to take part in forming it,"[111] and suggests that the church should continue the task of Puritanism in desacralizing political power, building democracy, and extending the field of human rights. But this does not lead him to a discussion of the structure of power. Instead, he emphasizes the need to desacralize politics.

109. Martin Luther, Thesis 26 of the "Heidelberg Disputation," in *Martin Luther: Selections from His Writings,* ed. John Dillenberger (Garden City, N.Y.: Doubleday, 1961), p. 503.

110. *The Church in the Power of the Spirit*, pp. xiii and 1. The English title is misleading because the word translated "power" is *Kraft* which is best translated "strength." Power in English can be used to translate both *Kraft* and *Macht*, but the latter has connotations of domination which Moltmann clearly wants to avoid in connection with the church. Since he equates power (Macht) with force, it should not be used to describe the work of the spirit. See discussion on pp. 208-11, above.

111. Ibid., p. 178.

In fact, more than in the earlier works, Moltmann now adopts a dialectic of means:

> Participation in the apostolic mission of Christ therefore leads inescapably into *tribulation, contradiction and suffering.* The apostolate is carried out in the weakness and poverty of Christ, not through force or the strategies of force.[112]

The power of politics is to be opposed with the weakness of Christ. Returning to his adaptation of Hegel's trinitarianism in *The Crucified God*, Moltmann says, "God experiences history in order to effect history. He goes out of himself in order to gather into himself. He is vulnerable, takes suffering and death on himself in order to heal, to liberate and to confer new life."[113] The church must recognize its own experience as part of God's experience in creating history.

The closest that Moltmann comes to discussing a new order of power is when he maintains that the fundamental task of the church at large is to found grass-roots Christian communities or "to found congregations at the lowest level, congregations which independently discover their powers and potentialities in the liberating history of Christ."[114] Had Moltmann begun here and followed the lead of Calvin and the Puritans in addressing the questions of ecclesiology in terms of political power, he might indeed have provided a base for the organization of marginal peoples that would have revolutionary potential. If marginal peoples form communities of power, they will attend to questions of justice and law, and to the institutional structures required to secure human rights. The potentialities so discovered might well be called "revolutionary" by those who are in power.

Such analysis is not forthcoming. Moltmann's adaptation of Hegel requires him to see political power as the alienated moment in God's becoming. It is the historical manifestation of God's separation from himself, and it is the cause of his suffering pain and death on the cross. The "Power of the Spirit" that drives the church toward the Kingdom of God is the power of unification, of love that overcomes

112. Ibid., p. 361.
113. Ibid., p. 64.
114. Ibid., pp. 328ff. and 357.

secular power, suffering, and death.[115] The church's movement toward the Kingdom of God is the overcoming of politics in the name of eschatological love and play.

RECAPITULATION

It is to Moltmann's great credit that he recognizes the religious nature of revolution and the central importance of the problem of evil. In this, he takes seriously the claims of revolutionaries. To the extent that part of the task of Christian theology and ethics is to motivate people to act and to direct attention to the problems that require action, Moltmann's writing is a powerful contribution. The analysis I have offered here does not adequately portray the power of his writing for eliciting from privatized faith a concern for the political.

Nevertheless, his political theology is strangely antipolitical. At no point is this more obvious than when he tries to connect Christian practice with revolutionary practice. There it may be said that he fundamentally misconstrues the revolutionary process. Because political power is always alienated power, he concentrates on criticizing it rather than on offering alternative power structures that might give shape to the experience of marginal peoples. The absence of such an alternative in a revolution almost surely means that marginal peoples would turn to other paradigms for organizing their experience, whether dualistic, Marxist, or nationalistic. And it is exactly such a resolution that Moltmann wants to avoid.

Even if the Christian does have some paradigm derived from the life of the church, Christian involvement in a historical revolution can never be a matter of total involvement on one side of the fray, as Moltmann at times suggests. There may of course be a powerful presumption in favor of those who have been oppressed in a revolutionary situation, and more important, it is surely the task of the Christian, long before the dialectics of power yield a revolutionary crisis, to point out the existence and support the cause of those who are oppressed. But the eschatological identity of the Christian creates some distance from those whose identity is determined by the internal dynamics of political and social structures. Since there is not a complete congruence between Christian

115. See ibid., pp. 50–65, "The Church in the Trinitarian History of God."

and non-Christian marginality and identity in a revolution, the Christian intervenes in whatever revolutionary dialectic exists.

Moltmann implicitly recognizes both the distance and the intervention when he has recourse to just war principles. These principles are not used to determine when a person or state has a right to self-defense (as they were in the just war tradition) but to determine when a Christian should intervene in a revolution and to distinguish between good and bad revolutionary actions. Further, the guilt that Moltmann says the Christian must bear in revolution is not so much the guilt of violence but the guilt of not being able to guarantee the outcome of the revolution. Therefore the notion of praxis, borrowed from Marx, begins to dissolve and to include more traditional modes of moral analysis. Or else praxis is derived from the Christian eschatological dialectic formed in the life of the church. But that dialectic, in Moltmann's analysis, is a dialectic of means, contrasting suffering love with political power.

Can one take seriously the claims of revolutionaries and avoid these results? I suggested in chapter 2 that the analysis of the structure of scientific revolutions yields no preference for either normal science or revolutionary science. The work of normal science makes scientific revolutions possible and necessary by the discovery of anomaly. On the other hand, normal science is dependent upon the insights afforded by the new paradigms that emerge in scientific revolutions. The Hegelian master-slave relationship *may* be read just as neutrally. It has probably been read more often as a justification of mastery, giving the master the dominant beat in the rhythm of history. In any case, Hegel himself used the encounter for interpretive purposes and not as a directive to action. The revolutionary critics of Hegel attempted to direct action by focusing on the slave, the contradiction, as the energizing principle of history. We may say that they gave a syncopated reading of the rhythm of history. Feuerbach criticized Hegel for inverting subject and predicate; Marx knew that Feuerbach could be criticized only on Hegelian grounds and proceeded to do so. Many critics of Marx have argued that he had only one blind spot: "Like Hegel himself he did not subject his own theory to a dialectical critique."[116] That critique is now carried on by various branches of neo-Marxism, and it is probably inevitable

116. Avineri, *Marx*, p. 258.

that theologians should find it necessary to subject them in turn to a dialectical Christian critique. Each of these successive critiques has looked for a universal, Archimedean point for directing human action in history.

But it is possible to approach revolution using the more neutral model of scientific revolutions rather than the intricacies of dialectic. The results for ethics may be more promising than attempting to locate the dominant beats of history. In the postscript to his book on scientific revolutions, Kuhn discusses the difficulty of communication between two incommensurate views of the world.[117] There is no one solution to the difficulty, but scientists working from two different perspectives may at least try the complex task of translating the language of one perspective into another by resorting to "shared everyday vocabularies." The point for Christian ethics may be simply put: if Christians do not articulate the principles and institutions of justice with care, they will have nothing to translate when confronted with competing paradigms for distributing human suffering. The everyday work must go on if the extraordinary challenges are to be met.

117. Thomas S. Kuhn, *The Structure of Scientific Revolutions*, 2d ed., enlarged (Chicago: University of Chicago Press, 1970), pp. 200ff.

6

Evil, Ethics, and Revolution

> . . . and establish thou the work of our hands upon us,
> yea, the work of our hands establish thou it.

Psalm 90

Political and social revolutions are acts of immense human energy and imaginative reconstruction. The world is seen from a different vantage point, and the new perspective gives the participants a sense of high exaltation. Because the reconstruction concerns the nature of evil, revolution has a religious quality and easily takes on the language of new creation. All is to be made new; the enemies, the oppressors, the foes of God or the foes of humanity are to be forever buried.

Camus remarked that "revolution destroys both men and principles. . . . In fact, if there had ever been one real revolution, there would be no more history. Unity would have been achieved, and death would have been satiated."[1] Cruelty is so much a part of revolution not only because revolutionaries are, in their exaltation, so sure of their cause but also because after the revolution evil persists when it ought to be buried. The desperate attempts at final burial constitute the Terror. Conversely, if history goes on (and if some evil is tolerated), it is because principles such as justice and and institutions such as government persist.

That evil and ethics both persist, as if connected, after the revolution—this may seem something of a paradox, and their connection must be carefully worked out.

REVOLUTION AND ETHICS

Let us recapitulate the conclusions of the preceding three chapters. The dualist revolutionaries give the clearest example of the resistance of revolution to moral justification. Because evil is to be eradicated,

1. Albert Camus, *The Rebel* (New York: Vintage, 1956), pp. 106 and 107.

223

revolution is its own justification. This revolution is not especially innovative: the revolutionaries replace the dualism of their oppressors with a dualism of their own, simply inverting the terms. This inversion, this conversion, provides exactly the passion and conviction necessary for waging the revolution: the revolutionaries are absolutely convinced of the inevitability of their victory. Yet the very source of this conviction precludes success, for the dualist has no paradigm for explaining evil after the revolution and therefore no foundation for organizing human affairs on a continuing basis. This last observation is, of course, made from an external vantage point—it is not of immediate interest to the revolutionary dualist and, indeed, might undermine the revolutionary's singlemindedness were he to become convinced of its truth. The person who is conscious of the larger processes of human history in which revolution plays only a part remains distant from the person for whom the revolution is all. He can be sympathetic to the revolutionaries' cause, but he can never be one of them. To the extent that sympathizers support or encourage the revolutionaries, their involvement amounts to intervention in the revolutionary process, yet they must hope and work for an outcome other than the stated goal of the revolution—with the risk of not being able to guarantee the result for either the revolutionaries or society as a whole. What comes after the revolution may be as bad or worse than what went before.

Hegel is the man of insight who applauds both oppressors and revolutionaries without the risk of involvement. Marx takes the vehicle of this insight, the Hegelian dialectic, and transforms it through his notion of praxis in order to combine insight with revolutionary passion. This account turns on the notion of a historically new marginality, a kind of negative universality which Marx supposes to be characteristic of the modern proletariat. But his attempt to give a coherent account of negative universality fails, and the revolutionary transition from potential to actual universality requires external direction from those who do have insight. Further, there is a hidden theodicy in Marx, in spite of his intention to do away with all such notions. The struggle of the human species with nature not only serves to explain human disorder but also provides a foundation for organizing society after the revolution, even if not along universal lines.

A theological transformation of Hegel and Marx permits Moltmann to define marginality and universality in terms of the dialectic of cross and resurrection, and to substitute the liberating work of God on the cross for the liberating work of the human species in mastering nature. But dialectic and marginality thus rendered make no direct connection with the historical forms of marginality that arise from the internal dynamics of authority and domination. Moltmann's Christian must therefore reconstrue the revolutions waged by the marginals of the world, and this also amounts to a kind of intervention in the revolutions of others, a point which Moltmann tacitly admits by his application of just war principles to revolution. Furthermore, Moltmann's Christian revolutionary praxis chiefly involves the criticism of existing institutions. The possibility of articulating new forms of political and social organization is undercut by the identification of political power with the negativity that is to be overcome.

In light of these criticisms it may be tempting to conclude that the Christian, and perhaps others, must remain outside the revolutionary process, developing an ethic of intervention based perhaps on just war principles but with a presumption in favor of the oppressed. Revolutions happen, and when they do the Christian simply struggles as best he can to limit the damage and effect some reconciliation even while working for the liberation of the oppressed; in short, he tries to transform the revolution into something like a citizens' rebellion. It may be that those who intervene from outside have no choice other than to follow such a course. It is doubtful, however, that many people are ever in a purely external relation to a revolutionary process, even when they feel themselves to be so. Those confronted by a highly dualistic situation may find it especially difficult to identify with either side (I think here of the attempts of outsiders to make choices in relation to the highly volatile racial conflicts in southern Africa), although parties in a position to intervene have probably already had some involvement in the process itself.

Several other considerations prevent adoption of an ethic of intervention as a solution. There is the practical and strategic problem that the intervener will have great difficulty in making his position heard in the heat of revolution. The just war principles grew out of a specific tradition of political theory and when applied to revolution depend, as I suggested in chapter 1, on the model of the citizens' rebellion in the name of the universal rights of man. To try to so transform a revolution is not unlike trying to make the revolutionaries go through a course in medieval political theory and the Enlightenment. It hardly need be said that revolutions under way do not afford the luxury of time, energy, or (most often) the historical context such education would require (Marx's "Men make their own history, but they do not make it just as they please" is pertinent here). And such attempts would surely be perceived by the revolutionaries as a threat to their goals.

More important, such an approach depends on a foreshortened view of revolution that seriously distorts the nature of human activity in relation to the revolutionary process as a whole. The development of an ethic of intervention or the use of just war principles to choose among revolutions betrays a crisis mentality and portrays revolution as an event with little history. Revolutions are a long time in the making. As in scientific revolutions, anomalies do not appear overnight but accumulate over a long period of time. One form of revolutionary marginality does not suddenly develop and threaten a pattern of domination. Rather, as Marx realized, there are many forms of marginality that accumulate over years and even centuries. They appear first as inconveniences rather than as serious threats, and many of them may disappear if the ruling theodicy is flexible enough to adapt. But the more obstinate marginalities retain their revolutionary potential. At one time confidently circumvented by dominating groups, they now move to the center of a society's attention.[2]

Further, the emergence of a new paradigm to explain marginality and suffering, essential if potential revolution is to become actual, is also a long process. In the case of the millenarians, for example, the dualist symbols of the apocalyptic tradition had long existed before finding their revolutionary application in the political and social circumstances of the Middle Ages. Marx's notion of the struggle with nature helps him articulate a theory of the emancipation of the proletariat, but the notion of mastery of nature was established in philosophical thought long before Marx.[3] The development and

2. Cf. George Steiner, "Life-Lines," in *Extraterritorial* (New York: Atheneum, 1971), p. 172. The article first appeared in *The New Yorker* in 1970.

3. The notion goes back at least to Francis Bacon. See Richard Kennington, "Descartes and Mastery of Nature," in S. F. Spicker, ed., *Organism, Medicine,*

coming together of the various elements needed to produce genuine social innovation is filled with anticipations that first go unnoticed, with false directions and premature proclamations of change, with stubborn resistance—in short, a process in which the revolution and its resolution are only the very last stages.[4]

What would someone concerned about the plight of the poor and oppressed, about social justice, or about the human good be doing during this process of preparation? Let me reemphasize that most persons are not Hegelian spectators but are a part of the process itself. What they do depends on their particular situations and involves an immense variety of acts. To be quite mundane about it, one person's response to human suffering may involve taking a neighbor with a broken leg to the hospital, visiting and comforting another who is bereaved, pleading on behalf of a third who has been callously laid off from work, contributing money to the cause of migrant workers—the list could go on and on. Another person may be doing far more heroic work on the streets of a ghetto or resisting the violence of a repressive regime in Latin America. Someone else may be trying hard, at some personal risk, to rethink the racial policies of his or her own labor union.

Now these various persons engaged in even more various tasks may disagree with each other on many things, but they also have a great deal in common. It is likely that they interpret their service to the neighbor within a general framework of common values and principles, that they see their attempts to alleviate suffering as part of what it means to keep implicit and explicit promises, to be faithful to one's calling, to pursue truth, to be motivated by a concern for justice. These commonalities suggest a common task, a concern for a moral world. Further, even serious disagreements, such as about which particular tasks are most important, or about who is to be counted as a neighbor, are likely to reside in different convictions

and *Metaphysics* (Dordrecht: D. Reidel, 1978), pp. 201–23, for a discussion of this notion in seventeenth-century philosophy and its culmination in the problem of theodicy.

4. See Thomas Kuhn, *The Structure of Scientific Revolutions*, 2d ed. enlarged (Chicago: University of Chicago Press, 1970), chaps. 6 and 7, for discussion of the preparation for scientific revolutions. On anticipation in science, see pp. 75–76. For a more detailed statement of the stages of revolution, see p. 216, above.

about what it is that causes injustice, or what it is that *prevents* the keeping of promises and the telling of truth in human society. They are not disagreements about the importance of creating a moral world or about the values and principles themselves.

These observations suggest some of the reasons why claims that Christian activity is revolutionary activity or, as in Moltmann, that the paradigm for the moral act is revolution are seriously misleading about the nature of both moral activity and revolution. For one thing, without careful qualifications such claims radically impoverish our sense of responsibility in the face of suffering. The variety of creative response is reduced to a single idea.

More important, if revolution takes place after a long and fitful process of accumulating anomalies and marginalities and after a new paradigm has emerged to interpret them, then directives to embrace solidarity with the oppressed or to embrace contradiction and the negative may not be very revolutionary at all. It is a seductive idea that the task of the Christian is to identify anomalies and marginalities before they come to occupy the attention of those who hold power and authority. But this gadfly view of the Christian role in society not only places the Christian outside the revolutionary process; it may well prevent revolutionary innovation, for two reasons.[5]

On the one hand, anomalies in the form of social marginality are not simply the mechanical products of impersonal forces of domination but arise in part because of the attempt to make a given paradigm for evil work. This is analogous to the work of normal science. Just as the normal work of science is what makes anomalies recognizable, so also those who seriously attempt to establish justice and moral community within the framework of a given paradigm are the ones most likely to discover experiences of suffering and evil that cannot be comprehended by the paradigm. Kuhn's analogous point on scientific revolutions is instructive:

5. What I have called the gadfly view of Christian activity is, of course, a reputable Christian position with many proponents in the history of the church. I do not agree with it for reasons that I hope are apparent and because I think it entails certain illusions about the ability of Christians to attain the degree of distance from the power structures of the world that being a gadfly requires. But my point in the text here is that such Christians should not call themselves revolutionary.

Novelty ordinarily emerges only for the man who, knowing *with precision* what he should expect, is able to recognize that something has gone wrong. Anomaly appears only against the background provided by the paradigm.[6]

In the social arena the precision is likely to be less, but those who have attempted to establish justice within a given paradigmatic framework are likely to have more clarity about the nature of the anomalies thus encountered than those who, from without, identify anomalies in general fashion as "the negative." They may also be more resistant to change than those who are eager to identify all anomalies as the negative. As Kuhn points out, those who attempt to make a paradigm work develop "a considerable resistance to paradigm change." A great deal is invested in the paradigm, and it is not easily surrendered. But "resistance guarantees that scientists will not be lightly distracted and that the anomalies that lead to paradigm change will penetrate existing knowledge to the core."[7] This is not an appeal for conservatism (and one should never confuse mere appeals to the past with active attempts to make a paradigm— the tradition—work) but a description of how effective thought proceeds. Consistent appeals for change and vague invocations of a "permanent revolution" involve little insight into the specific causes and character of anomaly and marginality. Such appeals betray not so much nausea over evil as disenchantment with order.[8]

On the other hand, a revolution will take place, if it takes place at all, when someone articulates a new paradigm able to give order to marginal peoples. It is easy to forget, and is too often forgotten, that what plagues marginal peoples, if they are genuinely marginal, is not order but disorder. They do not have a meaningful place within a theodicy, and this is true even if they are suffering under the "order" of a dictatorial or racist regime. Therefore a genuine concern for the marginals of the world, for the poor and the oppressed, must include attempts to structure a community for them. If no one attends to this, and if marginality reaches crisis proportions, then the most likely paradigm to emerge will be a form of dualism.

6. Kuhn, *Scientific Revolutions,* p. 65 (Kuhn's emphasis).

7. Ibid., pp. 64–65.

8. Julian N. Hartt, *A Christian Critique of American Culture* (New York: Harper & Row, 1967), p. 425.

Again, the people most capable of articulating a new structure for marginal peoples are those who have already had experience with making structures work, that is, those who by virtue of having taken seriously the task of making a specific paradigm work have become painfully aware of its failure to account for increasingly obstinate anomalies. It is no accident that the leaders of a revolution are almost always renegades from the ruling class: it is they who understand power and are best equipped, having rejected an old paradigm, to engage in innovative reconstruction.

These considerations confirm what a colleague said to me in passing: that the Christians who have had the most revolutionary impact on history are not those who have used revolutionary language but those who have attended to institution building. One thinks particularly of the influence of John Calvin, whose politics were in no way revolutionary but whose careful attention to discipline and law, as well as to the orderly functioning of ecclesiastical and political institutions, provided an organizing framework that carried revolutionary power in the midst of the immense upheavals and anomie of the sixteenth and seventeenth centuries. The effects of Calvin's training in law persisted through his conversion and his rejection of the institutions associated with the medieval church.[9]

In chapter 5 I showed that Moltmann came closest to recognizing the need to structure the lives of marginals when he advocated the founding of congregations and churches for the poor and oppressed at the local level. But the effectiveness of this proposal was undercut by his insistence (at least in connection with his explicit discussion of these churches) that the power of politics is contradicted by the weakness of Christ and by his consistent theme that all political institutions are alienating and must be resisted. This dialectic of means cannot lead to the articulation of new paradigms for ordering human community, because it overcomes the political by associating human suffering with political power in general.

Now lurking behind all of this is what theologians call a nature and

9. See Michael Walzer, *The Revolution of the Saints* (New York: Atheneum, 1969), and David Little, *Religion, Order, and Law: A Study in Pre-Revolutionary England* (New York: Harper & Row, 1969). These books are discussed in chapter 2. I might add here that Marx was so successful in creating a theory of social innovation because he took the work of the classical economists so seriously.

grace issue: to what extent does grace (redemption) alte the structure of human nature and nature in general (creation)? We have discovered that for Moltmann creation takes place through redemption, that the cross and resurrection together are the paradigm for the dynamics of creation. This implies that what changes in revolution (since the cross is a revolutionary event) are not simply human relations and the human understanding of them (this much is what Marx claimed) but the very structure of being itself. When Moltmann says that in the modern world evil has become political he does not mean simply that our understanding of evil has taken on political dimensions, or that political institutions have become more dangerous or inhuman; he means also that the structure of evil itself changes as the (re)creative process continues. If there are ontic changes in evil, then there is no reason to assume that prerevolutionary structures, including political ones, will persist after the revolution.[10] The political can be overcome by the weakness of Christ.

This is why Moltmann (and others who have espoused a revolutionary view of the cross and of Christian activity) spends so much time showing how most traditional Christian ethics—especially natural law ethics and ethics based on notions of order—are static. But the dialectical solution to the problem of ethics is excessively murky. It leaves conveniently hazy what it is that changes in revolution and what it is that persists. It gives only the general impression that human moral activity undergoes dramatic change, but exactly how is not clear. Moreover, proponents of this position are quite capable of inconsistency on exactly this point, as we saw in Marcuse's adoption of a moral calculus and Moltmann's adoption of just war principles (without supporting argument) to evaluate revolutions.

Providing an alternative to this dialectical view of nature and grace is a theological task going well beyond the scope of this work. But the event of revolution does illuminate the issues in connection with moral activity. Using Kuhn's analysis of scientific revolutions, I have sketched the way in which revolutionary innovation *depends* on the normal work of human ethics, and this suggests that the choice is not merely between revolutionary ethics and static moral systems. There is an alternative that sees the moral task as intimately bound up with

10. For discussion of this point in Moltmann, see pp. 218–20.

the possibility of revolution. It depends on the notion that in a revolution evil is not so much overcome as reconstrued, thereby persisting after the revolution. Such a view not only better accounts for the dynamics of revolutionary change as displayed in actual historical revolutions; it also is more suited to understanding the moral task insofar as (1) it is more able to explain the fact that revolutions are most often occasioned by those who give structure to human life (the dialectical tradition must always account for an embarrassingly large gap between what is intended and what is accomplished); and (2) it makes this creation of structure directly responsible for the possibility of innovation (rather than giving the moral task ironic significance by announcing in advance its dialectical death).

In what follows, I shall support these contentions by looking at how evil can be said to change in revolution. This requires a further examination of the notion of theodicy, which I have argued is at the center of revolutionary transformation. I shall try then to show how that change is connected to man's enduring moral task.

REVOLUTION AS CHANGE IN THEODICY

In chapter 2 I examined an ambiguity in the use of the term "theodicy." Theodicy proper belongs to the Judeo-Christian tradition, referring to the attempt to justify God in light of the tension between God's goodness and the facts of human suffering, wrongdoing, and evil. But it is used by sociologists after Weber to refer to all religious attempts to give meaning to experiences of suffering and disorder, including the suffering and disorder connected with inequality and domination. Up to this point I have ignored this ambiguity, using the term in its functional-sociological sense. It is now necessary to resolve it.

Revolution is a quest for a moral universe, a quest that is linked historically and conceptually to the Judeo-Christian theodicy. What Weber calls ethical monotheism holds that there is one principle of being and that that being is good. But because so much of human experience contravenes this belief, monotheism also gives rise to the moral demand to correct what is in the name of what ought to be. This moral demand can be expressed in many different ways. It can, as in the Book of Job, be coupled with claims of human innocence and aimed at God: God should correct what is. As in the Augustinian theodicy, it can be aimed at sinful human beings along with an assertion of God's innocence. It can also be aimed at enemies of God, enemies who must be overcome. But however the demand is expressed, and to whomever it is made, it renders "what is" morally unacceptable and in need of transformation (most often expressed in the symbol of the Kingdom of God).

In contrast, Weber's two other major types of theodicy make "what is" a complete warrant for human fate. The Indian doctrine of Kharma with its strict notion of causation leaves no possibility for viewing what happens in this or the future life as unwarranted. What can be changed is not one's present life but one's existence in a future incarnation. As Berger points out, such a theodicy, against which no empirical evidence could ever count, "constitutes the most thoroughly conservative religious system devised in history."[11] Zoroastrian dualism gives more flexibility to personal fate in this life: one can be on the right or wrong side. But again, what happens in this world does not count against the theodicy itself: things that cause suffering, disorder, and darkness are attributed to the principle of evil, those that create harmony and light to the principle of good. In these two types of religious legitimation, the question of theodicy proper cannot even be raised; no tension is felt between what is and what ought to be.[12]

The Judeo-Christian theodicy is "highly vulnerable to empirical disconfirmation"[13] because it alone sees experiences of suffering and disorder as evil in the sense of being antithetical to God and as counting against his goodness and justice. But one might equally as well say that those living within the Judeo-Christian tradition are compelled by its theodicy to attend to empirical questions of disorder, suffering, and injustice in a way that members of the other religious traditions are not. Certain apparent solutions, such as postponing the

11. Peter Berger, *The Sacred Canopy* (Garden City, N.Y.: Doubleday, 1967), p. 65.

12. Therefore Berger's statement that biblical monotheism "stands or falls with its capacity to solve the question of theodicy, 'How can God permit...?'" is misleading in its implication that biblical monotheism has more difficulty answering the question of theodicy than other religious traditions. Rather, biblical monotheism alone has to answer the question because it alone gives rise to theodicy. See ibid., p. 73.

13. Ibid., p. 70.

confirmation of God's justice until the afterlife or to a distant historical future, combined with accounts of the Fall, Original Sin, and predestination, do not make the problem go away. At most they make the tension between what is and what ought to be reappear in different guise, such as in the question of why God ordains some to salvation and others to damnation, of why God permitted (or caused, depending on one's theology) the Fall to happen, of why the eschaton is delayed, and the like—questions any teacher of theology has learned to expect from students struggling with Augustine, Aquinas, and almost every major theologian of the tradition. And none of these "solutions" entails an absence of moral earnestness about this life.[14] Resistance to evil is part and parcel of theodicy proper.

Now it is not just the case that the Christian theodicy as a whole is subject to empirical disconfirmation. Rather, within that theodicy there are competing paradigms for evil, articulated as a necessary part of the quest for a moral world, and each of these is likely sooner or later to yield anomalies that are potentially disconfirming.[15] This point has not merely to do with the intellectual difficulty of understanding, for example, how an earthquake can be understood as a consequence of sin (theologians learned early to distinguish between natural and moral evil[16]) but with the practical (moral) problem that the paradigm no longer guides the moral quest in fruitful directions.

It is important to recognize that paradigm solutions for evil within the Judeo-Christian theodicy do not emerge in a vacuum, nor are they simply given dogmatically. They arise in the context of a

14. The exception is the tradition, very minor, of libertine sectarians.

15. The only case in which this may not be true is in a totally otherworldly Christianity. The fact of the matter is that very few Christians are totally otherworldly. Most groups that have emphasized a heavenly salvation have also posited some transformation in this world, certainly in the lives of individual believers and in the life of the church, often also in the institutions of culture. The theological reason for this is the doctrine of creation and the Christian theodicy itself: there is one principle of being and it is good. To ignore completely the transformation of this world calls into question these basic beliefs. Therefore those Christians who have taken an almost completely otherworldly stance always court the heresy of Manichaeism or a similar form of dualism in which part of the world is given over to the power of evil.

16. Although, as suggested in chapter 2, some theologians have viewed natural evil as a punishment for sin.

religious framework that asserts the goodness of God, that requires the believer to keep God's commandments, to do justice, love kindness, and walk humbly with God, to love the neighbor and the enemy in short, to work for the Kingdom of God. A paradigm solution for evil in this framework is that which explains *what goes wrong*, that is, why efforts to establish the Kingdom fail or remain incomplete. At the same time, such paradigms serve the purpose of structuring questions for the continued effort, of suggesting how to proceed. It is in this latter connection that they produce anomalies.

Let us take an idealized example. A child who steals comes from an urban ghetto. The person who believes that most disorder and human suffering are consequences of personal sin will link the stealing to the child's original sin, and this notion will direct his attempts to deal with the child's behavior. Someone else beginning with the same assumption but at the same time motivated by a love for justice and mercy may be troubled with this explanation, particularly if attempts to convert the child fail and yield the conclusion that this child is lost to God's love. Close work with the child may reveal how much the resistance to conversion comes from the character of the child's parents, or from the fact that the slums offer so few opportunities for human beings to flourish. Such findings are anomalies for the paradigm-induced expectations. The paradigm may be stretched to cover the case and appeals can be made to biblical pronouncements about God's wrath visiting unto the third and fourth generations of those who hate him. Still, someone who does not merely have an interest in exposing sin but also has confidence in a moral universe may be rightly troubled by this stretching. And if someone likewise concerned about justice produces an alternative explanation that seems to account as well or better for why things go wrong (why the child steals), we have a competing paradigm for evil, or at least for some form of it.

Now the Marxist paradigm does just that. It offers not only a social class explanation for why the child steals but by the same token opens up an entirely different set of questions to be answered and new avenues of approach for working with the child. Questions that had been at the periphery now move to the center of attention. The patterns of relationship in which the child had always lived are reconstrued, still other patterns are discerned, and new disciplines emerge to study them and the

questions they raise.[17] When this new paradigm is able to interpret
not just isolated cases of children stealing but the condition of
whole social groups who find the explanation of sin to be at odds
with most of their experience, we have a revolutionary situation.

I called this an idealized example because the processes it refers
to are self-evidently more complex than the example alone suggests.
And historically the Judeo-Christian theodicy has embraced some
diversity of paradigms for explaining resistance to the Kingdom of
God, ranging from fundamentalist conceptions of personal sin and
the devil to liberal views of the negative power of ignorance. The
traditions defined by these paradigms may not have the same precision of definition and method as the various scientific traditions
with their exemplary paradigms, but the parallel is instructive.[18]
Each of the exemplars does have explanatory power—it would not
otherwise long be held by a community. To say that paradigms have
explanatory power means that they have not only the capacity to
interpret evil and its origin but also the capacity to generate questions about suffering, wrongdoing, and disorder that are productive
for the group's action. It follows, however, that some have more
explanatory power than others. To return to the child who steals: if
he is black, the view that his suffering and wrongdoing are a function
of racism has considerable explanatory power. If this view is held
unreflectively, however, it offers little more direction for human
action than a dualist paradigm for evil; indeed, it becomes that. If
racism is interpreted at least in part in terms of social psychology and
class, or even in terms of sin, it has another kind of explanatory

17. See Steiner, "Life-Lines," pp. 174–75, on the emergence of new disciplines after revolution. The point is implicit throughout Kuhn's work.
18. See Kuhn, *Scientific Revolutions*, chap. 5, for the relation between
paradigms and the definition of scientific communities and traditions. I say
that religious communities and their paradigms for evil *may* not be as precisely
definable as scientific communities, but I am not sure this is the case. On the
one hand scientific discourse and method seem far more carefully specified
and controlled than theological discourse. On the other hand, Kuhn's book is
controversial exactly because he shows that this discourse is not as neatly
defined and controlled as often supposed. It would at least be interesting to
study religious communities with respect to their paradigm views of evil and
how these limit and inform what they do in the social arena. Something like
this was done by H. Richard Niebuhr in *Christ and Culture* (New York:
Harper, 1951).

power and directs action accordingly. Which has the more explanatory power is exactly what paradigm competition and revolution are
about. There is no direct method of comparison, because the
interpretation generated by the paradigm is itself dependent upon
the paradigm for verification of its efficacy. By the same token, an
exemplar may be deficient in explanatory power—the position that
says the child steals because institutions are alienating is capable of
generating few productive questions.

It may seem to be the implication of this account that the unique
status of sin in the Christian tradition has been undermined, replaced
by something akin to a dialectical unfolding of sin and evil where
later paradigms (such as the Marxist) subsume and replace the
earlier.[19] But I do not think this is so. What is implied is that sin by
itself cannot account for all experiences of evil, and that changes in
our perception of evil are compelled by the theodicy in which sin
plays a role. The fundamental points may be stated as follows.

First of all, there are theological reasons to be circumspect in making claims about the nature and cause of evil. Paul Ricoeur reminds
us that

> the faith of the Christian believer is not concerned primarily with
> an interpretation of evil, its nature, its origin, and its end; the
> Christian does not say: I believe in sin, but: I believe in the
> remission of sins; sin gets its full meaning only retrospectively,
> from the present instant of "justification," in the language of St.
> Paul. . . . It follows that the description of sin and the symboli-
> zation of its origin by means of the myth belong to the faith only
> secondarily and derivatively, as the best counterpart of the gospel
> of deliverance and hope.[20]

What the Christian finally says about sin and evil must follow from
other claims in faith. This is a restatement of my earlier suggestion

19. For Hegel's own assessment of his work in this regard, see Emile
Fackenheim, *The Religious Dimension in Hegel's Thought* (Boston: Beacon,
1970), pp. 129-33.
20. Paul Ricoeur, *The Symbolism of Evil*, trans. E. Buchanan (Boston:
Beacon, 1969), p. 307. Most theologians would agree with this point insofar
as it specifies theological control over what is said about evil, but they may not
agree on what derivative means, or on how evil is derivative. Moltmann, for
example, makes evil derivative from an eschatological point of view.

that the Judeo-Christian theodicy's interest in evil is derivative, following from its central interest in establishing a moral world. To make dogmatic claims about sin and evil as a way of positing what is possible and what is not possible in human affairs is to give them creedal status and make God's goodness the anomaly. Since evil is the derivative category, that which is to be explained, it may be argued that *the Judeo-Christian theodicy is in principle open to revolutions in its conception of evil*, just as science is in principle open to revolution in its paradigm solutions.[21]

Second, what sin means has manifestly changed historically. This does not mean that there are no fixed points in the tradition but that there has been and still is disagreement about the cause, scope, and effect of sin and its relation to other forms of evil.[22] It may even be that the special place sin occupies in the Judeo-Christian theodicy can be interpreted by viewing sin as a betrayal of the theodicy itself. For example, sin may be the denial that Judeo-

21. Cf. David Tracy, *Blessed Rage for Order* (New York: Seabury, 1975), p. 6, on the principled openness of science to revolution. Many philosophical attempts to work through the theodicy problem wind up arguing for a revolution in the conception of God: since evil manifestly exists, one of the premises (about goodness or about power) about God must be wrong. Some theological discussions do much the same. I think it is implicit in Hegel that there are revolutions in both the conception of evil and the conception of God. Moltmann's position as discussed in chapter 5 clearly argues for a revolution in the conception of God over against culturally held views of the divine. It is less clear whether his trinitarian view of the history of God involves revolutions in the human conception of the divine on the part of those who participate in the history of promise and fulfillment. I think it is extremely important to make it clear that theologically the *principled* openness is toward revolutions in the conception of evil.

22. Ricoeur's *Symbolism of Evil* is an excellent phenomenology of evil. John Hick's *Evil and the God of Love* (London: Macmillan, 1966) works out an Irenaean theodicy in contrast to the more traditional Augustinian theodicy. For a recent restatement of the Augustinian theodicy, see Austin Farrer, *Love Almighty and Ills Unlimited* (Garden City, N.Y.: Doubleday, 1961). For a theodicy constructed from the standpoint of process theology, see David R. Griffin, *God, Power, and Evil* (Philadelphia: Westminster, 1976). Systematic attempts to link discussion of evil with moral action are rare. The classic work is still Reinhold Niebuhr, *The Nature and Destiny of Man*, 2 vols. (New York: Scribner's, 1941). But compare his very interesting and undeveloped typology of evil in the preface and last chapter of *The Irony of American History* (New York: Scribner's, 1952).

Christianity is in principle open to revolutions in its conception of evil. This would, I think, be a fairly precise statement of what has traditionally been called the sin of pride and idolatry, in this case the claim to have solved the problem of evil.

Third, the relationship between old and new paradigms in science is complex and may be instructive for theological reflection on evil. In some cases the old must be discarded, but in others it is incorporated in the new.[23] Often, the old paradigm remains part of common discourse because for a large part of human experience it does the job quite well. The overthrow of Newtonian mechanics by quantum mechanics did not push Newton's laws of motion from school textbooks or undercut their importance for understanding how most things work. In addition, the new paradigm must explain not only the anomalies but also what the old paradigm succeeded in doing. If it does not do this, the two paradigms would have to exist side by side in some kind of complementarity. Finally, the old paradigm exerts its influence by having set the agenda for the new: were it not for the work of the old there would have been no need for the new.

Fourth, the structure of scientific revolutions may be suggestive of how perceptions of evil change. In chapter 2 I indicated that while scientific revolutions are irreversible and unidirectional, they do not necessarily yield progress toward a specific goal. Science is a process of "evolution-from-what-we-know" rather than "evolution-toward-what-we-wish-to-know." The revolutions in science do not yield closer and closer approximations to truth but analogously with evolutionary selection yield paradigms and theories better fitted to solve the puzzles that confront them. "The net result of a sequence of such revolutionary selections, separated by periods of normal research, is the wonderfully adapted set of instruments we call modern scientific knowledge."[24] So the historical conflict among competing paradigms for evil in the Judeo-Christian theodicy may be understood to have yielded a complex and "adapted" view of evil

23. Cf. Steiner, "Life-Lines," p. 174; and George Lindbeck, "A Battle for Theology," in *Against the World for the World*, ed. Peter L. Berger and Richard J. Neuhaus (New York: Seabury, 1976), pp. 20–43, especially 31–39, for similar points about applying Kuhn's notion of paradigm shifts to radical shifts in theology.

24. Kuhn, *Scientific Revolutions*, pp. 171 and 172.

that is the "fittest way" to approach present-day problems of disorder, suffering, and wrongdoing. This portrayal of the relation among
competing paradigms suggests that successive efforts at establishing
a moral world are likely to yield their own anomalies, along with
new aspects of evil. And there is always the possibility that certain
directions taken in the quest for a moral world are best abandoned.

Moreover, the unidirectionality and irreversibility of revolution are
manifest in the fact that the Christian concerned about establishing
justice, and about what it is that frustrates the establishment of
justice, cannot, for example, work without the Marxist paradigm.
This does not mean embracing a communist program. After all, the
Marxist paradigm has almost as many versions as does the Christian
understanding of sin; those who do any kind of social class analysis
(and much else in social science) have already accepted some version
of the Marxist paradigm. Nor does it mean that the Marxist paradigm
is "right" in any absolute sense of the term. It too may eventually
yield in whole or in part to other paradigms, and the fact that some
Marxists ironically invoke the devil and others worry about new
forms of injustice in communist societies indicates awareness that
consistent attempts to apply the Marxist paradigm also produce
anomalies.[25] The point is that the role played by patterns of domination connected with the productive processes has been thrust powerfully onto center stage. It has been thrust there as part of the quest
for a moral universe, and it is on center stage because it does have
explanatory power. Our perceptions of what causes evil and what
frustrates justice have been forever altered as a result, even if the
Marxist account does not exhaust our experience of evil.

To say that patterns of domination are now at the center of attention does not mean that domination did not exist previously, or that
the forms of domination are now evil whereas at one time they were
not, or even that they are now more profoundly evil. The actual positions of the earth, sun, planets, and stars did not change when
Copernicus found a new way of looking at them. Evil may be

25. See Leszek Kolakowski, "A Stenographic Report of the Devil's Metaphysical Press Conference in Warsaw, on the 20th of December, 1963," in *A
Leszek Kolakowski Reader, TriQuarterly* no. 22 (1971), pp. 139–152. One of
the earliest and best-known studies of the persistence of old problems in new
guises in communist society is Milovan Djilas, *The New Class* (New York:
Praeger, 1957).

reconstrued in the same way. Patterns of domination are now recognized as contributing to what is called evil, and problems of human suffering, disorder, and wrongdoing that were at one time attributed to other causes are now attributed to or connected with domination. People who were considered the naturally existing poor are now perceived as victims of unjust distributions of wealth and power. Problems are regrouped or reclassified, and words are employed in different ways. The world itself is cut to a different pattern.[26]

The change in evil is, then, fundamentally cognitive rather than ontic as implied in much of the dialectical tradition (Marx excepted). But this does not mean that the change is purely intellectual, divorced from the dynamics of human relations. On the contrary, the most powerful contribution of those who put domination at center stage is to have shown that a cognitive change also involves a structural change in human relations. If a shift in paradigm in science requires the restructuring of the methods, vocabulary, and approach of the scientific community, a shift in paradigms for evil requires a restructuring of the methods and vocabulary of ethics. Such methods and vocabulary do not live a disembodied intellectual existence but are imbedded in the institutions of culture. Political and other institutions represent in their structure the social attempt to achieve justice and deal with the problem of evil. This is exactly the point of Peter Berger's contention, discussed in chapter 2 and adopted in this work, that every social structure has an implicit theodicy. That patterns of domination in a society exert a powerful influence on human cognition is an insight that informs the entire tradition of social theory, beginning with Marx and culminating in various branches of contemporary thought.

It follows from this analysis that the Marxist paradigm for construing evil is neither the first nor the last word on the subject, not because of some unfolding dialectic but because it arose within the broader framework of the quest for a moral world. There have been

26. As Kuhn frequently notes, the cognitive change in scientific revolutions has the effect of giving opponents the sense that they are actually living in two different worlds, and in a very real sense, they are. See, for example, *Scientific Revolutions*, pp. 192–93. Yet the fact that the world is genuinely experienced as a different world after Copernicus does not change the fundamentally cognitive character of the revolution.

and will continue to be competing paradigms for interpreting the human experience of evil, of what it is that hinders the quest. However, this account of the origin and significance of the Marxist position differs from the Marxists' own understanding of these issues. Moreover, and in language independent of the point of view that I have adopted, the idea that ethics and particularly justice are constitutive of human cognition has long been present in the Western moral tradition. It is implicit in the Jewish belief that keeping the law is the fundamental vehicle for knowledge of God; it is more or less explicit in the writings of Aristotle, Kant, and Rawls. In short, the Marxist paradigm for evil is one exemplification of the constitutive nature of justice, one extraordinarily powerful way of construing what it is that hinders the quest for justice. Without the quest for justice, and without the institutions and inquiries established and undertaken in that quest, the Marxist paradigm could not be discovered.

Now this revolutionary process is one that has a coherent history: new paradigms are possible because they answer questions that, although not answered by the old, were nevertheless raised against the background of the old. But many revolutions occur not within a given tradition but as a consequence of the conflict between two separate traditions which may well be asking different kinds of questions. Does this mean there are two different kinds of revolution? This question has been implicit at critical points throughout the preceding chapters. It made its appearance in Hegel's characterization of the Orient as stagnant by comparison with the dynamic West; it reappeared in Marx's suggestion that India was incapable of a liberating revolution without the oppressive intrusion of British attempts to master nature; it reappeared theologically in Moltmann's difficulty in connecting his theological dialectic with the dialectics of marginality; and it was present in the observation that conflicts between cultures were the most likely setting for dualistic revolutions.

A revolution or conversion that takes place in the setting of a conflict between cultures—say, a colonial situation—does not involve competition between competing paradigms of the same theodicy but between two theodicies that are systems in the sociological sense. This might be comparable to a conversion from a nonscientific to a scientific view of the world. In any case, the incommensurability of the two world views would seem by definition to be more extreme than the incommensurability of two paradigms within the same tradition.[27] Any marginalities created in the conflict are not generated by the internal dynamics of one system but arise from the conflict itself. To take just the case of conversion to Christianity: the converts in a non-Western culture will find that their newfound Christian understanding of evil does not have a special relationship to the traditional explanations for evil in their own culture. Moreover, as converts they suffer from a form of marginality and anomaly in relation to the traditional culture that is not a product of the internal dynamics of that tradition.[28]

The extreme nature of this incommensurability may make translation between the conflicting points of view even more difficult than that between the paradigms of the same tradition. For this reason alone recourse to dualism is more likely, although even in these cases translation is not impossible. But before examining what facilitates and what hinders translation I want to put forward several ideas about the role of Christianity in non-Western cultures as topics for further study.

First, we know enough about the appearance of Christianity in non-Western cultures to recognize that in most cases each culture will give it a distinctive stamp. The new Christian's situation is not so anomalous as to have no continuity with the indigenous cultural past. This does not differ greatly from the fact that Judeo-Christianity did not develop in a vacuum but through interaction with pagan cultures. So while the Judeo-Christian theodicy may, with its particular paradigms for evil, compel certain questions about the nature of human suffering and wrongdoing, it does this with a vocabulary and a set of ideas drawn from other sources as well. Not all of the old structures are overthrown in revolution.

Second, Christian conversion does have revolutionary potential insofar as it involves asking a set of questions about the nature of human suffering not asked by the indigenous culture. The revolutionary voices from the churches of the Third World attest to this

27. To my knowledge, Kuhn does not address the question of what is involved in a shift from a nonscientific world view to a scientific one.

28. It is important to note that the marginality created by the entrance of one cultural system into another may feed upon or reinforce marginalities already existing in the indigenous culture. Christian converts are often made among, but not limited to, the socially disaffected in a culture.

potential. It is, nevertheless, only a potential. Whether conversion actually yields revolution depends on a host of variables in the indigenous culture and in the way Christianity is presented. What is of most interest here is that this potential is present quite independently of the intentions of those who have been converted and of those who have done the converting. The evidence for this seems to me to be overwhelming—one has only to look at the number of revolutionary leaders who have been products of missionary schools.[29] Further, Christian missionaries most often go into other cultures as bearers of Western culture on a scale much broader than narrowly conceived religious ideas. They accompany other institutions such as business and government and teach ideas that include attitudes toward work, politics, nature, economics, and the like, ideas which may have an unintended effect.

This leads to yet a third notion, more speculative but worth mentioning. If the convert is influenced not only by explicitly religious ideas but also by Western social theory, that, too, may have a revolutionary potential. I have already noted the ambiguity of borrowing the term theodicy from Judeo-Christianity to refer to all psychocultural constructs for handling inequality and disorder. This application of the term involves conceptual imperialism. It is one thing to say that every religion orders anomic phenomena and experiences of suffering in such a way as to give them meaning. Suffering, if given a meaning, is tolerable. But to call this ordering a theodicy entails a meaning of a very particular religious and moral sort, one that is not necessarily present in the indigenous culture.

This conceptual imperialism underscores the extent to which much social theory is itself a theodical enterprise, a quest for a moral world. Since Hegel's philosophy of state and society is both the origin of one branch of social theory[30] and, in his own words, a theodicy, the rise of that social theory in the West may be interpreted without exaggeration as the attempt to work out the theodicy problem after Hegel, to look under (or beyond) what is for what ought to be. The interpretation I have given of the relation

29. Just a sample: Mao Tse-Tung and Chou En-Lai were pupils in Protestant schools in China; Ho Chi Minh was schooled by Roman Catholics in Vietnam before going to Paris; many leaders of African liberation movements are graduates of missionary schools.

30. See Herbert Marcuse, *Reason and Revolution: Hegel and the Rise of Social Theory* (Boston: Beacon, 1960).

between the Marxist paradigm and the Judeo-Christian theodicy would support this proposition, but determining its validity as a statement about social theory in general would require extensive philosophical and historical analysis.[31]

In any case, it would seem that the application of the idea of theodicy to non-Western religions and cultures has itself a revolutionary impact. Take, for example, the phrase that Max Weber uses to describe the basis of religious theodicy, "the incongruity between destiny and merit."[32] We must imagine whether someone immersed in a non-Western belief-system such as the Hindu caste system could read Weber and, taking him seriously, remain part of this system. The theodicy of the caste system gives meaning to his status and any suffering involved in it, but Weber's theory raises the question of whether the entire system does not mask a discrepancy between destiny and merit. It implants the notion that things could be otherwise, and it introduces a normative judgment on the caste system by interpreting the question of suffering as a question of evil and indirectly as a question of justice.

Another way of making the same point is to ask whether a person reared in the theodicy of the Judeo-Christian tradition would respond to the critical nature of social theory in the same way as someone in a non-Western culture. There is empirical evidence that social theory can undercut all religious beliefs much as Marx thought it would. But I have argued that it is possible for someone who accepts the Judeo-Christian theodicy to appropriate the critique offered by social theory as corroboration of the gap between what is and what ought to be precisely because this critique arose as part of

31. Marx, of course, thought he had overcome the so-called is-ought dichotomy. See Richard J. Bernstein, *Praxis and Action* (Philadelphia: University of Pennsylvania Press, 1971), p. 75. In chapter 4 I argued that he did not succeed. It is incontestable that moral passion inspired the studies of the great "classical" sociologists, such as Durkheim, Weber, Simmel, and others. Not all modern social theory has its origins in Hegel and Marx, of course; a major branch traces its ancestry to Hobbes. But the English tradition represented by Hobbes is also dominated by the notion of mastery of nature and the theodicy problem. See Kennington, "Descartes and Mastery of Nature."

32. Max Weber, "The Social Psychology of the World Religions," in *From Max Weber: Essays in Sociology*, ed. H. H. Gerth and C. Wright Mills (New York: Oxford, 1958), p. 275.

the demand for a moral world.[33] It is not clear that the same theory can be appropriated in the same way by someone from a religious tradition that demands a meaningful but not necessarily moral world.

For all these reasons, having nothing to do with a directly revolutionary program, Christians and others may be unwitting bearers of revolutionary potential in non-Western cultures. Marx saw this point clearly: he knew that England brought to its colonies not only new methods of production but a new attitude toward nature and culture. There is a certain irony, then, in the claim that Christians *should* be revolutionary. It is more to the point to inquire *how* they are revolutionary, and to understand how revolution is connected to the enduring task implied in the affirmation, "Thy will be done on earth as it is in heaven."

WHAT ENDURES IN REVOLUTION

My final interest, then, is to render more precise our understanding of what does not change in revolution. There is obviously something called science that persists through scientific revolutions. According to Kuhn, it involves (1) a consistent commitment to puzzle solving and (2) methods and values that are not derived from a particular puzzle-solving paradigm. Even though competing paradigms in a revolution are incommensurable, involving an element of conversion when allegiance is transferred from one to the other, these common commitments, methods, and values make translation possible between competing paradigms, along with rational persuasion, even when the usual forms of logical demonstration and empirical proof do not work.[34]

33. For an example of the adoption of social theory to corroborate the Christian theodicy, but in a direction very different from that taken here, see Jacques Ellul, *The Ethics of Freedom* (Grand Rapids, Mich.: Eerdmans, 1976). Ellul uses Marx, Freud, and other social theorists as proof of human determinations and the refusal of human beings to exercise their freedom in Christ; see, for example, p. 34. His construction leads him to a dualistic position: "As is the normal lot of Christians in all aspects of their lives as such, we are thus faced with an austere work which carries no visible recompense and offers no palpable satisfaction on earth. The entire work of freedom can only dash itself against the wall of incomprehension, refusal, and judgment" (p. 274).

34. Kuhn makes these points in refuting critics who have charged him with irrationality and relativism. For the positions of some of the critics, see Imre

I have shown that the parties on either side of a revolution often use similar language and profess allegiance to similar values, especially a commitment to a moral universe symbolized by the Kingdom of God. (This point does not mean that all involved are equally committed. Both sides may abound with hypocrites, scoundrels, opportunists, and the vicious.) Further, both parties may share a belief in freedom, justice, honesty, and other fundamental human values without agreeing on the meaning of these values, or on how they are to be applied, or on their relative importance. As I suggested earlier, all this depends in large part on convictions about what it is that prevents the Kingdom of God from being realized. For example, someone who refers all falling short of the Kingdom of God to individual sin will handle newly discovered cases of injustice in terms that have to do with personal failure. The person who refers all falling short of the Kingdom of God to power relations will be induced by that paradigm to reexamine them when confronted by new cases of injustice. Further, what counts as a case of injustice will not be the same from both perspectives. The person who is convinced that power relations are the chief obstacle to the realization of the Kingdom of God will also put more weight on questions of justice than will the person concerned chiefly with sin. Revolution is a battle between perceptions like these, and adherents of opposing sides tend to talk past each other even when discussing the same cases and the same values.

Therefore, in the first part of a revolutionary conflict it seems that the opponents really do live in two different worlds and that the choice between these is highly irrational. But in fact the opponents most often share a common vocabulary and common values. The vocabulary and the values are not so much abandoned (each side always charges the other with abandoning the moral enterprise) as reconfigured, and it is therefore possible to translate between two paradigms much as it is possible, if difficult, to translate between two languages. Since there is rarely a one-to-one relationship between terms in two languages, translation involves an imaginative leap into

---

Lakatos and Alan Musgrave, eds., *Criticism and the Growth of Knowledge* (Cambridge: Cambridge University Press, 1970). For Kuhn's response, see his "Reflections on My Critics" in the same volume, especially pp. 266ff., and his postscript to *Scientific Revolutions,* especially pp. 198–205.

the world of the other, and this imaginative leap invariably means compromising one's own world view; what is expressed in one language cannot be exactly reproduced in the other. Something is lost, but at the same time something is gained. Through translation people come to see things they have not seen before, and once they have in fact begun to see them in this new way they find that they have "slipped into the new language without a decision having been made."[35]

The element of conversion lies in the fact that coming to see the world in a new way is not a question of rational proof but involves an imaginative leap, a gestalt shift. But those who take this process seriously should at least be able to determine how paradigms differ from each other and, more important, become aware of the peculiar strengths and weaknesses of each for generating productive questions about the problems it confronts. These latter provide reasons for choosing among paradigms, even if they do not constitute proof. More important, they provide a climate in which the conversion is not simply more likely to take place but to take place in a way that permits those involved to see the continuity between the tasks before and after the revolution; that is, to avoid the dualistic assumption that a revolution is a complete break, that recreation involves total destruction of the old, that the choice between two paradigms is totally irrational.

This continuity is exactly what is denied by the dualists and by some dialectical views of revolution. To return to the relation between nature and grace: if grace and redemption radically alter nature and creation, then to the extent that revolution exemplifies the transition from nature to grace, the tasks before and after the revolution are contradictory rather than continuous. This would be similar to a claim that what Newton accomplished does not count as science whereas what Maxwell, Heisenberg, and Einstein accomplished does. The conflict between their respective views of the world would not be a conflict between two incommensurable paradigms within the tradition of a common endeavor but a conflict between two very different endeavors. There would then be no need to translate, no reason to show why or how the values and

---

35. Kuhn, *Scientific Revolutions*, p. 204.

commitments of those working post-Einstein are the reconfigured values of those working pre-Einstein.

This point seems clear enough with respect to the dualists but perhaps not so obvious as a characterization of the dialectical tradition. Yet a look at just one set of issues supports the resemblance and makes it seem less of an exaggeration. That set of issues concerns the relationship between the two kingdoms, between church and state, divine and human justice. The fundamental question to be asked is whether there is sufficient similarity between their tasks to make translation between them not only possible but fruitful.

The dialectical position on this question will become clearer if we typify a series of views on the origin of human (political) justice. It is possible, first of all, to link human justice and government chiefly to the Fall. Without the Fall there would be only love or the perfection of divine justice, equated with love. Within this position the variations range from the millenarians and radical sectarians who would connect political justice solely to the Fall to positions holding that the institutions of government have been so corrupted by the Fall that politics and justice have a paradoxical or contradictory relationship to the Kingdom of God and love. In this case, political justice is so closely associated with evil that divine justice can be understood simply as the overcoming of evil. Although scholars do not agree on the point, the view that government is irretrievably corrupted by the Fall is one interpretation of Luther's view.[36]

A second stance is to link justice fundamentally to finitude. The exigencies of time and space, the fact that we cannot foresee all the consequences of our actions, the variations in abilities and gifts both among persons and within the lifetime of a single person—in short, "the elementary necessities of this earthly life"—all of these things require that human activity be ordered by justice and the institutions that support it. This position can also be attributed to Luther.[37] Its central motif is the connection between justice and necessity, with

36. The basic source for Luther's views on secular government is the treatise, "Secular Authority: To What Extent It Should Be Obeyed." See John Dillenberger, ed., *Martin Luther: Selections from His Writings* (Garden City, N.Y.: Doubleday Anchor, 1961), pp. 363ff., but references to the connection between sin and the secular government abound in other writings.

37. This is Paul Althaus's interpretation of Luther. See *The Ethics of Martin Luther,* trans. Robert C. Schultz (Philadelphia: Fortress, 1972), pp. 47–48.

the implication that when the exigencies of temporal life are over, justice (and the political) are no longer necessary.

A subtype of the stance linking justice with finitude is the association of justice with the structure of economies, the human activity connected with the management of scarcity. Scarcity is a function of finitude, but the more one views the fundamental problem of finitude in economic terms, the more it is possible to think of overcoming at least certain kinds of justice problems by overcoming scarcity. There is an element of this notion in Marx's thought, although it would be wrong to say that it exhausts his account of human activity. It is a sufficiently powerful element in his work to explain in part why he devoted so much of his attention to the productive dimensions of human activity, to the overcoming of the limits imposed by nature.

Third, justice may be found to be a consequence of particularity in the sense that as persons and groups achieve distinctiveness and identity both individually and historically, politics and principles of justice are required for the adjudication of inevitable differences in vision, volition, and the like. It is important to distinguish this view, in spite of superficial similarities, from the one linking justice with finitude, for a reason that derives from analysis of what is meant by the Kingdom of God. If fellowship and the covenant with God are possible only for *persons*, then the particularity implied in personhood suggests that justice is still a virtue of the Kingdom of God; or, perhaps better put, that there is a fundamental continuity between human justice and the justice of the Kingdom of God, a suggestion that would not seem as obvious to someone who made only the link between justice and finitude. Among secular writers, John Rawls's theory of justice may fall under this position,[38] and Hegel is close to it in his discussion of "abstract justice."[39] The connection between justice and particularity is also related to scarcity, but not with scarcity understood simply in terms of natural resources. Particularity entails the scarcity concomitant on choice in the sense that the choice of one thing precludes the choice of another. In theological

38. John Rawls, *A Theory of Justice* (Cambridge, Mass.: Harvard University Press, 1971), pp. 1–17. Most deontological or formalist theories of justice would fall into this type.

39. See sections 34–40, "Abstract Right," in Hegel's *Philosophy of Right*, trans. T. M. Knox (Oxford: Clarendon, 1957).

terms, this involves the recognition that the creative process is not a matter of both/and (everything is possible) but of either/or (while anything may be possible, not everything is possible).[40]

When justice and political activity are connected with the development of particularity, we move toward still another type of stance. Justice and the political may be understood much as it is in Aristotle as a precondition for the emergence and development of human association. In this sense, justice is not simply a means of adjuticating conflicting claims arising from finitude and scarcity or the fact of particularity but is itself a constitutive element in what makes particularity or personhood possible. Justice is a precondition for human debate about the good, or for human association in relation to a common good, or for communion with God. In this view, which seems to include theologians such as Aquinas and Calvin, justice is the form of creation itself, a necessary component of what it means for God to have a world, created or *re*created, capable of a covenantal relation with him.[41]

40. The idea that what it means to have a human world involves an either/or, a choosing of something at the expense of something else, also runs through the work of Sigmund Freud: to have civilization entails saying no to some instincts. For example, this passage from *Civilization and Its Discontents* (Garden City, N.Y.: Doubleday Anchor, n.d.), pp. 42–43: "Sublimation of instinct is an especially conspicuous feature of cultural evolution; this it is that makes it possible for the higher mental operations, scientific, artistic, ideological activities, to play such an important part in civilized life." Freud's theory of sublimation can be understood as an attempt to work out a theory of the human world in connection with an expanded definition of scarcity, that is, expanded beyond its usual association with economic production. But his brooding pessimism about the consequences of the choice for civilization links him more with the view that justice is a function of necessity, of finitude.

41. Calvin, for example, says of civil government that "its function among men is no less than that of bread, water, sun, and air; indeed, its place of honor is far more excellent." See John Calvin, *Institutes of the Christian Religion,* trans. F. L. Battles (Philadelphia: Westminster, 1960), bk. 4, chap. 20, section 3. But he also said, "Had we remained in the state of natural integrity such as God first created, the order of justice would not have been necessary. For each would then have carried the law in his own heart. . . . Hence justice is a remedy of this human corruption. And whenever one speaks of human justice let us recognize that in it we have the mirror of our perversity, since it is by force we are led to follow equity and reason." *Commentary* on Deuteronomy 16: 18–19; quoted by Sheldon Wolin, *Politics and Vision* (Boston: Little, Brown,

Now the first of these types stands apart from the others in linking human justice with a particular conception of the nature and origin of evil, the Fall. It alone begins with an explicit theological judgment about evil. The consequence of this judgment is twofold: on the one hand, all the other things to which justice can be connected—necessity and scarcity, particularity and vitality—tend to become associated with evil. There is no place for them except as that which is in opposition to God. It is for this reason that extreme positions of this type approach dualism: finitude itself stands in opposition to God. On the other hand, divine justice stands in opposition to human justice. Divine justice is the eradication of evil, including occasions for disorder and suffering that other positions might not label evil. While divine justice is perceived as the eradication of evil, human justice is *at best* an organized disorder (Augustine). There is no interest in justice as the institution by which benefits and burdens connected with scarcity are distributed or by which claims growing out of particularity are adjudicated. If persons who hold such a position are revolutionaries, then it is clear that much that is perceived as evil will persist after the revolution—and the Terror will not be far behind.

It is instructive to compare this linking of human justice and the Fall with the dialectical tradition. The dialectical tradition has no notion of the Fall except insofar as the Fall symbolizes the alienated moment of God's (or human) becoming. But the *except* is critical. The tendency of the dialectical tradition is to subsume all forms of evil under "the negative." The negative of the alienated moment is the occasion and cause of suffering, disorder, even sin. The alienated moment is akin to the Fall. This means that although the dialectical tradition has much in common with the position that evil is a function of finitude, its view of justice has far more in common with the radical sectarian's. Human justice and the institutions connected to it must be overcome by the divine. And insofar as suffering and disorder connected to particularity persist, the dialectical tradition must declare a "permanent revolution."

1960), p. 463, n. 41. Such passages are proof against proof-texting the Reformers and other theologians. Their positions on politics must be constructed from a fabric of themes on power and coercion, nature and grace, justification and sanctification, love and justice, and so on.

In other words, positions that associate human justice with the Fall and positions that have only a dialectical interest in justice foreclose for theological reasons the connection between evil and politics: where you have politics you assuredly have evil. The attack on evil is thereby also an attack on the political, or on human justice. To be sure, the dialectical tradition is far more subtle than the dualists in talking about the overcoming of the old. Nevertheless, whether in the more tragic Hegelian form or the progressive Marxist form or the eschatological formulation of Moltmann, political institutions and human justice stand as a kind of resistance to the attainment of the Kingdom of God. In purely religious formulations, what government is up to (having to do with power) and what the church is up to (having to do with opposition to power) are different things. Translation between their competing paradigms does not hold interest, since the movement from one to another is not simply a cognitive shift but a movement from one mode of being to another, where the second transcends and abolishes the first.

But consider the type of stance that links human justice and political institutions to the development of human particularity as constitutive value. This involves no prior commitment to a special view of evil and is therefore consonant with the position that evil is a derivative category, following from the quest for a moral world. It thereby permits consideration of the continuity between the task of government and the task of the church. This does not mean collapsing church and state. On the contrary, the historical fact of the existence of two separate governments requires explanation (it is part of the theodicy problem), and that explanation would necessarily include reference to what it is that frustrates the establishment of justice or the creation of a moral world. Such an explanation would include warnings about the idolatrous potential of political power, but it would not single out political institutions as being uniquely prone to idolatry by virtue of their being political. Rather, it would recognize, as Karl Barth and others have reminded us, that the church represents a new order that is decidedly political: it is the *Kingdom* of God.[42]

42. See Karl Barth, *Community, State, and Church*, ed. Will Herberg (Garden City, N.Y.: Doubleday, 1960): "Of one thing in the New Testament there can be no doubt: namely, that the description of the order of the new age is that of a political order. Think of the significant phrase: the Kingdom of

This linking of human justice with particularity and the development of persons establishes what Sheldon Wolin has called a "continuous realm of discourse" between the religious and the political.[43] Political power in its many manifestations is not to be overcome and replaced by something else but is constitutive of any conceivable human society. The church must attend to questions of power not merely in order to understand itself as a human institution (as if being this were a concession to frailty and even evil) but to understand its role as representative of a kingdom. In this role its task is not to flail at all patterns of domination but to articulate principles for ordering power, to establish which forms of power are just and which unjust not merely in society at large but in the church.

If the language of politics is a part of the church's discourse, then those in the church are competent not merely to criticize power but to engage in the difficult task of translating among competing theories of why it is that justice fails. They will have to engage in that task if for no other reason than that the very existence of two governments, state and church, is likely to entail differing theories about the nature of evil. But this does not mean that they are engaged in different tasks. Further, both may be said to proceed according to the best lights of their own paradigm solutions to the problem of evil. Often they may proceed on their separate paths without a great deal of conflict. But if the church's commitment to the quest for a moral world is more than perfunctory, if its primary interest is not in protecting what it has (which amounts to claiming it has solved the problem of evil) but in continually addressing that which still needs to be done, then its own attempt to structure human relations, to establish just power, may well run afoul of the official policies or unofficial power structure of the other (secular) government.

God. . . " (p. 124). Much of what Barth says in these essays corresponds to the analysis I have given here, but his strongly Christological position takes him in directions different from what follows. But see also this: the state is to "*a certain extent* . . . a kind of annexe and outpost of the Christian community" (pp. 133–34); and, "The real Church must be the model and prototype of the real State" (p. 186).
43. Wolin, *Politics and Vision,* p. 179. Wolin is discussing Calvin.

Consider the church that has worried about its predominantly white membership and has come to the conclusion that some form of Marxist class analysis offers the most powerful explanation for the fact that "eleven o'clock on Sunday morning is the most segregated hour in America" in spite of years of effort to change it. No matter that some or all may want to include sin in the picture, either as a complement or in translation. If class analysis comes to explain why it is that the church as a community of believers is not racially inclusive, then that analysis directs the church in its action. But the church alone cannot take action, because the patterns of power involved extend far beyond its own community. The church is now a potentially revolutionary community not because it has chosen to be revolutionary or uses revolutionary language but because of the structure of its moral commitment.

The word *potentially* is important. It is clear that if the church takes its moral task seriously it will find itself at times embroiled in revolutionary conflict. This is both a historical report and a statement of probability, given the nature of many societies in the world today. And I should hasten to add that this probability in no fashion depends upon adoption of the Marxist paradigm. On the contrary, there may be places where marginalities and anomalies are not essentially a function of class dynamics, and in such cases importation of Marxist analysis may be quite unconstructive. This is why it is essential that the weight of attention be given to the positive task of creating just human institutions. Only then will the points that resist justice be evident and will the church know, through painful change on its own part, whether it is called to revolution—rather than itself continually calling for revolution.

But revolution may not be forthcoming, at least not in the sudden, violent form most often meant by the word. My purpose here has not been to promote revolution or to make it predictable but to make it comprehensible. If the church has consistently attended to questions of power and justice, it may well find responsive partners in the larger society. The task of translation can be a continuing process rather than one born solely out of crisis, but this depends on whether a continuous realm of discourse has indeed been established. In such cases, the demand for change and the resistance to change may be less destructive of human beings because the discourse and the climate exist for recognizing and talking about the deep conflicts that may arise. Moreover, societies may exist with several competing theodicies side by side—this may be the essence of what is called the pluralistic society.[44] Here the dynamics of change are likely to be far more complex than in a society with a more monolithic structure. But in such pluralistic societies also the church's role in whatever change takes place will be more constructive if it is prepared in both inclination and skill to address questions of power and to build institutions.

The idea of a continuous realm of discourse between the religious and the political then assumes a continuity of tasks, vocabulary, and values before and after the revolution. The nature of these tasks, the way the words are used, and the way in which the values apply may be reconstrued, and a new vocabulary may develop, but the fundamental change is in the paradigm solutions to the problem of evil. When that changes, what counts as justice changes, not because old definitions of justice are totally abandoned but because the problems to which the principles of justice apply are regrouped.[45] The vocabulary of power also remains, but in reconstrued form: there is a shift in what counts as legitimate power, in what is coercive and what noncoercive, because new forms of power are detected and new patterns perceived. But the notions of justice, of power, and of many other traditional normative and political categories remain and are important to the translation process between competing views of what is evil. They are the vocabularies that permit opponents to discover that they cannot agree on what justice means because they have different views of what frustrates justice. But that in turn permits them to recognize that the very idea of justice is constitutive of the discovery of different views.

This point is implicitly recognized by revolutionaries when they themselves use moral language and claim to be more just than their

44. If a pluralistic society is one without consensus on the nature and cause of evil, it follows that there is also lack of consensus on the human good.

45. I think it can be argued that each major *substantive* principle of justice (such as "to each according to works," "to each according to need," or "to each the same thing") has an implicit corresponding theodicy, a view of what prevents justice. For a discussion of substantive principles of justice in relation to the formal idea of justice, see Chaim Perelman, *The Idea of Justice and the Problem of Argument,* trans. John Petrie (London: Routledge and Kegan Paul, 1963), pp. 11–29.

oppressors. It is implicit in the fact that Marx used both Hegel and the classical economists to construct his own theory before rejecting them; and it was implicit in his recognition that the growing organization of workers was the most revolutionary fact about them. It is just short of being explicit in some of the recent dialectical work of critical theory.[46] But none of them takes the final step of assuming that the normative task of achieving justice is the constitutive framework for the possibility of having revolutions.

From a Christian perspective, this step must be taken first and foremost by the institution of the church itself: it is an ecclesiological task. The point here is not to abandon God talk for political talk, or even to translate God talk into political talk, nor to discern the political and worldly implications of the Gospel. All of these assume the division between the Gospel and the political. The point is rather to find a form of discourse in which it is recognized that the society of Christ, like any society, has power relations and thus needs to ask what patterns of authority are just and what unjust. And although I have spoken here almost entirely of politics and power, the same is true of exchange or market relations: they too exist in the society of Christ. Such a continuous realm of discourse has long been absent from most at least of the Protestant churches, and refinding it will not be an easy task.[47] But only if the church forms its life and discourse accordingly will it have the tools to address similar questions in the larger society and to participate in articulating forms of justice appropriate to power in its many forms.

46. One finds especially in the recent work of Jürgen Habermas an almost Kantian point of view in the notion of the "ideal speech situation" which is implied or anticipated in all human discourse. Actual communication among persons is usually distorted by power relations, but any speech presupposes a normative ideal. See "On Systematically Distorted Communication" and "Towards a Theory of Communicative Competence," *Inquiry* 13 (1970): 205–18 and 360–75. The background work is Habermas's *Knowledge and Human Interests,* trans. Jeremy J. Shapiro (Boston: Beacon, 1971). See also, *Communication and the Evolution of Society*, trans. Thomas McCarthy (Boston: Beacon, 1979).

47. Perhaps the fact that mainline Protestant churches rarely, if ever, practice excommunication indicates their incapacity to deal with questions of justice, power, coercion, and the like. I do not say this to plead for excommunication but for attention to the issues of power lying behind the doctrine and practice. On the positive side, Christian analysis of power and justice might begin with the Eucharist and the patterns of power and exchange permitting and denying access to the table.

If the poor and oppressed are formed in such a society, they too will be able to engage in the task of ethics. They will move from being what sociologists call the "sociologically incompetent" to being among the "sociologically competent." And in the continuous attempt to correct cases of injustice they may well find instances that resist correction so powerfully that they are forced to reassess the reasons they have depended upon for explaining the failure of justice. More important, the structure of their own existence may be an alternative to the implicit understanding of why justice fails in the larger society. If they have attended to these normal tasks of ethics with rigor, they will know with some precision why the moral quest has failed and will thus have a hand in the translation process essential for new interpretations of evil to yield new formations of justice. If they have not engaged in these tasks, it can be said with certainty that revolutionary paradigms, if required, will be constructed by others.

This sketch of an alternative to the dialectical view of revolution itself exemplifies what has been said about translation: there is no neutral ground on which to stand to demonstrate that one view rather than another is correct. What I have attempted to do is to translate between the moral points of view represented by those who would approach revolution as just another moral problem and those who adopt a dialectical-critical position, but this translation is not demonstrably correct. Nevertheless, there may be good reasons for accepting this alternative, and I want to review briefly what these are.

First, one could offer theological reasons, but I have not done much of that here. The nature and grace issue alone might occupy chapters or even volumes. What I have tried to show are the points at which certain theological issues are critical to the argument, and some of my own predilections have been obvious. Having said this, I would want to add that theology is not, I think, something done independently of the kind of analysis done here. If theology pertains in part to human activity (I do not want to say praxis) it must at least account for the questions that have been raised.

Second, all the alternatives must be able to account for the phenomena they purport to discuss. In this chapter I have tried to show that the alternative based on the structure of scientific revolutions is the one most suited to actual revolutions. I shall not rehearse what has already been said, but one point requires some comment. If the dialectical tradition in its more theological forms is committed to the idea that evil and the Kingdom of God are part of a process in which there is change in the very structure of evil within the history of being (or God), then an account of that change must go beyond a report on what has happened in human history. The history of the cosmos, after all, greatly exceeds the span of human life. The problem of holding together human (cultural) history and the history of nature goes back to Hegel and is embedded in dialectical assumptions, but I shall confine myself to one observation: every theologically dialectic approach to revolution of which I am aware discusses the progressive overcoming of evil only in terms of revolutions in cultural history. Therefore the nature/grace problem is almost always translated as something like Marx's prehistory/history problem, and God's unfolding is far more the unfolding of human history than of the history of creation as a whole.

Part of the persuasiveness of the alternative I have suggested is that it accounts better than the dialectical tradition for the changes in human cultural history by emphasizing the cognitive aspect of revolutionary change in evil (which is at one and the same time a change in human relations), and by assuming that political institutions are constitutive of that cognitive change and thereby endure through it all (which history, at least so far, bears out). But there is another side to its persuasiveness: that by working with language and conceptual constructs that also refer to significant changes in science we avoid assuming or implying a split between what happens in cultural history and what happens in natural history. This does not mean that there are no differences. It is simply a way of not foreclosing the possibility that some of our experiences of evil are connected to natural processes. Nor does it foreclose the possibility that there is continuity between the cognitive processes pertaining to nature and to culture.

The third and most important reason supporting my choice of alternatives must derive from their implications for human action: how do they induce us to proceed? Here I am most concerned about proceeding in the face of suffering and oppression, for it is most often the poor and oppressed who lie at the heart of revolution. Certainly when one is confronted by the brutish conditions of severe poverty, of human life on the margins of social institutions, of people rejected through either active prejudice or powerful indifference, the temptation is strong to attack the institutions that have ostensibly caused the suffering or that are manifestly incapable of doing anything about it. The motivation for quick and dramatic transformation is born out of an acute sense that things have gone desperately wrong and that continuing on the present course is insane. This negative revelatory element is present in every revolutionary perception: there is a sense of being face to face with evil, with resistance to justice and God.

But it is at least sobering to reflect that most often poverty and oppression have been caused by other sudden transformations: nations committed to overnight modernization, individuals and groups in a hurry to move up in the world, premature closures on what is evil and who is among the elect. Why should the sudden transformation of the marginals be different? To be sure, plunging into revolutionary action is one way of joining the ranks of the "sociologically competent": you learn quickly about certain forms of power, much like the nonswimmer thrown into deep water may quickly learn enough about swimming to keep his nose above water. But there is no guarantee that this immersion in revolutionary struggle will yield wisdom about just and unjust forms of power.[48]

Those in the dialectical tradition who are sensitive to this dilemma have therefore always urged extreme caution. Marx was forever worried about whether the time was ripe for revolution. Simone Weil is not far wrong in claiming that for Marx "a revolution takes place when it is already nearly accomplished."[49] Moltmann counsels warning younger brothers against the errors of their elders and not opposing "honest rationality"; and he finally counsels some very straightforward traditional moral analysis.

At its worst, then, the dialectical motif encourages antinomian and anti-institutional rage. In this situation, it is revolutionary only in the sense that Marx said capitalism was revolutionary: it is permanently revolutionary, tearing down everything that impedes

48. For a sobering view of the effect of rapid modernization under both "left" and "right" ideologies, see Peter Berger, *The Pyramids of Sacrifice* (New York: Basic Books, 1974).
49. Simone Weil, *Oppression and Liberty*, trans. A. Wills and J. Petrie (Amherst: University of Massachusetts, 1973), p. 148.

it.[50] At its best, the dialectical method permits attention to many of the concerns I have expressed about the need of the poor and oppressed for a meaningful structure. But even at its best this tradition will not take that one step more and look at the political and the moral as constitutive of the very possibility of revolution.

Would this make a difference? I think so. On the one hand, the position I have sketched is more accurate in describing the actual response of people when confronted by injustice and suffering: they do their best to correct these conditions. On the other hand, attention to the normal tasks of articulating principles of justice within a given paradigmatic framework and trying to shape human life accordingly gives some guarantee that marginals and those concerned about them will develop a community of justice that consistently calls attention to what must be presupposed for any human association. While there is no guarantee that this will lead to insight into the power relations hidden behind the given form of justice (within the church such insight would follow, if at all, from the role of love), it offers some chance that the constitutive elements of human society and well-being will not be taken for granted if a revolution comes.

There is no quarrel, then, with Marx's dictum that the philosophers have only interpreted the world, while the point is to change it. And I take seriously the painful lesson that human attempts to establish justice and to interpret the world may come up against obstinate realities that require radical rethinking about the nature of evil. But I do quarrel with any interpretive scheme that by celebrating the disjunctions of history detracts attention from the tasks at hand. That prevents significant change.

50. Marx, *Grundrisse,* ed. and trans. David McLellan (New York: Harper Torchbooks, 1972), p. 94.

Index